PENGUIN AFRICAN LIBRARY AP10

Edited by Ronald Segal

South West Africa

RUTH FIRST

RUTH FIRST

South West Africa

GLOUCESTER, MASS.

PETER SMITH

1975

First published 1963
Copyright © Ruth First, 1963
Reprinted 1975 by Peter Smith Publisher Inc.
With the kind permission of
Penguin Books Limited.
ISBN: 0-8446-2061-0

Contents

Introduction: The Bare
Bones of Conflict   11

PART ONE: THE ANTAGONISTS

      Masters and Servants   25

  1 The Servants   27

  2 The Masters   49

PART TWO: THE HEAVY HAND OF HISTORY

  1 Explorers and Elephant Hunters,
     Missionaries and
     Traders   61

  2 The Old Colonialism under
     Germany   69

PART THREE: THE LEAN YEARS OF THE MANDATE

  1 White Man's War   87

  2 Sacred Trust   94

  3 Punitive Expeditions   98

  4 Land Rush   106

  5 The Tribes Retreat   110

CONTENTS

PART FOUR: THE SCORE – IN BLACK AND WHITE

Black and White 119

1 The Wrong Side of the Line 121

2 The Dignity of Labour 129

3 'You are a Black Spot' 140

4 Wealth Accumulates, but Men Decay 151

PART FIVE: THE WORLD AS REFEREE

1 The League of Nations:
On the Geneva Carpet 169

2 The United Nations: Retreat from
the Twentieth Century 175

3 Points of Law 185

4 How the People Organized 196

5 Sharpeville and the Sixties 209

PART SIX: NEXT ROUND? 229

Appendixes

A What is Protection? 245

B Table of Land Ownership 247

C Table of White Settlement 248

D Foreign Investment in South West
Africa 249

E Education in South West Africa 253

References and Sources 255

Index 263

Maps

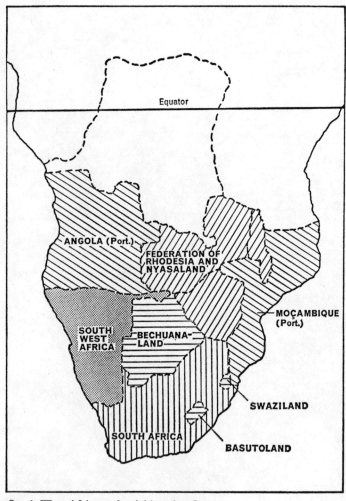

South West Africa and neighbouring States

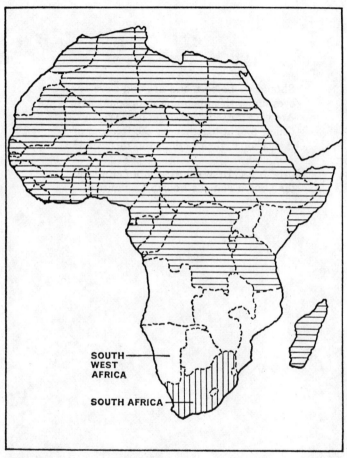

The independent States of Africa (dependent States unshaded)

Should we be born and live and close our eyes under this unending imprisonment? Are we a cursed generation because our Chiefs fought together for the freedom of their people, their nation, and their land?

CHIEF DAVID WITBOOI, in a Petition to the United Nations Fourth Committee

Introduction: The Bare Bones of Conflict

'What exactly do you think you're doing?' the Archivist in Windhoek demanded, calling me into his office. 'Collecting material for a book,' I said. He could stop me, he said aggressively. We argued the toss; he produced the Archives Act, and then compromised. I could work there, but he would decide what material I could not see. From the reports on the table he withdrew all those dating from the end of 1946.

That was the year South Africa rejected the United Nations Organization's request to put the mandate of South West Africa under international trusteeship; she has defied the world body ever since. South West Africa is South Africa's property: trespassers will be prosecuted.

The week before I left for South West Africa, the newspapers had announced that the borders were being manned to block any threatened United Nations invasion. (The Special Committee on South West Africa had asked for access to the territory so that it could examine conditions there for itself.) I was no invading force, only a journalist bent on collecting the facts and feeling of the South West African situation. But I knew that questions were not encouraged, interviews with U.N. petitioners were seen in official eyes as preparation for subversion, and I had a political record of close association with the Congress movement in South Africa. So it seemed prudent to anticipate police bans (to keep me out of the territory), and scrutiny (to frighten off interviewers), by taking as devious a route as possible.

The train crawled painfully over the barren, stony, drought-stricken south. In the coach were four men, travelling to the capital in order to give evidence in a murder trial: an assistant magistrate, sergeant, constable, and doctor, who whiled away the hours with bottles of brandy. The sergeant was talkative. He had been on duty in Ovamboland for six months in 1961, at the height of the Angola troubles. 'We raided the kraals with machine guns,' he volunteered, 'looking for agitators.'

The Angola-South West border cuts families, villages, the tribe, in two. Ovambos who have for generations crossed from one country to another continue to do so. But pass books and permits issued by one government or the other, not family ties and village origin, today determine a man's right to be in South West Africa or Angola. 'When we found an agitator in Ovamboland who was really from Angola,' said the sergeant, 'we gave him back to the Portuguese.' The Portuguese had their own ways of dealing with trouble-makers, he said: they were put into a plane and dropped into the sea. I must have wrinkled my nose in distaste. 'But they are not people,' he said firmly.

I had no way of checking the sergeant's story; it was his attitude that I found most revealing.

'They are different.' Africans are not like Whites. That is the heart of apartheid. If peoples are not the same, they cannot expect the same treatment.

Not that Simon Legree, whip in hand, struts the streets of Windhoek. Nor is apartheid everywhere visible as a ceaseless series of brute, sadistic acts. Its influence is more insidious.

Nationalist theoreticians and spokesmen have changed their ground. They no longer say openly that Africans belong to an inferior race and so cannot be allowed equality with Whites. The courtesy may sit uncomfortably on many Nationalist lips, but it is considered good political form nowadays to insist that 'Bantu' culture is such a precious – and different – thing that it must be given ample scope to flourish. The imperative need, therefore, is to demarcate separate areas, where Africans may develop along their own lines and live happily ever after.

But whether Africans must be made to 'develop' outside the White areas because they are inferior (the version accepted by the police sergeant), or just because they are different (the version for export abroad), the policy drives Africans and Whites apart. It drives Africans into the wilderness; creates not one South West Africa, but two, one privileged and the other deprived and both in never-ending conflict; and it dubs as treasonable any attempt to bring the two South West Africas together.

I had four clear days unhampered by political police scrutiny in which to attempt a meeting with the African South-West. Then suddenly the Special Branch (as the political police are called) woke up with a jerk. There was an outsider in town, talking to Africans, asking questions, taking notes, riding about in the conspicuous salmon-pink American car of the Herero Councillors, asking for government reports in the Archives.

The police state in operation is not noisy or dramatic, except in time of emergency; it can be relaxed, even slovenly. The detectives on duty that first week-end wore shorts and rugby socks, and childish smiles on their faces as, in the prowling police car, they outdistanced me, the footslogger, on the way to an appointment. In the beginning there were two, later four, and even five and six on duty, working in pairs, padding along the pavement six paces behind me, or on the opposite side of the road, sitting at the next table of the open-air coffee house. There was, this time, no midnight thump on the door. On the contrary, there was even an uncomfortable air worn by the more intelligent of the detectives, as it became obvious that talks to White town councillors and Herero Chiefs, businessmen and administration servants, with walks down main streets and to historical monuments, constituted a normal enough programme for a visiting journalist.

But the scrutiny never faltered: the trail to the dry-cleaner and the shoemaker, the skulking next to the telephone booth, both ends of the road and every exit of the hotel patrolled, detectives following me to the airport, to the post office to buy stamps, watching me at breakfast, interviewing people I had seen – 'What does she want from you?'

Most Whites were too polite to comment on the chase. They remained accessible, but were guarded and reticent.

Africans were bursting to talk. Bystanders in the street showed by smiles and winks that, if the Special Branch was on my heels, they were on my side.

The Chase soon achieved part of its object. Premises that had been initially available for interviews with Africans were withdrawn, regretfully but firmly; officials were tighter than clams (though that is official second-nature in this country); Africans came to interviews glancing over their shoulders at sudden uninvited attendants. 'I know I will be a fugitive when my words are published,' wrote one old man in a note smuggled into my hotel.

Interviews were conducted on street corners, in motor-cars, under a tree, in crowded shops; some had to be cancelled: for this is a community where passers-by look askance at any conversation between a White and an African. Where flimsy cords of communication between the colours are spun, intimidation severs them instantly.

Whites and Africans meet, of course, but as administrator and headman, constable and convict, master and servant. In the Windhoek of 1962 there are three White men who from time to time meet Africans on a basis of equality to talk over the territory's problems. There is not a single political organization in South West Africa to which both Whites and Africans belong; there has never been a forum in the country for both White and non-White speakers.

It is not that relations between the two South West Africas are strained; beyond the mere master-servant relationship they do not exist. Whites alone sit in the Legislative Assembly. Whites enjoy a monopoly of debating, voting, budgeting, administering, planning, and deciding. All policies in South West Africa are shaped by them, for their own benefit. When the policies come under fire, the Whites themselves feel assailed; their acute sensitivity to criticism is as characteristic of them as of their political parents in White South Africa.

'Give the Africans a share? But they are not fit, not ready for it,' is the answer.

And from the White man's viewpoint it may seem so. He sees

Africans as illiterate, uneducated, untrained, and from this he draws the conclusion not that African education has been neglected, but that the African cannot be educated.

When the White looks at the African on the land he sees a ragged shepherd, a farmer whose stock comprises no more than a few bony goats. And he sees this as proof positive that the African does not know the rudiments of farming, not as the result of landlessness, overcrowding, lack of capital, absence of all agricultural help. The Africans about him in the towns do the labouring work, have no skills and little training. What further proof is required that they are inferior?

The White sees Africans as an aimless, dispirited, disunited rabble, rent by feuds. He knows virtually nothing of their organizations, their political leaders. White supremacy fed by law and custom develops a swollen capacity for comfortable thinking, for seeing the facts of an unequal situation, but only one possible explanation. The African people and the African areas are backward. But progress costs money, and the South West White has spent almost all of it on himself.

Government race policies, like their results, are cruel and twisted, but not, curiously, all the people who benefit from them. They are bluff, hospitable, jovial – till you discuss politics, and that means the 'Native Question'.

It is incomprehensible that the African does not see what the South West White so easily can: that he is richer, better educated, just plain superior, and the best judge of what is good for the country, for the African; a far more competent judge than the African is himself of what he wants and how long he will have to wait for it. White South West Africa is blinkered by self-interest, and by *fear*.

There is fear that the Africans will 'swamp the Whites' (though no one has yet explained why a majority should not be expected to outnumber the minority).

There is fear that the African will turn the tables on the White, exact retribution, take revenge. Every day of White supremacy makes such a possibility greater, but there are very few able to see this.

Above all, there is the fear of the Whites who have no other place to go. South West Africa is their home. Afrikaners feel this especially. For if White South West Africa goes, will not White South Africa follow very soon? Even the German is better off: he could conceivably return to Europe.

So White South West Africa digs its trenches for survival, as its Algerian and Congolese counterparts did so many corpses ago.

What of the other South West Africa?

There are Africans walking about Windhoek's old location who recall the day when no White man could settle in the country without the permission of their Chief. Their lives span the four score years of White occupation: the German conquest, the betrayal of the mandate, the dead-end of discrimination today. They hold emphatic views as well: the work of the last eighty years must be undone, and a fresh start made.

African South West Africa has an undying distrust of everything that the South African government does and says. It conducts a silent and undeclared war of non-cooperation. Offers of money for development are rejected because the Africans fear that the money is conditional on their acceptance of apartheid. Africans refuse to move from the tin-can slum of Windhoek to the new Katutura township; the new housing is better, but it is apartheid housing.

This intransigence of the political organizations and the United Nations petitioners bewilders and irritates White men who profess sympathy for some African claims, if not all. The spirit of the African movement eludes them. It wants not crumbs or even slices of bread from the table of the government, but a hand on the knife that cuts the loaf. It cannot see in new townships or clinics any attempt by the authorities to change an inherently unjust system. It is distrustful of a government that seeks to ridicule and weaken and if possible destroy all African political organization.

African South West Africa refuses to believe the doctrine of its own inferiority, refuses to resign itself eternally to a lower order of society. Apartheid offers no recognition of this, no concessions, only an unwavering repression. Accordingly, African political attitudes have hardened in recent years to a rigid hatred of the South African government and the South West African administration. Battle has been joined, and one may not treat with the enemy.

African claims to independence are all the more emphatic because the South West tribes refuse to acknowledge the South African government as their conqueror. South Africa was given the country to administer as a mandate in trust; the trust has been betrayed; and as the mandate was bestowed on South Africa by the nations of the world, those nations must now come to the rescue of the wards. The patient faith in world justice still held by a people for so long dispossessed of their heritage is not without pathos; but it shows a firmer grip on the essentials of the South West African conflict than does the campaign of the Nationalist Party to represent the United Nations as a trespasser upon the sovereign rights of South Africa.

The terms of the mandate, the legal issues, have been buried in the noise of a campaign to represent the U.N. as assaulting the sovereignty of an independent state. There have at times been such concerted attacks on the U.N. that it seemed the government was softening up opinion for South Africa's withdrawal from the world body altogether. South Africa's delegates to the U.N. have abstained, for months on end, from committees and debates. But even an intransigent Afrikaner nationalism cannot risk complete isolation and, jerk by painful jerk, has been compelled to turn its face towards the world.

South West Africa is no longer the obsession of a lone, whimsical priest. In sixteen years it has grown to be a major international issue, more central to the survival of the world body than ever Michael Scott or the Hereros dreamed.

The simple basic facts have been endlessly repeated in the voluminous records of the World Court, the United Nations General Assembly, its Fourth Committee, Trusteeship Council, and Special Committees.

No amount of ingenious chicanery can obscure the simple basic facts about South West Africa, commented a London

Times editorial in September 1960, entitled ' Theft of a Mandate '.

It was a German possession fiendishly abused. It was placed under the mandate system of the League of Nations in order that its wretched tribesmen might be given a new deal in the light of decent world opinion. Instead of fulfilling this obligation of honour, the South African Government, quibbling barefacedly about the succession from the League of Nations, has swallowed South West Africa into its vile schemes of apartheid and has, adding insult to injury, taken advantage of its misdoings to strengthen its parliamentary majority. The Nationalist Party has helped itself to extra seats out of South West African voters. There is only one verdict possible in this sorry business. A mandate has been stolen and the thieves are vainly protesting their innocence.

The South West African case arouses passions not only because an international trust has been betrayed, but also because South Africa herself is the delinquent nation of the world, the rogue elephant among the countries pledged to the U.N. Charter's principles of brotherhood and equality, an embarrassment to her allied nations of the West.

It is bad enough that a mandate is withheld from international supervision and a dependent people blocked from development to independence under the tutelage of the world body. It is a thousand times worse that the country which has betrayed the trust should have become a by-word in the twentieth century for obscurantist racial philosophies and fierce discrimination against peoples on the grounds of their colour.

Apartheid has become anathema to countries widely different in their social systems but at one in their detestation of racialism. There are few issues which so fire international unity as this one does. South West Africa is a challenge to an age that recognizes the right of nations to independence and acknowledges the principle of international accountability for the problems of underdeveloped communities. It is the sole remaining territory still administered under the mandate system of the League of Nations, whose people are no nearer self-government and independence than they were more than forty years ago. The territory is a constant recrimination to the more advanced nations who delivered up the trust in the first place, and a crude affront to independent Africa and Asia, who see their special protégé held captive by a government and political system that they detest.

South West Africa is a test case of U.N. efficiency. Principles have been proclaimed, but action persistently deferred. The resolutions have been strong enough, but Dr Verwoerd, a past master in the use of words, is not afraid of them. South Africa has used evasion, procrastination, boycotts, and sulks; now open defiance, now niggardly negotiation; but after sixteen years her stubborn refusal to budge before near-unanimous United Nations decisions presents a challenge to the whole authority of the world organization.

Two attempts have been made by the U.N. to tackle the issue, not from behind the debating tables of the glass-fronted building in New York, but in Africa itself. Both sharpened the crisis for the world body, committed in principle to action but paralysed by its internal conflict.

The first attempt took place in 1960, when the U.N. South West Africa Committee announced that it would enter the territory in accordance with the General Assembly resolution that it should investigate conditions on the spot. South Africa's Minister of External Affairs, Mr Eric Louw, threatened the Committee with arrest if it crossed the border, and then Britain refused the Committee access to Bechuanaland (where petitioners were waiting to be heard) unless it undertook not to try and enter the mandated territory from British soil. From Salisbury the Committee had to fly north and homewards, instead of advancing south.

As a member of the U.N., Britain was bound by the 1960 vote; she undermined it when power considerations in Africa and her links with the South African government triumphed over her allegiance to U.N. decisions.

Verwoerd's apparent arrogance is inspired by his belief that the bi-partisan diplomacy of the big powers will reduce the world body to ineffectiveness. The 1961 U.N. resolution on South West Africa was the strongest ever passed; again the world body pressed for its Committee to be allowed access into the trust territory. This time Dr Verwoerd made a slight tactical retreat and permitted two members of the Special South West African Committee to tour for ten days under the aegis of his officials, on condition that they first reported their findings to him, and that the inspection by the two men would not be regarded in any way as an admission of U.N. authority over the territory. It was a climb-down by South Africa: a few months earlier she had refused even to answer questions about South West Africa. But it was clearly a calculated one, designed to gain time and win influential friends. The Nationalists admitted this. Their cause would lose nothing by letting representatives of the hated world body into South West Africa, they consoled their followers, because Britain, France, and the United States would stand by South Africa in New York and prevent any really effective action from being taken against her. With powerful friends at court, Dr Verwoerd was prepared to try the role of the big-hearted negotiator.

For all the simulated cockiness of the Nationalists, they know that South Africa must do something to stem the surge of international hostility that threatens to engulf her. Her mishandling of the mandate is her Achilles heel, and she knows it. That is South Africa's dilemma: White supremacy can survive only through the practice of apartheid, but it is the imposition of apartheid on South West Africa which must sooner or later force South Africa's grip from the territory. . . . And a crack in Nationalist control over South West Africa would inevitably spread across the border into the Republic itself.

If the South West African issue expresses the essential dilemma of the apartheid state, it also touches the exposed nerves of the U.N.

How many years can the U.N. survive the routine of vigorous denunciation and resolutions every autumn, followed by eleven months of inertia and undercover manipulation to nullify the resolve?

Can the world body act to rescue the mandate from apartheid? Can international intervention, with the weight of moral, even legal argument behind it, be evoked in an area where actual fighting and bloodshed are not taking place?

What of the reluctance of powers with interests in Africa to allow U.N. intervention in South West Africa, for fear that this should set a precedent for action to end colonialism in the rest of settler-dominated East, Central, and Southern Africa?

Dr Verwoerd hints that he is always prepared to negotiate on 'reasonable' terms. A negotiated agreement on the mandate would avoid the terrible consequences of conflict. But is there room for negotiation with South Africa? Can a government dedicated to perpetual White supremacy change its ways, move far enough under international pressure? Or is it ten years, forty years, too late? The answer is the record of South Africa in the mandated territory of South West Africa itself.

*

This story of South West Africa goes up to the end of 1962, and so must leave unfinished the chronicle of the legal case at The Hague, the latest chapter of events at the United Nations, and the outcome of the Commission appointed by Dr Verwoerd, South Africa's Prime Minister, to recommend a five-year plan for the accelerated development of the African people – this latter step a belated response to United Nations pressure and the need of the South African government to repulse criticism. The story is unfinished, but the early patterns described here are fixing later ones.

The factual material draws heavily on available government reports. Some figures, especially of budget expenditure, put the best possible complexion on the government record, for they quote estimates, not actual expenditure, for the most recent years. Many of the statistics are incomplete and so tell only part of the story; some are contradictory, because the government version often is. Much of the published material on South West Africa is cracked with age, or distorted, not least by the total omission of the African side of the story. Even the history of the territory is still a matter of contemporary political controversy.

If this book strains after any version, it is that of the African people of the territory, told to me in person.

A brief note on terminology is needed. I have used the word *African* as the general term for the tribes (singled out as Ovambo, or Herero, where these are specifically dealt with). But where government sources are quoted directly, I have kept to the official usage of *Native* or *Bantu* for the sake of accuracy of the quotation. I have used *Nama* not *Hottentot* because the Nama people dislike that term. I have rejected *Bastard* for *Rehobother* for the same reason. *Whites* has been used instead of *Europeans*, the more popular South African usage. Where Africans, Nama, Rehobothers, and Coloureds (of mixed descent) are grouped together, the term used is *non-White*. It's all very confusing, but colour discrimination tends to be!

Many South West Africans and South Africans, and others, have helped: Jariretundu Kozonguizi, Zedekia Ngavirue, Toivo Ja Toivo, Mburumba Kerina wrote from afar from their present homes in London, Sweden, Ondongua in Ovamboland, and New York respectively. In Windhoek my visit would have failed without the help of Werner Mamugwe, Chief Hosea Kutako, Clement Kapuuo, and others too numerous to mention. Winifred Courtney in the United States made available to me notes and records of the United Nations sessions. M.R. helped with the German material. Julius Lewin's encouragement spurred this book on as did Ronald Segal's from London. 'Rusty' Bernstein read the first draft and suggested improvements. My thanks to Mary Benson, who read the proofs. The book's shortcomings are all mine, of course.

Part One: The Antagonists

Masters and Servants

Two-thirds the size of South Africa or larger than France and Great Britain put together, South West Africa is a great slab of territory fringed by desert and occupied by just over half a million people. It is the sparsest populated country south of the Sahara.

This was the only mandate entrusted to an adjacent power The coastlines of the two countries are extensions of one another; the land boundaries are barely distinguishable. And South Africa has treated the country as a projection of herself. Here Afrikaner farmers and their sons have found *Lebensraum*, side by side with the German settlers of an earlier conquest.

One in seven of South West Africans is White, but the Whites have the exclusive use of twice as much land as the Africans. Six thousand White farmers, cattle ranchers in the north and sheep raisers in the more arid south, own sprawling farms each the size of two English counties.

Africans, when they are not labourers in White-owned enterprises, live in closed Reserves, or in the territories outside the Police Zone, that administrative area established in German times and preserved by the South African government for White occupation.

The world knows much more about the issues and legal arguments that rage round South West Africa than it does about the people who live in the land. They are Herero, Nama, Berg-Damara, Ovambo, Rehobother, Bushmen: and Coloured, the non-Whites, the subjects, the servants. And they are South African (English- and Afrikaans-speaking) and German: the Whites, the rulers, the masters.

25

1. The Servants

The Herero

The Herero were cast for the leading role in the South West Africa drama, and they have played it superbly. A measure of their success is the resentment, swollen sometimes to hatred and anger, and yet underlaid with grudging admiration, that they have earned from successive administrations and their touchy White rulers.

'Do you have Herero labour too?' I asked the American manager of the Tsumeb mine. 'Hereros! working in a mine!' he snorted. 'Hereros won't work in a mine, they think they own South West!'

They certainly walk the streets as though they own them, but for a people so imposingly tall and stately this is not difficult. Long-limbed, erect, with oval faces, high foreheads, aquiline noses, they must be among the most handsome peoples in Africa: composed, elegant, and proud, if also somewhat aloof. Their women dominate their surroundings in Victorian dress of carefully studied fashion detail: sweeping, ankle-length skirts, with many underskirts, short bodiced waistcoat, mutton-chop sleeves, long strings of necklaces, braid, pearly buttons, and draped shawls, all a faithful replica of the dress worn by the wives of the Rhenish missionaries in the nineteenth century; on their heads high padded turbans replace the three-pronged leather tribal head-dress of earlier days.

According to their traditions, the Herero people once lived in 'the land of the fountains' to the west of Lake Tanganyika. A branch of the great Bantu-speaking group, they took part in the migration southwards from Central Africa, but then branched off westwards themselves, driving their herds into what is now South West Africa, in the mid sixteenth century. Some settled in the Kaokaoveld (where the Ovahimba and the Obatjimba still live), others continued south.

Misnamed the Damara by a confusion of the Nama word for them, they are skilled and devoted cattle farmers; their cattle wealth was the talk of all who saw their herds in the nineteenth century. Land was the property of the whole nation, and whilst no boundaries set the limit to individual grazing grounds, every head of cattle had its owner.

For the sake of their cattle [wrote a former administrator, Gorges, in a report to the British government] no labour was too great. For long hours beneath a scorching sun the Herero would draw water bucket by bucket from the water holes or wells for his animals to drink. They dug their water holes at the cost of infinite labour, the sharp horn of the gemsbok being the substitute for a pick and a gourd serving for a bucket. For days and weeks he would persevere despite terrible hardship and privation in search of one lost or strayed animal. His whole object in life was the increase and preservation of his herds which, in the favourable climate and environment of Damaraland, thrive wonderfully.

After the Herero-German war of 1904, these people were prohibited by government ordinance from owning stock, but the great drama of their history lies not only in their long success-ful struggle to remain cattle-raisers, but in their very survival as a people. Their rebellion against German rule precipitated four years of bitter warfare, from which the Herero emerged shattered. Germany's reprisals against subjects who had dared challenge her were savage: if ever there was a case of genocide this was it, for the 80,000 strong Herero tribe was reduced to a mere wander-ing 15,000, and only very slowly over the years (at times, during the early days of the mandate, the death-rate overtook the birth-rate) has the Herero population risen to 40,000.

This resilience is one of the strengths of the Herero. Dr Gunter Wagner, who studied the economic aspects of Herero life for the South West African Native Affairs Department, commented on the 'undiminished ability of the Herero to recuperate from setbacks'. Contrary to the inherent conservatism of most pastoral people, he discovered, the Herero practised a cattle economy 'well advanced on the road to adapting itself to present-day requirements.' The keeping of large numbers of unnecessary stock was no longer based on religious notions. Dr Wagner found that cattle were used to produce other forms of wealth; and despite the scepticism of officials, the Herero had shown a striking initiative and talent in organizing a dairy industry. In areas where the rainfall was better, the Herero, always considered an exclusively cattle-breeding people, had even taken to plough cultivation.

South West Africa is predominantly stock-raising country, and there is no doubt that, given proper facilities, the Herero could be as successful – and perhaps better – at cattle farming as any others.

A portion of the tribe – two-thirds as many as live in South West Africa – endure exile in Bechuanaland, the descendants of the remnants who survived the desert flight at the end of the Herero-German war. One community is in Bamangwato country, where Chief Samuel Maharero was given refuge and his son Frederick lived after him. Another colony, with flourishing herds, live around Sehitwa near Lake Ngami, among the Batawana. In 1947 there was a move among the Bechuanaland Hereros to return to the land of their forefathers, and a formal request was made, through the British government. But South Africa replied that there was no land for them.

The South West Administration seems to think that it has enough trouble with 40,000 Herero on its hands, for though a minor tribe in the territory, their sense of grievance and history, their disciplined, vocal, and dignified advocacy of their cause, has been a rallying-point for all the others.

The presiding genius of their cause is the venerable Chief Hosea Kutako, in whose ninety years are compressed all the main phases in the history of his people: their prosperity as

29

independent cattle farmers; their costly war with the German Army; their slow recovery from defeat and near destruction; and their tenacious efforts to have nine decades of wrong righted with the help of the U.N.

Stockier than most Herero, vigorous of voice, with only the wrinkled skin around his eyes bearing witness to his ninety years, Chief Kutako seems as immovable as a mountain. More than anything else, his unwavering leadership has made the Herero what they are today. He has been herdsman, a member of Samuel Maharero's inner circle, major in the Herero army – he was wounded in the cheek at the battle of Hamakari – prisoner-of-war, fugitive, school-teacher, foreman of a railway gang, bookbinder, and, finally, recognized head of the Herero. Though officialdom makes great play of the so-called divisions and rivalries among the different tribes in South West Africa, it is significant that the Administration asked Kutako, the Herero head, to visit Ovamboland and persuade Ovambos to enlist in the South African forces during the Second World War.

Gradually the old statesman is ceding his leadership of the tribe to Clement Kapuuo, the personable young teacher whom the tribal councillors cluster about in close conclave, for pronouncements must be those of the tribe, not of the individual, however royal of blood and prominent in the tribal hierarchy he may be.

Herero tribal cohesion was shattered by the 1904 war, and, though it has risen again, government policy is designed to undermine it. When Frederick Maherero was alive, the government refused to let him return from exile to lead his people. Only when he was dying, and asked for a permit to enter South West as he wished to be buried at Okahandja, did the government relent, granting him his request on condition that he assumed no political leadership. Two weeks later he was dead.

The tribe is dispersed over eleven different Reserves – the government once explained that 'by placing groups of them in a number of districts, there was a great opportunity for many more of them to work outside the Reserves' – and no tribesman may move from one Reserve to the other without a permit. No official recognition is given to any tribal leader higher in status than a headman. Of late the Nationalists have manoeuvred through their system of Bantu Authorities (government-approved tribal councils) to spread dissension among the Herero and encourage a major tribal split. Singularly, the Administration permitted Chief Munjuku II, the head of the Mbanderu – many of whom dispute the office of Herero Paramount Chief – to return to South West Africa from Bechuanaland, and officially installed him with all picturesque ceremony, to the deep distrust of the Herero tribal heads. Munjuku II's public statements have been contradictory, and his followers are said to be divided, with one section seemingly more intent on contesting Hosea Kutako's claims to leadership than on preserving the vital political unity of the tribe. Yet, for all the acrimony that the tribal dispute has engendered, Munjuku II staggered hopeful government circles when he, too, arrived to meet the Carpio two-man U.N. Commission in May 1962 with a demand for full independence at once. The Herero may have their internal tribal differences, but their political aims are one.

Each year in August the Herero take out their threadbare, military uniforms and stage a ceremonial parade before the graves of their Chiefs at Okahandja. They cling to their role as history-makers, but do not brood on the past. 'How do you feel about the Germans in South West Africa?' I asked Clement Kapuuo. 'Is there still much bitterness?' He replied: 'The Herero-German war was not the first we fought. We were accustomed to war and have taken defeat. But we do hold something against the Germans – today they support the Nationalist Party!'

The Nama

The Nama clans (called by the Whites Hottentots, a description they dislike) were once the sworn enemies of the Herero, and the two peoples swept down on one another's lands and herds, jostling for position in the central region of the country. Today their Chiefs jointly sign petitions to the U.N. When Chief Hendrik Samuel Witbooi comes to Windhoek, he and Chief

Hosea Kutako are closeted together in consultation, and both old men sit on the Chiefs' Council, which is one of the instruments by which petitioners at the U.N. have kept in touch with their people back home.

The historian and the politician of White South West Africa make much of the Herero-Nama wars to illustrate their contention that the two peoples, mortal enemies for so long, can never live together in peace; that once the safeguard of White rule is removed, the country will again be plunged into inter-tribal war. Chief Witbooi conceded: 'The Herero people and we fought many battles against one another. ... But,' he added, 'since then we have declared that we have become brothers; that is, we have now made peace. Since then, and up to today, we live as brothers.'

That is one result of German and South African rule over South West Africa: old enemies on the tribal battlefield have become allies in the fight for political rights.

The Nama clans are generally grouped into two sections: those who settled in the country after their migration southwards, long before the arrival of the other tribes; and the Orlams peoples, who passed through the country on their way into South Africa, lived south of the Orange River for a while, and then returned, before the pressure of White settlement, speaking Cape Dutch and using horses and rifles, in the eighteenth and nineteenth centuries. The old clans were the Bondelswarts in the Warmbad area; the Fransman Namas of Gochas; the Red Nation of Hoachanas; the Veldschoendragers, the Topnaars of the North.

The Orlams (from a Malay word meaning 'foreigner') included the Witboois, the peoples who settled at Gobabis, Berseba, and Bethanie; and the Afrikanders, marauding for cattle and land under the leading Orlams Chief Jager Afrikaner and later his son Jonker Afrikaner, who commanded a formidable war organization and who half-way through the nineteenth century was ruling from Windhoek. It is on the site of his capital that the fine houses of the town are now built.

Most impressive Nama leader was the famed Hendrik Witbooi,

guerilla leader, evangelist, statesman, and accomplished diarist, who from his headquarters at Gibeon foresaw the pattern of White occupation and, having united the Nama people behind him, died in struggle against it.

His grandson lives at Gibeon today, the rallying-point still of all the clans, though the rifle and guerilla war have been replaced by the fountain pen and the petition.

Nama unity goes back to the agreement, known as 'The League of Nations', signed by all the Chiefs in 1858, when they pledged themselves not to allow mining in their territory without the knowledge and concurrence of all; not to sell their land to any Whites from the Cape Colony; not to send a commando against the Herero without 'legitimate cause'; and to consult one another once a year.

By tradition each Nama clan had a ruling family from which the Chief's line came, but the Chief himself was elected, and his authority was limited, for he undertook little without the consent of his council and the approval of the tribal gathering. Chiefs today are little better than foremen, the Namas say.

In the days when the Namas had the south to themselves, they were prosperous, with large herds of cattle: their wars with the Germans reduced them to a savage poverty.

The drought which ravaged South West in 1931–2 prostrated a people already on its knees. The stock census of 1930 in the Bondelswarts Reserve counted 2,300 head; in 1934, after the drought, the number had been reduced to seventy-three. One Chief was left with a single goat; most of his people had nothing at all.

Today the Nama Reserves are ludicrously small islands in the stretch of White-owned sheep farms. Their problems are those of an unrelieved poverty, of scraps of land which are far too small and water-starved to be farming areas, and so remain sad and neglected rural slums.

An American Methodist Episcopal Minister who supervises his church schools and knows the Reserves of the south well, said:

The people are sick, tired, cross. The land is too small, yet pieces have been cut away over the years to make White farms. Some people own three goats, that is all in the world. Sometimes they eat mealie meal porridge once a day. School feeding for the children was stopped. The houses are of clay and tin. The men must get passes to go to work, and then they work for two or three weeks at a time and earn a few pounds. The only future before the men is to become shepherds. The people have to pay grazing fees, and the money goes into reserve funds for improvements; but often the people on the land are too poor to pay the fees and must write to their sons who have gone away to the towns to ask them for money.

The people want to help themselves. How can they, if there is no money, no water? The people are crying for water. I know a man who wanted to dig a well. He had to get permission from Windhoek. Help? They get not a shilling from anyone. Chief Witbooi was told that if he accepted the government controlled Bantu Authorities, he would get help from the government. This is blackmail. The people want a new government. They are no longer afraid, as they once were.

The Nama petition to the U.N. has a tragic lilt to it.

On the 'White man's claws of oppression', a petition said:

It is extraordinary that a race such as the Whites in South West Africa, professing education and superiority, living in a land where ringing bells call child and parent to the Church of God, a land where Bibles are read, and Gospel truths are spoken and where courts of justice are presumed to exist ... can make war upon us the poor defenceless blacks. ...

The Nama have a wistful and saddened look: perhaps their slight stature, pale apricot-yellow faded skins, and quiet movements give this impression. Those in the towns seem to show in their faces that they are regarded as enemies; their 'place' is in the shrunken Reserves of the south, or in the kitchen or shearing shed, out of sight and hearing.

The Berg-Damara

The Berg-Damara (also known as the Damaras or the Bergdamas) are a people of mysterious origin, difficult to classify. Some say that they vie with the Bushmen for first claim to the country. Missionary records report that they have lived over wide areas, lack a central tribal organization, and over long periods have been taken into servitude by, and shared the

34

territories of the Namas, the Herero, and others. Seligman, in his *Races of Africa*, says that the Berg-Damara are a group of true Negroes long isolated from others of their stock. They speak Nama but also use expressions which are not Nama and which, one theory goes, are derived from languages in the Sudan. Their ceremonies show both Nama and Bantu influences. They are skilful copper and iron smelters, and this art they are said to have learned from the Ovambo. One exotic theory maintains that the Nama are descendants of the ancient Phoenicians and the Berg-Damara, that they inherited from the latter their language and from the former their colour.

The important South West Africa Government Commission of 1936 on the future of the territory contains exactly 135 words on these 30,000 people.

For many generations they have lived mainly by serving others, and they are doing that now, under probably more favourable circumstances than they have ever enjoyed before. They made no complaints to us except that their wages were inadequate. . . .

One gets the impression of a blank in history, of a still, voiceless people, from the records.

Not so from Fritz Gariseb, Windhoek spokesman of the Berg-Damara, who set down his story for me.

I am an old man, born on Aukeigas during the days of the great rinderpest, long before the White man. During this time we were living as a free people and we lived wherever we pleased. Our flocks, and we had many livestock, used to graze everywhere. I was, to cut a long story short, a free man. The first time I ever came face to face with a European was during the German occupation, in the town today known as Windhoek. At this stage we also made our first acquaintance with prisons, and other White customs like the public mass executions. Passes took the form of metal number plates, of which every town had its own. Ever since the administration was handed over to the South African government, we have had no say in our fatherland. We are the true owners of this land, but we have no freedom of speech (you saw this yourself when you tried to speak to Africans); there is no way of expressing our grievances and complaints. Our lives are controlled by passes. These are the chains of our lives, the chains that strangle us. And besides, we have to pay taxes, though we have no say at all in government. All the money from White taxes as far as I can see is used in building for the Whites – the new rugby stadium, the air terminal buildings, the new state hospital for Whites, the new English medium school for Whites, the new Hardap dam at Mariental for the benefit mostly of the White farmers there.

The only way that the non-White is helped is by the building of such apartheid schemes as Katutura location and the new Coloured township. On the White farms the worker may own five or six cattle, and if there is one who has more than that number, he must sell the rest to the farm owner, at the price fixed by the farmer. Male calves are taken by the farmer because, he says, they eat his grass and drink his water. So the farm labourer loses even the little he has. And if he objects he is immediately told to leave the farm.

And so the grievances went on and on.

There is a struggle for leadership of the Berg-Damara people between the government-recognized headman David Goraseb and men like Fritz Gariseb, U.N. petitioner, who recounts with scorn how David Goraseb, asked by his people to travel to Windhoek to help them get better schooling facilities, tele-graphed: 'Bantu Affairs Commissioner will reply your Tele-gram.' His angry subjects retorted: 'This is the way our Chief represents our people. Whose purpose does he serve?'

Leading Berg-Damara contested the appointment of David Goraseb. Would he in fact be *their* Chief? they queried. They were told that a portion of the Chief belonged to them, and the other portion to the Administration. They replied, said Fritz Gariseb, that they could not have a Chief serving both the people and the government.

The main Berg-Damara Reserve is Okombahe, to which they were moved in stages from their former land at Aukeigas; but they also live in Otjimbingue, side by side with the Herero. In Okombahe the Berg-Damara were promised a Canaan. 'But what have you today?' they ask. 'A "paradise" of rattling skeletons and hunger ghosts.'

The Berg-Damara people have for decades been caught between the advance of White occupation and stronger tribes like the Herero and Nama, and they have been pressed into servitude by all. Their last influential chief, Cornelius Goraseb, was granted German protection from the Herero, and the Okombahe Reserve, in return for an annual levy of labourers to the German government. When the Herero-German war broke out, he refused to fight with either army. He died in 1910, prophesying 'I know that when I am no more, my people will be scattered like chaff in the wind.' There is a barely a place in South West Africa where Berg-Damaras are not working as labourers.

Vedder (*The Native Tribes of South West Africa*) prints a literal translation of a song by a Berg-Damara whose hunting-grounds had passed into the possession of a farmer at the beginning of the century:

> My hunting grounds have become even like
> unto a waterless land, since he who has
> settled here deals with me in such imperious
> manner.
> Know ye not, ye women, of a land to which
> we may go?
> A waterless land is this where I am driven
> way from the water!
> Know ye not, ye women, of a fount to which
> we may wander?
> I shudder at the hard word for I hear it again
> and again.
> Ye say: 'None we have seen!'
> 'Tis well, I shall go forth and search.

The Ovambo

Without Ovambo labour, few wheels would turn in South West Africa. Ovamboland and the Okavango between them make up only one-twentieth of the territory's total land area but carry half the population, and supply most of the muscle and brawn. The 1960 population estimate for South West Africa was 73,000 White and 477,000 Africans. Of the Africans almost a half were from Ovamboland alone.

A population density map of South West Africa symbolizes the White minority's nightmare: great spreading blobs of black

37

humanity pressing heavily down from the northern territories, held off by laws which decree that no Ovambo may step out of the northern areas except when possessed of a work contract for a stipulated period. Ovambo women are rarely seen outside Ovamboland, apart from the very few who have been allowed, in recent years, to visit their husbands working on the mines or in large labour centres, where the men live a twelve- to eighteen-month-long bachelor existence in closed compounds.

Ovamboland is shut fast to the outside world. An Opposition member in the South West Africa Legislative Assembly told me: 'Ovamboland is a closed book. We don't know what happens there.' No one knows, except for senior government officials in Pretoria and the people themselves, sealed off by rigorous control of their borders. For, while no Ovambo may enter the Police Zone except under the aegis of the labour-recruiting organization, Ovamboland itself is forbidden territory to all non-Ovambos, and especially all Whites. Only the handful of government officials stationed there, and the missionaries who have done the only education and health work in the entire area, constitute a White presence.

The Ovambo fall into seven tribes: the Ondanga, the Ukualuthi, the Ongandjera, the Ukuanyama, the Ukuambi, the Ombalantu, and the Ukolonkathi and Eunda, grouped together.

Said to be amongst the oldest settled people in Southern Africa, the Ovambo were part of the great migration southwards from the lake districts of Central Africa. Being an agricultural people, they settled on the lands watered by annual floods, while the Herero migrated further, herding their cattle before them in the search for new pastures.

The Ovambo live on the flat, grassy stoneless plains intersected by 'oshanas', broad dry water courses that are a feature of the region. In the rainy season, the floods rush down to submerge great stretches of the land; in the dry season, the country has a parched and sterile look, with grazing and stock deteriorating fast under the urgent sun. A type of millet is grown on raised mounds of soil between the oshanas.

The agriculture of these people who crowd the northern

areas is barely a subsistence one, and there is periodic famine. When there was no boundary with Angola to the north, no Police Zone barrier in the south, and no rigorous restrictions on movement beyond the Reserves, the people would migrate to better rainfall areas in time of drought. Now there are no new lands. Now when there is famine, grain supplies alone can secure survival. In the early days of the South African Administration, when the tribes were still heavily armed, the Native Commissioner collected guns in exchange for grain, at times of famine. Now the government sells relief grain for the savings of migrant labour.

Explorer Galton's early encounter with the Ovambo found them plump and well-fed, men of polished demeanour, quiet, sociable, and with a cool and fearless bearing. The maze-like Ovambo kraal that fascinated him is still built today, behind palisades; and the home of a Chief spreads to innumerable compartments: entrance, space for religious ceremonies, zig-zag path to main living quarters, butter room, grain basket, goat kraal, smith, the beer pantry, and the rack for cattle-horns.

After their experiences with the Herero and the Nama peoples, the Germans were nervous of clashing with the well-armed Ovambo tribes, and in 1906 – though individual Ovambo were still permitted to travel south for work in the mines – the German government by proclamation forbade entry to Ovambo-land except by special sanction of the Governor.

The first official incursion into the northern areas was that of the South African army in 1915. The mission of the Commanding Officer was clear: 'to notify the Chiefs of South African occupation of South West Africa, and *to invite them to cooperate in encouraging their people to come out for employment on the railways and elsewhere*'. The Commanding Officer's first cable back to Windhoek, dated 28 August 1915, read: 'Received cordial welcome from Chief Martin of Ondonga District ... have received assurance his cooperation with regard native labour which anticipate will meet all requirements.' The story of Ovambo-land's place in South West Africa proceeds from this point.

Ovambo men keep the two multi-million-dollar mining corporation towns of Tsumeb and Oranjemund going; they can the pilchards at Walvis Bay; shepherd the precious karakul on the farms in the south; work on the railways; service the municipalities, dig the roads, work on building and construction projects, and keep the white housewife happily free from chores.

The picture that shines brightest in official eyes is the one of Ovamboland as an untroubled tribal back-water, home of the 'natural savage' in all his quaintly primitive charm. This is illustrated by the touching story of the Native Commissioner in the northern areas who had to organize a parade for a Royal Visitor and, in order to present the state of nature unspoilt, had all Christians pushed to the back of the crowd for the Royal viewing!

Herero, Nama, Reheboth, and Berg-Damara petitions to th e U.N. are discounted by government spokesmen as the work of 'agitators'. If proof were needed of non-White contentment, officials cry, the Ovambos, who constitute the clearly major tribe, supply it. Yet, if you scour the records of the U.N., you will find traces of another viewpoint. In 1956 the Tribal Congress of the People of Ukuanyama – in a letter mailed, of all places, from Angola – petitioned, curiously, that South West Africa be placed under the trusteeship of Canada. The U.N. reply to the petition was burnt by the Commissioner, the Tribal Congress complained in the following year.

A petition signed by eighty Ovambo said: 'We are supposed to be satisfied because we have not lost our land.' It then went on to demarcate that portion of Ovamboland which had been lost to the tribes ... including the Tsumeb mine which 'belonged to Ovamboland, for it was worked by the Ondanga before the White people came.'

Apart from one or two clashes with White government, Ovambo tribal society was not warred against or conquered. Without prior experience of it, the Ovambo and associated Okavango tribes approached White rule, on the whole, with tolerance and trust. The effects of labour migration, of taxation, of government interference in tribal rule (through pressure on the Chiefs and headmen), and of contacts with the wider world are only now beginning to be seen.

Nowadays White South West Africans remember with apprehension that the Ovambo people live on both sides of the border with rebellion-torn Angola. From the first signs of trouble in Angola in 1961, South West African police did patrol duty in the villages along the border, searching for arms and ammunition and political organizers. They even erected a fence as a stronger barrier than boundary markers to cut South West Africa off from Angola's province of Lower Cubango. So now Ovambo villagers on the Angola side climb over the fence to visit, or be recruited for work, or worship in church on Sundays, for many of the people in the border area are Anglicans, and the Anglican Church is not recognized in Angola.

Ovamboland seems, on the surface, to be placid enough. But who can tell what stirs below, apart from the Ovambo themselves? Angola displayed a flat silence until the sudden rebellion. All may be said to be well in Ovamboland, till the surface breaks.

The Rehobothers

Just south of Windhoek in a strange Cinderella 'republic' (a republic by obstinate inclination, if not status) live the Rehobothers. Speaking a patois Afrikaans, they call themselves the Basters – meaning, strictly, 'Bastards', but more accurately and less offensively, 'those of mixed origin' – for they want to flaunt not forget their origins. The old names Campbell, MacNab, van Wyk, Diergaardt, Bezuidenhout, and Beukes run like blue veins through the Rehoboth families. By the rules of South Africa's human studbook these people, closely related by blood and marriage to the ruling Afrikaners, are yet rejected by them. And how the Rehobothers hate and resent the relatives who have become their masters!

Ask them what they think of government policy, of the laws on immorality and mixed marriages, of race classification, and the spokesman could be Hermanus Beukes, tall, gaunt, with burning eyes under a wide hat, looking like one of Steinbeck's dust-bowl characters. As he talks, the words flare like tongues of flame.

What is left of the former independence of the Raad [Council] of the Rehoboth Gebiet [Territory]? Independence? Yes, we are independent, as far as the government leaves us alone, gives us nothing. That is our independence! [He pauses, and then adds] It has got to this point. The schooled [educated] Rehobother is today in less of a position to rule himself than were our people in the last century.

Their 'independence' is their constant cry. Sovereignty, they call it, and the arguments have not flagged over forty-five years, have leapt countless hurdles of constitutional interpretation, the close legal scrutiny of treaties, like high-spirited horses before the branding iron.

The Rehobothers do not care what the special South African Government Commission found in 1926: they repeat what their grandfathers intended when they negotiated for their land in 1870, when they signed their treaty with the Germans, what their fathers were told by General Botha in the First World War. If arguments demolish their legal claims, they furiously fall back on their moral ones; and if the moral ones do not move the authorities – as they obviously will not – they retreat into a stubborn self-devouring resentment that flares at times into boycott.

Show them the South West Africa Affairs Amendment Act, the whole South African statute book, and they will wave it aside and refer you instead to their own Ancestral Law, the *Vaderlike Wette*, almost a century old. Fifty-seven miles away in the Windhoek Archives is a copy ink-written by several different hands on fifteen sheets of faded blue notepaper, a simple archaic set of common-sense rules for dealing with thieves, murderers, and errant spouses. It may not measure up to the sophisticated code of more complex societies today; but, the Rehobothers will tell you, again with that fervent gleam in their eyes, it gave them quite as much 'justice' as they get today.

The 'Baster' communities first made their appearance in the

second half of the eighteenth century. Afrikaner trekkers, farming on the frontier, had married Nama women, and their communities – '5,000 souls with 700 muskets' – spread along the Orange River boundaries of the Cape for close on 600 miles. In 1865 the Land Beacons Act of the Cape government required occupiers to prove their title to land. The half-caste communities found themselves displaced by the pressure of White farmers higher in the social scale, and forced all at once to pioneer further fresh lands.

To the 1870 meeting at Okahandja, where an uneasy peace was being concluded between Herero and Nama, came a deputation of Basters under Hermanus van Wyk. An approach had already been made to Chief Swartbooi, head of the Nama tribe last in possession of the Rehoboth territory, and Swartbooi had permitted the Basters to settle there, for as long as his own people did not need the land, at a rent of one horse a year. The 1870 meeting approved the arrangement (though the counter claims to the land were complex, and more than one horse was given to more than one Chief), and by the following year the Rehobothers – eighty to ninety families, and 800 souls in all – were in occupation.

Like the Herero, the Rehobothers gave Palgrave, the British Special Commissioner, preparing for the annexation of the territory by Britain, a mandate for British Protection; but when the German government took over the country instead, they seem to have had no qualms about concluding a treaty with it. The seven-clause agreement, as negotiated between two governments, offered German protection to a sovereign Rehoboth community, while pledging the community not to dispose of any land or make any other treaties without asking the German government. The Rehobothers were specifically granted exclusive jurisdiction in civil and criminal cases.

The German government could have had little cause for complaint about Rehoboth loyalty, for the community supplied fighting men for the German wars against errant tribes, and crack shots they were reputed to be.

When the Herero were driven by despair to battle, Maherero

43

wrote for help to his former enemy, Hendrik Witbooi; but the Rehoboth captain into whose hands the letter was given passed it on, instead, to the German Governor.

The Rehobothers abandoned their loyalty to the German government only with the outbreak of the First World War and the invasion of South West Africa by Union troops. As they reminded the Germans, they might fight wars against African tribes, but they would not be conscripted where both battle lines were White!

The Rehoboth episode in the war, the encounter with South African troops and their general, the switching of sides, all played an important part in the South West Africa of the 1920s, as they still do, for the Rehobothers cling tightly to their treaties, and fight today the battle of the broken promises as vigorously as they fought it then.

They concentrate on what are, to them, the essential facts. They had independence once under the Germans, and the point had not yet arrived – by the time that the German occupation was cut short – when the German government had tried to alienate it. They had broken their treaty with Germany and had risen to fight; they were, they regard themselves, part of the conquering forces that expelled Germany from her former colony. Victors should gain and should at least not lose by their victory. Yet Rehoboth independence of today is a mere shadow of its former substance. The ancestral law has become a curiosity for historians; the old Council is still called a Council, but a magistrate, a White government servant, presides over it. The Council members deliberate, but they have no power to legislate, and may only advise. And when they complain of their poverty and their government-neglected lands, they are reminded that they have 'independence' and the right to do something for themselves.

The Rehoboth territory is one of the few in South West Africa that retains almost intact its pre-German boundaries, though slices of land have been lost here and there, and the Rehobothers still have individual title to their land, in contrast with the practice in the Reserves. Yet possession of their original home is not enough; indeed, it carries reproachful memories of what, from this distance, seems like former glory. Change, unless it glows with the promise of complete sovereignty, is rejected with suspicion. The Rehobothers feel that nothing any South African government has brought them has ever been any good.

When in November 1961, therefore, the Rehobothers were offered a loan and new constitution 'for greater autonomy *within the framework of government policy*', they turned the offer down flat. For, despite all the antagonisms within the Rehoboth community (and these linger on in disputes over Church control) the overall picture is a war of attrition between Rehobothers and the government.

Rehoboth political passion is intensified by a fire-and-brimstone religious fervour. Seventy-four-year-old Johannes Beukes is the father of Hermanus and grandfather of student Hans Beukes, who was refused a passport, but is studying in Oslo nevertheless. He is a tiny man, pale with a pixie face, and a thin gold ring in each ear. As he relived events in 1925, when government and Rehobothers were close to arms, he rose to his feet for effect. Behind him on the wall was a painting of Christ wearing the crown of thorns. The martyr strain runs through this family, and Hermanus Beukes rounded off the interview: 'I may not see the eventual day of freedom, because, from what I know of our Christian democratic government and its history, I've learnt that if you act for your rights, you are killed in cold blood.'

Meanwhile, the dispute is one of words and attitudes, with very little done. But of intransigence there is plenty, and suspicion and acrimony towards the ruling Afrikaners who sired this community and then cast them out.

The Bushmen

Prevailing attitudes to subject peoples are revealing. Government reports are spattered with 'findings' – more correctly, prejudices – against the non-White inhabitants of South West Africa. The Okavango are 'perverted and degenerate', spoilt by bountiful Nature in their tropical home; the Herero are 'sullen, morally degraded' – though they have 'force of character'; the Rehobothers are 'indolent and improvident'. Only the Ovambo are 'contented and happy'. It does not seem to have struck those who pass judgement so smoothly that it is those least touched by 'White civilization' whom they find to be the least degenerate!

Towards the Bushmen there is a curious generosity, as a people that has for centuries been pushed to the edge of extinction. 'Wild but interesting' is the verdict; and thirty years ago an ethnologist urged a government commission to set up a Bushmen Reserve on the grounds that language-study considerations alone justified the preservation of this primitive race; a time would come when philologists, physiologists, and ethnologists would be grateful if there were still Bushmen in the country whom they could study!

There is, in the White man's pointed patronage of these slight, hungry, gentle people something of the affection that Anglo-Saxons show towards helpless animals. Hostility towards the Bushmen would be out of place: they are harmless and have fled from the White order, never able to challenge it. Always they have fled, or been exterminated. Perhaps there are a score left in South Africa today. The deserts of South West and Bechuanaland shelter perhaps 50,000 (of whom some 20,000 are in South West Africa), but these are the recent estimates of scientific expeditions, revealing many more than were formerly reckoned to have survived.

In the arguments about who came first to Southern Africa, the Whites or the African (Bantu-speaking) tribes, it has always been conceded that the Bushmen were there before anyone else, roaming in family bands over the land, hunting with great skill and precision for their food, and whiling away any hours of satiety with dancing, mimicry, and inspired story-telling in their speech of soft clicking sounds. The cattle of the White or African interloper on their hunting grounds they saw as fat lethargic game, and joyfully they let fly their poisoned arrows. Every man's hand was turned against them, and they in their turn came to be hunted like game.

Inexorably larger and larger waves of settlement broke over The Bushmen hunting grounds. To survive at all, they had to withdraw into more remote areas, to the edge of and then into the hostile desert of thirst and the ceaseless sun.

Today in South West Africa small remnants of the Saan ('the gatherers') and the Heikom ('the people who sleep in the bush') roam the banks of the Orange River, the Namib desert, and the wastes of the north-east adjoining Ovamboland. But the greatest numbers struggle to survive in the Kalahari desert, the no-man's-land between South West Africa and Bechuanaland that no one else wants.

For long dismissed as unemployable because, it was said, they were too undisciplined, the Bushmen have nonetheless been pressed – often harshly – into work. Increasingly, nowadays, they work on farms in the north-east for a small cash wage during the winter and then escape into the desert to hunt and gather wild food in the summer.

Though the Bushmen roam far, their family bands, rarely numbering more than twenty members each, have specific territories, and they respect boundaries rigidly. They never understood the careless advance of cattle-keeping African tribes and encroaching White farm settlements.

Elizabeth Marshall, in her perceptive study of the Bushmen, *The Harmless People*, describes them as unaggressive and docile.

Bushmen would not try to fight because they have no mechanism in their culture for dealing with disagreements other than to remove the cause of the disagreements. Their hold on life is too tenuous to permit quarrelling among themselves. A Bushman will go to any lengths to avoid making other Bushmen jealous ... Their culture insists that they share with one another; without rigid cooperation they would never survive famine and drought.

They have not understood, but for the most part have accepted their displacement, and with it the belief that their displacers were superior. Was it not obvious, by show of strength alone?

Today the government can afford to pause and consider the little people with their remarkable powers of adaptation, who have taught all others a lesson in sheer endurance against physical odds; and there are plans to put the Bushmen, too, into a Reserve. Introducing the new Bushmen Affairs Commissioner to a meeting of Bushmen, the Administrator delivered a homily on the need for knowledge and hard work. 'You must be like other people, self-supporting. It would be very wrong of the government to allocate land to people who cannot use it properly, when so many other people capable of and only too willing to develop farms, are crying out for land,'* he said.

The Coloured People

Of mixed descent like the Rehobothers, but separate from that community with its singular history, is a Coloured population of some 12,000. Many are immigrants from South Africa (one quarter of the total obtained entry permits into South West Africa during the two years 1959–60,) and they work in the territory as teachers, artisans, and fishermen at Walvis Bay.

To the expressed disgust of the Rehobothers, a fairly new South West African Coloured Organization has accepted the government offer of a Coloured Advisory Council, government-nominated, and removal to segregated Coloured townships. Coloured people living in African areas are treated as Africans and are subject to all the restrictions of the pass laws. Rather than join in African political movements for the removal of disabilities like these, Coloured leaders are opting for separate residential areas, in the hope that segregation from the Africans will bring them a higher ranking in non-White society, and government favour.

POSTSCRIPT: In 1960, there were only two *Indians* recorded as living in South West Africa.

* *Bantu*, November 1961.

48

2. The Masters

The Germans were the old rulers of South West Africa, unseated in 1915; the South Africans, mostly Afrikaner farmers and Civil Servants voting for the Nationalist Party, are the new. Of the 73,000 Whites in the country, the Germans (17,000 in all) comprise just less than a quarter; Afrikaans-speaking Whites muster some 49,000, and English-speaking Whites a small minority of 7,000. The two sets of rulers, old and new, are partners in the most important job the White settler has in southern Africa: 'Keeping the kaffir in his place.'

When South Africa defeated the German forces in South West Africa during the First World War, and was given the territory in trust, the majority of German settlers remained there. The garrison was sent packing, and with it a number of Germans marked down as especially undesirable. A few left voluntarily, but the rest were left on their farms and to their businesses. It was not long before the Smuts government showed a touching solicitude for them, offering them automatic naturalization and equal representation in the Legislative Assembly. The key to Smuts's attitude can be found in a letter that he wrote to a representative of the German government: 'The Germans of South West Africa, whose successful and conscientious work I highly appreciate, will materially help in building an enduring European civilization on the African continent, which is the main task of the Union.' In the first election for the territory's Legislative Assembly, the Germans, then just over half of the White population, won seven of the twelve elected seats.

Amenable as the South African government was, however, to enlisting the help of all White men in fortifying race supremacy, strain characterized the cooperation between the old and the new rulers. The Germans did not take kindly to domination in a land that they had opened up as colonizers. There were clashes over the use of the German language and over naturalization, with deep resentment at the steady deliberation with which South Africans were brought in by the Administration to out-vote and out-number the Germans on the land.

Recognizing that, for as long as they fell out among themselves, their powers in the Legislative Assembly would be clipped, the conflicting White communities engaged in long negotiations during the thirties to compose their differences. They were on the verge of doing so when the leader of the United National South West Party (the counterpart of the United Party in South West Africa, but not formally affiliated to it) called for the mandate to be administered as a fifth province of South Africa. This alienated German support, and negotiations collapsed. For by now the rise of the Nazi movement in Germany, with its cry for the return of her former colonies, had excited Germans in South West Africa to hope that they might once again form part of a German empire. So, against the background of Europe in the thirties, all chance of reconciliation between Germans and South Africans, however strong their bond as White men in an African country, was – temporarily – lost.

A branch of the National Socialist Party had existed in South West Africa before 1932; but, until the party came to power in Germany, it had been regarded as of little consequence. Then, feeding on local grievances and foreign help, the local Nazi movement grew. Funds, instructions, and new party leaders arrived from Germany. Individuals were intimidated, loyalty campaigns conducted, political unreliables reported to Germany. A Territorial Führer supervised the Nazification of children in the German school. The processions and flag-waving demonstrations were poor mimicries of the real thing in Europe, but they frightened the antagonistic in Windhoek and Swakopmund.

After Munich, tension and German truculence rose in South West Africa. Young Germans left the territory to train as soldiers and pilots in Germany. South Africa's Minister of

Defence, Oswald Pirow, whose admiration for National Socialism was stronger than his allegiance to his own country's imperialist ambitions, admitted that if one of the African mandates had to go back to Germany, he would rather it were South West Africa than Tanganyika! The outbreak of the war found the South African parliament in special session, with the Cabinet split down the middle on the issue of neutrality. South Africa declared for war by a majority of thirteen precarious votes. Smuts gave the German Minister notice to leave, and interned hundreds of Germans in South West Africa.

The rise to power in South Africa of the Nationalist Party in 1948 made the post-war adjustment between the Germans and the new South African government especially easy. The Germans who had spent the war years in internment camps emerged from them bitterly resentful of the Smuts government and the United Party. The Nationalists had been vigorously opposed to the war, and to Smuts for even longer. It was natural that the two waves of opposition to the United Party government should meet and alter the balance of White party policies in South West Africa.

Until then the United National South West Party, with fifteen members to the Nationalist Party's three, had dominated the Legislative Assembly. In the 1950 elections sixteen Nationalists and two United National South West Party members were returned. Since then Nationalist Party strength has continued to grow, helped by Nationalist-rigged delimitations and a heavy influx of Nationalist-voting railwaymen and Civil Servants. The United Party can do nothing to arrest its own decline.

The German vote was a key factor in the 1950 swing. The Germans in the territory had adjusted themselves to a second defeat for Germany in their life-time. In the 1940 election campaign they had not bothered with nominations, for they held that the fate of South West Africa would be decided in Europe and that it was futile to take any further part in local squabbles. With the defeat of Germany, however, all hope that South West Africa, or any German colony, would be restored to the Fatherland was dashed. The Germans turned their attention to politics inside South West Africa. The United Party had not only interned them, but its spokesmen had threatened them with deportation after the war. No wonder Mr J. P. Niehaus, leader of the United National South West Party, told me ruefully: 'I can't get the Germans to vote for me; I drew up the internment lists!'

The Germans voted Nationalist not only to avenge themselves on the United National South West Party, but also because they felt themselves a community on sufferance. The last time that they had opposed the governing party, they had had cause to regret it; now they voted for the party which they judged the most likely to stay in power. And, of course, there were business considerations. If one voted for the governing party, one had better prospects of import permits, of preferential treatment when it came to government tenders, of a larger share in the economic cake.

Nationalist wooing of the German vote did not flag even after the party had won its massive majority. Three weeks before the 1958 elections, the Legislative Assembly passed a motion granting to the German-speaking population of the territory the language rights that they had enjoyed before the outbreak of the Second World War. (The Opposition, while not opposing the motion, tried unsuccessfully to have it postponed until after the elections!) Then immediately after the elections, the Legislative Assembly resolved* to bestow pensions on 'European' (i.e. White) veterans of the German army who had served in wars in South West Africa before 1920. It was estimated that under this measure some 270 Germans who had fought against South Africa would receive a total of £46,000 a year.

The German vote made South West Africa safe for the Nationalist Party in the mandate. It also helped to swell the Nationalist majority in the South African parliament when in 1949 the mandate was for the first time given representation there in a blatant manoeuvre to consolidate Nationalist strength. All six South West African representatives in the South African House of Assembly are Nationalists.

* Ordinance 31 of 1958.

There were hopes that the close political alliance between the Germans and the Nationalists might be undermined by the formation of the South West Party, launched at Windhoek, in July 1960, by 'Japie' Basson, the Member of Parliament for Namib, who had been expelled from the Nationalist Party for opposing the abolition of communal African representation in South Africa's parliament. The new party proposed minor reforms, offering vaguely 'some effective form of local administration for Africans living permanently in the White Areas, and rapid political and economic development of the Native territories'. But its vigour lasted barely a year, and in Windhoek nowadays the Whites pronounce its obituary notice. Some voters, especially Germans, had crossed over from the Nationalist Party. Even former Nazis had conducted an agonizing reappraisal. But any real readjustment had not lasted long. For some, the party had not departed far enough from the traditional patterns of White supremacy politics. Others were frightened by their own political boldness, when they saw that the small third party did not make spectacular gains. They were frightened even more by the propaganda use made by Nationalists of events in the former Belgian Congo, whose bogey of a savage Black Africa submerging the Whites seemed uncomfortably close in 1960 and 1961.

While most went back into safer political folds or lapsed into political lassitude, there remains a scattering of South West Whites, some in Windhoek, fewer in Walvis Bay, who are breaking from White supremacy politics. They are trying to get to grips, in discussions among themselves, with African grievances; and by looking into the facts of the mandate's history, they are adjusting themselves to the idea that the U.N. cannot be dismissed as dangerously meddlesome. It has standing in the South West African issue, and the South African government will have a difficult job defending itself from the current attack at the International Court. But this group is still very small and has not ventured to make public its existence.

As the U.N. took a sterner stand on South West Africa in 1960 and 1961, signs appeared of a greater awareness inside and

53

around the United National South West Party that the Nationalist government would not long continue to have everything all its own way, and there was some rethinking, though much of it singularly muddled. The leader of the United National South West Party announced that his party would cut adrift from the outlook of the United Party in South Africa and turn more progressive. Policy was to be reviewed at the next Party conference. It has at last dawned on the United National South West Party that it had gone down to defeat because it had presented a policy so close to that of the Nationalist Party that voters could make little distinction between the two, and had therefore chosen the more aggressive variation. Now the United National South West Party may even try its hand at opposition. Any reforms in policy, however, will probably be too few and come too late, for White attitudes have set firm over the years, and it will take a sharper shock than a rejuvenated United Party to shift them.

It remains a frightening fact that not a single White political leader in South West Africa has ever advocated a non-racial democracy. All political spokesmen announce programmes with their eyes glued to the (White) voters' rolls alone.

In general there is more uniting the Whites than dividing them. Differences between the Nationalist and United National South West Parties fade into insignificance, except at election time, when argument splutters over the fine distinctions between their respective formulae for handling the mandate and the non-Whites. The inhabitants of South West Africa may be forgiven for not always appreciating the distinctions. The Nationalist government will argue the case before the International Court of Justice in 1963 when South Africa's treatment of the mandate is put to the legal test, but the Nationalists have merely continued a policy initiated by the United Party forty years ago. The Nationalists gave South West Whites representation in the South African parliament, incorporated the South West Africa Native Affairs Department into its Pretoria-controlled black empire, and have for all practical purposes run South West as a part of South Africa (defying all the trust terms of the mandate). But the cry to make South West into a fifth province of South Africa was started by the United National South West Party leader in 1932, and though today that party acknowledges that the U.N. must be consulted before any change in the status of the mandate, it set the voters to chase the incorporation hare in the first place. The United National South West Party stands or falls on the policy of segregation; the Nationalists have taken that policy to further extremes. Both policies play on the fears, prejudices, guilt, and privileges of the White man in southern Africa.

When it comes to the push, then, Whites act as Whites, and tactical disputes between the two main political parties recede to triviality.

The Nationalist Party enjoys a virtually free political passage in South West Africa because the policies of the United Party are basically indistinguishable from its own; because no principled opposition of any size has yet arisen; and because the Nationalists brazen and bully it out from a position of strength and have frightened other Whites into leaving them a monopoly control over the affairs of state.

Certainly the German community has abdicated any significant claim to a share in the administration and Civil Service of the territory. As self-conscious and none too successful colonizers, they seem to have accepted with relief that a new set of rulers should have taken over the task of keeping the Africans in their place. They themselves can now get on with their businesses and their farms and their more elevated pursuits as the mainstay of any cultural life in the country. They have even abandoned the field of civic affairs and municipal politics. They once possessed the majority in the Windhoek town council, but the German councillors found the municipal officials and Civil Servants curiously reluctant to furnish them with official information, and, sensitive to resistance, withdrew from the contests altogether. The Nationalists value German votes, but prefer to run the territory alone.

Former tensions between Germans and Afrikaners (the Germans scorn the uncouthness of their successors) seem to have been driven below the surface by political exigencies. The German community keeps very much to itself after hours, socially and culturally; ensures periodic transfusions from Germany through visiting cultural groups and sends its young generation to study in German universities whenever economically feasible.

White political opinion, however, is moulded not by the sophisticated German element or even the townsmen, but by the patterns of frontier living: the trek away from the wider world, the withdrawal into insularity and rigid conservatism, the physical distance from and suspicion of other cultures. Isolation soon generates intolerance and hostility towards the strange. The farming frontiersman is threatened on all sides – by predatory animals attacking his stock; by the indifference of the towns, the areas of softer living; by the judgement of a world beyond. Fanatically he stakes his future on a system of race discrimination which will insulate him from the indigenous majority everywhere around and repel the influences of other nations and world bodies.

The frontier farmer in South West Africa is the 'man in the street'. The government has protected his interests and respected his views first and foremost. But farmer or townsman, most Whites think and act alike, in a compound of self-interest, prejudice, and rigid refusal to try and understand the history and aspirations of the Africans, whose conditions of life and challenge they dare not face.

Here, then, are the two South West Africas locked in conflict. The Whites, a monolithic political force (for the exceptions are too few to affect the pattern), heavily armed because South Africa is heavily armed, monopolize government and its various benefits. They are richer than they have ever been, self-assured, intransigent, and just a shade uneasy now at the changing world beyond their borders.

The African tribes and other non-White communities display an astonishing divergence in origin, customs, and history. But their common experience of White rule is shattering old divisions and shaping in their stead a common cause. They carry on their backs not only the burden of the White man, who lives his good life by their labour, but also the tragic burden of their history.

Part Two: The Heavy Hand of History

I. Explorers and Elephant Hunters, Missionaries and Traders

Even among colonies South West Africa is an anachronism. Under South African control it has steadily become not more but less independent; and, among Germany's former possessions, it is the only one in Africa, indeed anywhere, not to be placed under the international trusteeship system, let alone advanced towards independence.

One reason why South West Africa has limped so slowly through the twentieth century lies in the fact of her remoteness. This is more than just her geographical isolation at the foot of the continent, bordered by desert. It is also her place in the encampment of White-ruled southern Africa: that complex of South Africa, Angola, Moçambique, and the Rhodesias where White investment, industry, settlement, and self-interest are most deeply entrenched and least ready to surrender or compromise.

There is another reason, too, for South West Africa's tardy emergence on to the African and international scene. She was among the last countries in Africa to be colonized. International awareness of the country and, even more important, African awakening within it, got off to a very late start.

White occupation of South West Africa goes back only seventy-eight years, compared with the three centuries of her nearest neighbour, South Africa, and the four of Angola, on her northern border.

In 1889, when German troops set up the first garrison there, the last frontier war had already been fought in South Africa, and the tribes disarmed; only one final outburst, the Bambata Rebellion among the Zulus in Natal, was still to come as one last desperate bid against White authority by an African tribe. With its crushing, the 'native question' ceased to be a military matter; the chiefs were subdued and later put on the government payroll; and the discovery of diamonds on the Kimberley fields prompted the first hesitant emergence of African organization along modern political lines.

South West Africa lagged far behind. It was not that the world of explorers and navigators, commissioned by royal courts, the mission societies, and chartered companies, did not know of its existence. Once again, it had been the intrepid Portuguese who had left the first mark of the White man's power, in the shape of a simple stone cross, placed on a rocky crag, just north of Swakopmund, on the shores of South West Africa. That was in 1484, eight years before Columbus set foot on an island of the Americas. The Portuguese expedition must have stepped ashore just long enough to be deterred by the same sight that discourages sea travellers today: those endless high sand-dunes along the dreary desert coastline of the Namib, known to later seamen as the coast of dead ships. Two years later a better-known Portuguese expedition, that of Bartholomew Diaz, who went on to name the Cape of Good Hope, landed from his little fifty-ton ship at a narrow South West Bay which he named Angra Pequena. Except for occasional landings during the next few centuries, with cursory glances at the country beyond; whale and seal catching; barter between ships' crews and Namas along the coast; and a small ship repair yard at Angra Pequena, South West Africa remained untouched by White men. When they entered the country at last in any numbers and for any length of time, it was overland, from South Africa.

Rumours of copper in the interior drew them on. The Governor of the Cape, Simon van der Stel, hazarded a personal investigation to find the mouth of the Orange River; but though he guessed at it, he did not find it. Jacobus Coetzee, farmer and elephant hunter, killed only two elephants during his own investigation, but crossed the river that van der Stel had not reached, and brought back reports (proved inaccurate in later years) of black people, living beyond the mountains, who had long hair and wore linen clothes. A later expedition, in 1762, also sent out by a Cape governor, found none of these mythical people in the north, and, indeed, encountered rather more animals than humans (it sent the first giraffe skin ever to be seen in Europe to Leiden). Yet now reports from the interior told not of elephants or long-haired blacks but of the cattle-breeding Herero.

The travellers of the eighteenth century were, for the most part, officials, hunters, men eager for trade, men of action, not men of letters in the style of some explorers who went on epic journeys to open up other parts of Africa. The journeys of the following century were, however, to leave more coherent – if sometimes amusing – reports behind them. An officer of the Royal Horse Guards, Sir James Alexander, was invited by the Royal Geographical Society to prepare for an African Expedition of Discovery through the 'hitherto undescribed countries of the Great Namaquas, Boschmans and Hill Damaras'. The expedition set off with an impressive list of equipment for 'an absence of at least twelve months from civilized society'. It took

for offence and defence, three double-barrelled guns, rifles ... complete with bayonets and swords, three boarding pikes, seven rockets, one hundred pounds of canister gunpowder, six hundred rounds of ball cartridge, for a stand in case of being attacked; and ... for bartering with the natives .. red caps, tobacco ... brassware; musical instruments as a violin, tambourine, pan's pipes to keep our people alive and the natives in good humour.

Conscious of the White man's civilizing mission in Darkest Africa, Sir James records that, by taking a bath at Warmbad, he 'set the natives the example of ablution'. Alexander's expedition produced the oldest map of the territory, and the first list of fifty words in the Herero language. When he reached the capital of Jonker Afrikaner, the powerful Oorlams Chief, he was surprised to find 1,200 people living in huts in a well-ordered township. Here he first heard of the conflict between the Herero and Nama people which racked South West Africa for so long.

A cousin of Charles Darwin, Sir Frances Galton, led an expedition in 1851, deferring an attempt to reach Lake Ngami in favour of a search for the Ovambo people of the north. He and the Swedish naturalist Andersson found, after travelling through everlasting stones and thorns: 'their charming corn country yellow and broad as a sea before us ... a land of Goshen to us ... and at the sight of the agricultural opulence the wagon driver burst into exclamations of delight'. Galton found 'some of these savages magnificent models for sculptors', but most of the Hottentots (Namas) 'had the felon face ... the features so general among prisoners in England, prominent cheek bones, bullet-shaped head, cowering but restless eyes, heavy sensual lips ...'.

The first White pioneers to take a consciously greater interest not in animals and glinting metals, but in people – and then not as anthropological specimens but as souls – were the missionaries. They explored the country and the people with great purpose: charting the tribal occupation of land, learning the languages and starting their reduction to writing. As early as 1802 the London Missionary Society had posted its agents north of the Orange River, and after 1821 the Wesleyans, too, appeared. Missionaries ventured deep into the interior, struggling to cross rivers, to control fevers, and to convert and collect for the Church in the unknown. A missionary meeting held by the Reverend Joseph Tindall at one village brought in 'on the collection plate' six oxen, ninety-two sheep and goats, two koodoo skins, and nine sjamboks. The missionary's journal of conversion is interspersed with measurements of a female elephant, height, girth, sole of foot, length from tip of trunk to tail-end, and then the triumphant entries further on: 'Another backslider returned to the Lord!' and 'My mind dwelt on the northern tribes ... the time is near to give them the gospel.'

It was the transfer in 1840 of the rights of the London Missionary Society to the Rhenish Mission Society, with headquarters in Barmen, that made of German missionary endeavour an important stepping-stone to the German occupation of South West Africa. Bismarck said, years later: 'The missionary and the trader must precede the soldier.' And so it happened in South West Africa, with the difference that some of the pioneer missionaries combined religion and trade, attaching general stores to the mission stations, in order to help them pay their way. Later the Rhenish mission established an industrial and farming colony, to teach potential converts the virtues of hard work and efficiency, and not least to bear the financial burden of missionary work in South West Africa. Still, it is reported, it took thirty years of preaching and trading before the first Herero convert, a pious old lady of Otjimbingwe, allowed herself to be baptized.

Missionaries and traders set up business side by side (though the traders resented the missionary excursion into shop-keeping). Charles Andersson, who had taken part in Galton's Ovamboland expedition, became the richest merchant in the country. Soon the traders were coursing with their wagons up and down South West Africa, bartering clothes, tools, brandy, guns, powder, shot, and bullet-moulds for cattle and sheep and ostrich feathers. Missionary Kreft wrote of his experience with the tribe at Bethanie:

> The traders are coming into the land at present in such numbers that one wonders what is to become of it all. .... There is such lust for buying things ... [the people] will simply not believe that this aimless buying must reduce them to poverty; when a tremendous number of their cattle are done they begin to save. The killing of animals stops and they live entirely on milk and that makes it necessary for them to trek and wander about once more.

While the missionaries took to trade, combining the work of evangelist and shop-keeper, both traders and missionaries soon involved themselves in inter-tribal politics and warfare. The early records are cluttered with their intervention. Not a treaty was signed but traders and missionaries were there as witnesses and drafters, advisers and negotiators. The missionaries believed that it was impossible to raise a nomadic people in the scale of civilization, and so they made strenuous efforts to get the tribes to settle down and demarcate boundaries – at the very time when the Herero and Nama peoples were displacing one another's herds and encampments with periodic fervour. Heathens could not be left to govern themselves in sin and ignorance, so the pioneer Rhenish missionary Hugo Hahn became Maharero's

65

confidential adviser (and, in time, adviser to the Cape government as well). He supervised many of the abortive peace talks between the tribes, and several meetings even took place in his house. It was inevitable that the line between advice and influence should soon have become difficult to draw, for missionary and trader alike. Significantly, Jonker Afrikaner, the Oorlams Chief, proposed as part of a peace decree in later years that no traders should be entitled to residence, that the prices of goods should be fixed not by the sellers but by him, and that the missionaries should fall under the control of the tribal chiefs.

Jonker Afrikaner must have had some prescience of the role that the missionaries were to play in later years, when Germany came to depend on them as advisers and go-betweens. In 1891 it was a missionary inspector Dr Buttner who advised the German government to attack the Nama Chief Hendrick Witbooi when, after one of his defeats by the Herero, he was in retreat to the south. By then, however, the Nama Chief had shed any illusions that he might once have had. Five years before, in 1886, when the missionary Rust, on behalf of the German Commissioner, had presented a draft protection agreement to his father Chief Moses Witbooi for signature, the old Nama leader had grown so enraged that he had closed down the mission and taken to preaching himself.

The Whites were few in number, but they enjoyed great influence as purveyors of the new goods, and as representatives of the new influences radiating from other, powerful orders in a wider world.

At times they discarded advice for open intervention. In the 1864 war between the Herero and the Nama, the Herero were led into battle by the English traders Frederick Green and Haybittel, and by the traveller and trader Andersson, who had meanwhile achieved appointment by the Herero as 'regent and military commander for the period of his natural life or as long as he desired to hold office'! They defeated the army of Jonker Afrikaner and ensured a period of Herero ascendancy. But this blatant interference by outsiders on the side of the Herero was deeply resented by the Nama, and in 1868 a Nama raiding party plundered Andersson's shop and with it the Rhenish mission. Mission representatives went post-haste to Berlin and petitioned the King of Prussia for protection, but the outbreak of the Franco-Prussian War temporarily diverted attention from the incident. A petition of complaint was forwarded to the Cape government as well, through William Coates Palgrave, the former surgeon, who had been appointed the Cape's Special Commissioner in South West Africa, and who undertook several conscientious missions in the country, negotiating annexation or protection arrangements with chiefs.

For by this time White involvement in the country was beginning to cause complications, and none knew this better than the Herero Chief, Maharero. He was bombarded with advice by hunters and traders, urging him to invoke the protection of the Cape government, and was himself distracted by the difficulty of arbitrating in disputes between Herero and Whites. If he judged in favour of the White, he earned the suspicion of his own people; if he backed his own people, he incurred the displeasure of the traders, who were his sole source of arms.

Most ominous were reports that the trek wagons of Boers from the Transvaal were searching out new territory and coming uncomfortably close to Herero lands. The reputation of the Boers had preceded them. The Herero Chiefs wrote:

We have learnt with deep concern that a very extensive gathering of Dutch farmers has arrived . . . to settle. . . . They intend to make war on us and compel us to submit. . . . We have no unoccupied land for the admission of any other nation, more especially one who, we have been led to believe, has always looked upon the black tribes with scorn and indignation and who both recognize and practise slavery. . . . The Boers, like ourselves, have an irrevocable attachment for cattle. . . . They would require an extensive tract of country. . . .

Maharero's approach to the Cape government was tentative: could he have advice on how to govern better? Palgrave's missions were the result. The Commissioner spent four years in his labours, and by September 1876 he had in his pocket a document placing all Hereroland under the protection of the Cape government, and another from the Rehobothers agreeing to overseers.

Maharero had been warned that the occupation would cost money, and a tax had been fixed (though the following year he complained bitterly about it).

Only the leading Nama Chiefs, with the rugged independence that was to reassert itself again in later years, and a presentiment that White protection was not an end to interference but only a beginning, stayed away from meetings with Palgrave (who was keenly aware of their opposition and warned his government that, when the time came, Namaland would have to be invaded). They wrote to the Herero Chief:

> We would like to know your opinions on the subject of Palgrave. ... It is our firm determination to retain our country and our people. We will stand as one man for our country. ...

Palgrave's labours miscarried when the Cape parliament baulked at having to back annexation with a police force. The traders clamoured against taxes, and the echoes resounded through parliament, while in 1880 warfare broke out anew between the Herero and the Nama. It seemed that annexation would bring too many troubles in its wake. The only result of the Palgrave mission was the occupation of Walvis Bay – the one good harbour on the coast – by the British in 1878. (It later passed to the Cape and so to South Africa, which explains why today it is just geographically, not politically, part of South West Africa.) Maharero was to comment sourly: 'The British flag flew here. It waved this way and that; we attached ourselves to it, and we were waved backwards and forwards with it.'

The petition of complaint that sped to Germany after the Nama raiding party had plundered the Andersson shop and the Rhenish mission at Otjimbingwe was in time to have more effect than the one sent to Cape Town, though throughout the fifties and sixties the official German attitude to merchant and missionary work was one of *laissez-faire*. There was mission work but without official auspices; trade, but without state aid. State assistance and intervention had to wait for Bismarck and a united Germany.

2. The Old Colonialism under Germany

Germany was the last European power to acquire colonies and the first to lose them. In 1878 she possessed not one square foot of colonial domain. Twenty years later she owned huge areas of Africa, in the east, the south-west, the centre, and the west; islands and whole archipelagoes in the Pacific; and was looking forward to inheriting the possessions of Portugal and Spain. Most of the German colonial empire was the product of a single year: Togoland and the Cameroons in July 1884, South West Africa in August, New Guinea in December, German East Africa by May 1885. Twenty years after she had started her new career in earnest, Germany ranked third among the powers of the world in the extent, population, and resources of her overseas holdings, and second in the sinews of empire-building: a navy, a merchant marine, and commerce. Yet, after another twenty years had passed, her ships lay at the bottom of the sea, her flags flew only over the home country, and she had lost her colonies to her competitors: won and lost them during half the expected span of a man.

Bismarck, the reluctant colonizer, acceded to German nationalist demands for colonial acquisitions in time to join the scramble for Africa. Telling themselves and the world that they were liberating Africa from the Arab slave-trade, bringing peace and protection to the last continent unoccupied by European powers, the leading nations of Europe attended the Berlin Conference of 1884–5 and, by recognizing one another's rights in Africa, accomplished its 'peaceful' partition. Bismarck expressed the amity which inspired the powers of the West: 'All the governments share the wish to bring the nations of Africa within the

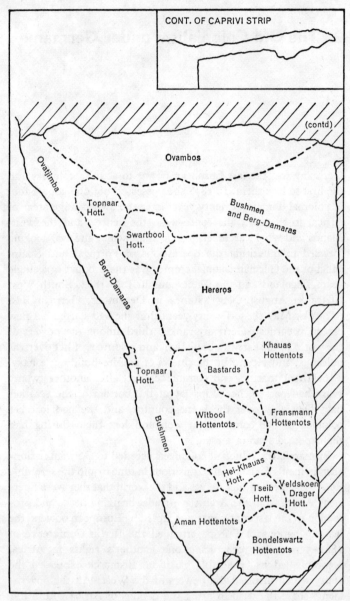

(contd)

Ovambos

Ovatjimba

Topnaar
Hott.

Swartbooi
Hott.

Berg-Damaras

Bushmen
and Berg-Damaras

Hereros

Khauas
Hottentots

Topnaar
Hott.

Bastards

Bushmen

Witbooi
Hottentots.

Fransmann
Hottentots

Hei-Khauas
Hott.

Tseib
Hott.

Veldskoen
Drager
Hott.

Aman Hottentots

Bondelswartz
Hottentots

Tribal areas in 1890 at the time of the German annexation.

pale of civilization by opening up the interior of the continent to commerce, by furnishing the natives with the means of instruction.' Philanthropy was the pretext for imperial expansion.

There was the assumption, never contested, that Africa could be carved up without reference to its inhabitants; that where there was no White government, there was no government at all. New political boundaries cut through tribes, even through villages. The powers of the West did not go to war, on this occasion, over colonial spheres of influence. Any engagements were fought instead against the inhabitants of the territories in Africa who knew nothing of, and certainly did not recognize, the Berlin settlement.

Germany was too late for much of Africa, but not for all. There were still vast areas unclaimed, and South West Africa was one of them. A Bremen merchant, Luderitz, with Bismarck's promise of support if he could find an unclaimed harbour, dispatched an agent to search for one – in a temperate zone, Luderitz stipulated – and bought the first tract of land, round Angra Pequena, from local chiefs in 1883. Bismarck handled the affair with subtlety. As early as 1880 he had sounded out the British government on the protection of German subjects in South West Africa, then only missionaries; next he had required protection for a German merchant and his warehouse. Germany's veiled notes suggested that she would prefer to leave the responsibility of protection to Britain. And by the time that the British government awoke to the purpose behind Bismarck's probings on the sovereignty of Angra Pequena, Germany had taken possession of the new outpost. Britain tried tardily to get the Cape government to assert its claim to land beyond the Orange River, but the Cape was preoccupied with a cabinet crisis and waited six months before announcing annexation. By then Bismarck had sent Luderitz an official proclamation of imperial protection. H.M.S. *Boadicea* sailed from Cape Town, but found a German gunboat stationed in the bay of the new empire.

Pro-British observers found Germany's entry into South West Africa vexing, for it blocked the possibility of a southern Africa securely British from the Cape to the Zambesi. There were even those who uncharitably accused Bismarck of having filched the territory from under the lethargic nose of a British Liberal administration. Gladstone was magnanimous. 'If Germany is to become a colonizing power, all I can say is God speed her. She becomes our ally and partner in the execution of the great purposes of Providence for the advantage of mankind.'

If the Cape and British governments conceded the contest with reluctant grace, trader and prospector Robert Lewis did not. Interpreter for Palgrave, widely known as an agent of Cecil Rhodes, and referred to by Bismarck in a Reichstag speech as that 'rapacious Mr Lewis', he had lived in South West Africa since 1858, where he had been given widespread concessions by treaty with the Herero Chief Maharero, in return for promising to ensure that the Transvaal Boers did not settle on Herero land. Lewis called himself the Prime Minister of the Damaras, and placed in safe-keeping at Cape Town the papers giving him Maharero's power of attorney, signed on 9 September 1885. The German treaty with the Herero Chief was dated six weeks later. When Lewis saw that the Germans had arrived with the clear intention of staying, he wrote a plaintive letter to Bismarck, explaining how his claims – the only legal ones – had been mislaid over the vital weeks. Passionately he urged the prince to inquire into his own German treaty and 'be governed by his sense of duty to that Higher Power who reigns over all earthly Kings'. There is no sign that Bismarck was moved by the appeal!

South West Africa was Germany's second largest colony, and the only one suited to White settlement. But it was costly to develop. The inaccessible coast needed harbours, mineral wealth was there but difficult to extract, and though the country seemed good enough for cattle-raising, there was insufficient water for wide-scale agricultural development. Settlers had to be tempted to emigrate from Germany.

The early years of German colonization followed the pattern set by the English and French. Chartered companies were granted concessions in exchange for capital, and the merchant missionaries replaced or supplanted by professional traders. But the Deutsche Kolonialgesellschaft lost a great deal of money in the first year and was unable to support a government of any kind. Bismarck was obliged to dispatch an Imperial Commissioner, one Dr Göring, whose son, as the Nazi air marshal, would help plunge Germany into the Second World War.

The Commissioner's first enterprise was to inveigle African Chiefs into accepting the 'protection' of Germany. Göring's early meetings with Maharero, watched by the ubiquitous missionaries and traders, are a record of parry and thrust between the two men. Göring explained that the Cape government had declined to bear the cost and responsibility of protection, and that the English and Germans had agreed not to interfere with one another. Maharero ruefully commented:

> I have as yet received nothing from either side to cause me to rejoice. I think all this talk about payment for concessions are but pitfalls for my destruction. It seems strange that whenever you big people come to me you always bring strife.

Maharero signed a treaty with the German government nevertheless. Then, under pressure from trader Lewis, he tried to repudiate it in 1888, threatening Göring and his staff that 'if they did not wish to see their heads lying at their feet, they should be out of Okahandja and well on their way to Germany before sunset'. Göring's party withdrew precipitately to Walvis Bay for Cape government protection, and from there sped to Berlin. The Herero Chief's threat came too late. By 1889 the first twenty-one German soldiers had arrived in the new colony under the command of Captain von Francois.

It was the Nama Chief in the south, Hendrik Witbooi, who dug in his heels and refused to sign any treaty. In 1888 he wrote to his hereditary enemy, Maharero, a moving and prophetic letter:

> You are to be protected and helped by the German government but, my dear Captain, do you appreciate what you have done? Do you imagine you will retain all the rights of your independent chieftainship after you shall have destroyed me (if you succeed)? You will have bitter eternal remorse for this handing of your land and sovereignty

over to the hands of White people. This giving of yourself into the hands of the Whites will become to you a burden as if you were carrying the sun on your back.

Witbooi had read Maharero's motivation well, for the Germans had promised soldiers to help the Herero against the Nama. Leutwein, governor of the colony for eleven years, wrote that he had used his

best endeavour to make the native tribes serve our cause and to play them off one against the other. Even an adversary of this policy must concede to me that it was more difficult but also more serviceable to influence the natives to kill each other than for us to expect streams of blood and streams of money from the Old Fatherland for their suppression.

By 1890, when only three of the twelve Nama tribes had signed protection agreements, Captain von Francois received instructions to give one of the tribes an impression of German power. Witbooi seemed the obvious man to take to task, for he was the main challenger of German rule, and his humiliation would inevitably influence the other tribes.

Once more the Germans offered protection. Witbooi cried, this time to the face of the German military commander von Francois: 'Protection, what is this protection? Everyone under protection is the subject of the one who protects him.'

The attack on Witbooi's stronghold at Hoornkrans was launched in secrecy. Witbooi, who seemed to have expected a formal declaration of war, was surprised while drinking his morning coffee. Women and children, together with the Chief's personal journal, fell into the hands of the German troops, but Witbooi and his fighting men escaped. He at once sent a lieutenant, Samuel Isaak, to the Herero at Okahandja to try and persuade them to fight with him. Then he withdrew into the rock-bound Naukluft mountains. When asked by the new German governor, Leutwein, to talk peace, Witbooi retorted:

Von Francois did not open fire on me for the sake of peace, but because I was at peace. He tried to shoot me not because of any misdeed whether by word or act, but only because I refused to surrender that which is mine alone, to which I have a right. I would not surrender my independence.

As reinforcements were on the way, Leutwein decided to 'put water in his wine' and offered an armistice. A few months' lull intervened. But by August 1894, fresh troops had arrived, and operations were resumed. His first line of defence was occupied as Witbooi unsuspectingly enjoyed the so-called armistice; then his stronghold was shelled and stormed by German troops. After three weeks, with his troops famished and living on locusts, he was forced to surrender and sign the protection agreement.

The Germans crushed risings by some of the smaller tribes, notably the Bondels people, who took to arms when their Chief was shot and who surrendered only several years later, when surrounded by 300 guns. Significantly, they rose again in 1923, this time against the South African government, in an episode that gave the mandate much unwanted publicity.

In addition to her troubles in South West Africa, Germany was embarrassed, towards the close of the century, by the outbreak of serious revolt in her East African colonies. Soon the entire coast was in insurrection, and the Reichstag reverberated with socialist assaults on colonial cruelty, graft, and scandal. It was in this atmosphere, with the heady colonial sentiment of the eighties and nineties replaced by the colder realities of colonial administration, that the German-Herero war broke out.

Germany's Merchant Administration lasted from 1885 to 1891, before steps were taken to encourage settlement, but even then there were very few settlers who did not find it necessary to be traders first, and then farmers.

Dr Paul Rohrbach, a highly placed official in the German Colonial Office, wrote:

The decision to colonize in South West Africa could after all mean nothing else but this, namely that the native tribes would have to give up their lands on which they had previously grazed their stock, in order that the White man might have the land for the grazing of his stock.

Palgrave, who had seen the thundering herds, thought it

impossible to estimate even approximately the cattle wealth of the Herero, 'though there is evidence enough to indicate that it is considerable'.

By 1903 more than half the cattle of the Herero had passed into German hands, through trading deals later described as 'unblushing theft'. The trader-farmers needed little or no financial aid from the State. They conducted their own cattle barter, drove hard bargains, and expected the government to act as bailiff for unscrupulous dealers. When the governor proposed cash trading instead of barter, the prohibition of credit deals and the establishment of courts where claims by Africans against traders could be adjudicated, a howl of indignation rose up from the settlers. At last Berlin passed an ordinance cancelling all credit after twelve months; but far from alleviating the position, this caused the traders to embark on an intensive debt-collecting round.

Maharero, builder of the Herero nation, had died in 1890, designated 'Paramount Chief' by the Germans, though his own people had never known the office. The Germans connived at the appointment of Samuel Maharero as his successor, whose pliability when under the influence of rum and brandy was well-known and valued. But his accession in the face of a stronger claim under Herero law caused a deep tribal split.

The Herero watched with consternation as treaties were abrogated, the rulings of their Chiefs and their old tribal custom ruthlessly replaced by the new German law, and Samuel Maharero coaxed or bullied into boundary agreements which led to the confiscation of trespassing cattle and the loss of their land. The tribes had no concept of private land ownership. Yet somehow the individual immigrants were acquiring farms – *luftschwebende* (farms floating in the air) Rohrbach termed them. The rate at which the Herero were losing their land disturbed even the government and the missionaries, and a reserve system was devised. Land on the fringes of reserved areas was to be used as a trading bank, while the reserved areas themselves were secured against alienation. But trader credit continued to mount till it reached the 'value' of a farm, and Chiefs could easily be manoeuvred into deals, so that the encroachment on tribal land continued. Slowly the Herero woke to the realization that the land they roamed and the water-holes they used now 'belonged' to somebody else. In 1896 a heavy cattle confiscation by the German authorities sped Herero resentment to war fever, but gradually the temperature fell. The year after, a terrible rinder-pest epidemic struck, depleting Herero cattle even further.

For a while the divide-and-rule policy pursued by the German administration reaped success. When Chiefs of the Eastern Herero demanded the return of some of their lands, the governor bluntly refused. As a result they rebelled three months later, and Maharero's followers, mollified on this occasion by a boundary concession, remained quiescent. The execution of Chiefs Nikodemus Kavikunua and Kahimemua, described by Captain Schwabe, served as a salutary lesson.

We had to travel through the entire village. There was no male Herero to be seen, but the women were rolling about on the ground, and covering their heads with sand and earth. From every house, every hut, every garden, the long drawn blood-curdling lamentations accompanied the distinguished Chiefs on their last journey. In silence, and drawn up in a great square, the guns unlimbered at the sides, the troops received us. Then we went on through the deep sand of the river bed to the place of execution. ... Halt! The condemned men were lifted from the cart. Proudly and with head erect Kahimemua walked to the tree to which he was bound; Nikodemus half-dead with fear had to be carried. The eyes of the two were then covered, and the firing sections ... marched into their places. ... Short commands: Present – Fire! The volleys rolled like thunder through the neighbouring mountains and two traitors had ceased to live.

Governor Leutwein was in the south dealing with a Bondels-wart uprising when the Herero at last took to arms. He wrote to ask the cause of the rebellion from Samuel Maharero, who had suddenly forsaken his brandy to unite and lead his people.

I did not commence the war this year [replied the Chief]. It has been started by the Whites. For as you know how many Herero have been killed by White people, particularly traders with rifles, and in prisons. And always when I brought these cases to Windhoek the blood of the people was valued at no more than a few head of cattle.

The war began on 12 January 1904 at Okahandja. By February all the Herero Chiefs were in the field, their forces instructed not to lay hands on Englishmen, Boers, Berg-Damara, Nama, or missionaries. Traders who had dealt honestly were left alone; one, taken prisoner, was placed on a horse and delivered to a mission. Leutwein wrote:

> It seems to have been the definite intention of the Herero leaders to protect all women and children. When in spite of this some were murdered, this is to be ascribed to the fact that everywhere inhuman people are found who do not confine themselves to such limits.

It was the turn of a Maharero to write to Hendrik Witbooi. 'Rather let us die together and not die as the result of ill-treatment, prison or all the other ways.' But his appeal never reached Witbooi; the Rehoboth captain asked to act as intermediary placed the letter in the hands of the governor instead.

The Herero went to war with some 7,000 fighting men, of whom only a third were armed with rifles, many of which were old and primitive, and with little ammunition. They were encumbered in the field by their women and children, their cattle and sheep. German reinforcements were summoned, and until they arrived in force, German control of South West Africa threatened to collapse at any moment.

The Huzzars campaigned for weeks, 'languid and with dull head', as described in Peter Moor's *Journey to South West Africa*, a German novel of the time purporting to be a soldier's account of the campaign. The book portrayed with poignancy the long trek through tired monotonous country naked of human beings. Then over a camp-fire the writer heard an old Afrikaner, long in the country, touch on the cause of the uprising.

> How should it be otherwise? They were ranchmen and proprietors and we were there to make them landless working men; so they rose up in revolt. They acted in just the same way that North Germany did in 1813. This is their struggle for independence. 'But the cruelty?' someone asked, and the speaker replied indifferently, 'Do you suppose that if our whole people should rise in revolt against foreign oppression, it would take place without cruelty?' And are we not cruel toward them?

By August the maxim and quick-firing Krupp gun had shattered the back of the rebellion. There were some sharp short engagements, and then the Herero withdrew into the Waterberg Mountains. There the decisive battle of Hamakari was fought, and the Herero made their desperate break through the German lines. The whole people took to flight: into the more remote mountains; northwards into Ovamboland; through the Omaheke, the waterless sandveld. Samual Maharero's party dashed east into the desert and exile of Bechuanaland.

Peter Moor wrote of the scene that met the eyes of a German scout:

... tracks of innumerable children's feet, and among them those of full-grown feet. Great troops of children led by their mothers, had passed over the road here to the north-west. ... I stood up and going to a low tree by the road climbed a few yards in my heavy boots. Thence I could see a broad moonlit slope, rising not a hundred yards distant, and on it hundreds of rough huts constructed out of branches, from the low entrances of which the firelight shone out, and heard children's crying and the yelping of a dog. Thousands of women and children were lying there under the roofs of leaves and round the dying fires. ... Still the thought went through my head: There lies a people with all its children and all its possessions, hard pressed on all sides by the horrible deadly lead and condemned to death, and it sent cold shudders down my back. ... Through the quiet night we heard in the distance the lowing of enormous herds of cattle and a dull confused sound like the movement of a whole people. To the east there was a gigantic glow of fire. The enemy had fled to the east with their whole enormous mass – women, children and herds. The next morning we ventured to pursue the enemy. The ground was trodden down into a floor for a width of about a hundred yards, for in such a broad thick horde had the enemy and their herds of cattle stormed along. In the path of their flight lay blankets, skins, ostrich feathers, household utensils, women's ornaments, cattle and men, dead and dying staring blankly. How deeply the wild, proud sorrowful people had humbled themselves in the terror of death! Wherever I turned my eyes lay their goods in quantities, oxen and horses, goats and dogs, blankets and skins. A number of babies lay helplessly languishing by mothers whose breasts hung down long and flabby. Others were lying alone still living, with eyes and nose full of flies. Somebody sent out our black drivers and I think they helped them to die. All this life lay scattered there, both man and beast, broken in the knees, helpless still in agony, or already motionless, it looked as if it had all been thrown out of the air. In the last frenzy of despair man and beast will plunge wildly into the bush somewhere, anywhere, to find water, and in the bush they will die of thirst.

The campaign was over. Leutwein might have negotiated peace, but he was superseded by General von Trotha, of Chinese Boxer Rebellion fame. Fresh from crushing the Arab uprising in German East Africa, he was not prepared to make peace in South West Africa until he had fought the war through to the end and made a salutary example of the rebels. Herero Chiefs, summoned from the field to discuss peace terms, were shot. A negotiated peace was impossible, stated von Trotha, since the Herero Chiefs had nearly all fled, or through their misdeeds during the rebellion had rendered themselves so liable that the German government could not treat with them. Von Trotha threw a cordon across the land to seal off all escape-routes and issued his notorious Extermination Order (*Vernichtungs Befehl*), still the cause of heated controversy in Windhoek.

The British government's atrocity Blue book of 1918 – officially declared destroyed by resolution of sensitive Germans when, during the mandate period, they obtained representation in the territory's Legislative Council – cites the order as having required the killing of every Herero man, woman, or child, and it turns the stomach with its detailed descriptions and photographs. Carefully it reports the killing of prisoners, wounded and unwounded, women, girls, and little boys, of men and women who had surrendered dying at the hands of soldiers and labour overseers in camps and by the lash. German General Staff records and commentaries of the day are more nebulous and claim that a counter-instruction to the extermination order was issued by Berlin. The argument does not erase the memories of Herero living in the Windhoek old location today. 'It came to the same,' Hosea Kutako told me, describing the killing of his young brother and sister, and of the baby on the back of a fleeing relative. What destruction the German troops did not inflict in battle or in blood-letting as retribution for Herero resistance, the desert and despair did. Remnants of the tribe roamed the country, dying of hunger and thirst, their land, herds, liberty, family life all lost, their tribal cohesion shattered. The official German General Staff record states that the number of Herero who surrendered, or were captured, amounted to 14,769, including 4,137 men. 'There remained those who had fled to Bechuanaland.'

The German army was still cleaning up the north when suddenly the south rose in rebellion. The Bondelswarts rising had at last been crushed, but when peace terms came to be discussed they appeared so alarming to the other Nama tribes of the south, and general dissatisfaction with the German administration had by then become so acute, that Chief Hendrik Witbooi, now eighty years old, rallied all the tribes of the south, except the Berseba people, repudiated his ten-year treaty with the Germans, and once more led his men into battle.

One year of desperate guerilla warfare followed. Then Chief Witbooi, on whose capture, alive or dead, von Trotha had placed a substantial reward, was killed in action near Tses. To prevent his body from falling into the hands of the enemy, his followers held back the advance of the Germans while they hastily dug a grave on the battlefield, buried him, and then covered the grave with stones.

Leutwein wrote of Witbooi:

A born leader and ruler that Witbooi was, a man who probably might have become world famous had it not been his fate to be born to a small African tribe.

After Witbooi's death, Jacob Marengo took his place at the head of the Nama fighters. The struggle lingered for another two years, but one by one the tribes in the south were forced to surrender. By 1907 active warfare had ended.

Herero and Nama defeated were herded together into prison and labour camps. The war had broken the resistance of the tribes. But it had also destroyed the colony's labour force, and von Lindequist, the first civilian governor (von Trotha was recalled in 1905), got missionaries to appeal to Herero still roaming the land to seek refuge in the camps. The Herero tribal domain had been declared government property and the Herero themselves forbidden to keep cattle, since, writes Vedder,* 'they no longer possessed grazing land, and everywhere there was a demand for them as labourers and herdsmen.' The starving survivors emerged from the desert, and their scattered hide-outs, and the supply of labour to the farmers could at last be resumed. Men and women prisoners were put to work building the harbour at Luderitz, or on the railways. Thousands were held on Shark Island, where prisoners lived in fenced enclosures on the beach; women, it is reported, were spanned in teams of eight to pull 'scotch' carts. Of 2,000 Nama prisoners placed on Shark Island in September 1906, 860 died from scurvy within the first four months.

Leutwein recorded the colonizer's post-war estimate: 'At the cost of several hundred millions of marks and several thousand German soldiers we have, of the three business assets of the Protectorate – mining, farming, and native labour – destroyed the second entirely and two-thirds of the last.' 'Two-thirds of the last' – a general's book entry. The Herero population had been reduced from over 80,000 cattle-rich tribesmen to 15,000 starving fugitives; more than half the Nama and Berg-Damara had died.

Hendrik Witbooi, Jacob Marenga, the Herero Chiefs in the field, were the last of the tribal warriors, heroic figures on horseback in an age of mechanized warfare. Skirmishing for grazing land, they were outflanked by the armed powers of Western Europe, busy manoeuvring for concessions, treaties, and strategic spheres of influence. Missionaries who traded bemused them; traders who advertised not only their wares but also the accompanying benefits of Christian civilization, despoiled them. Tragically divided among themselves by different origins and history, languages and customs, before the days of a unifying African nationalism (though Hendrik Witbooi, in his greatness, had visions of one), they did not see the common fate preparing to overtake them.

* *Cambridge History.*

With the rebellions against her rule at last crushed, Germany required all 'natives' over the age of seven to carry passes. No tribesman could acquire land or animals without official permission. Any 'native' without visible means of support was punished as a vagrant. The colony lived in constant fear of another rising. Governor Seitz warned against 'brutal excesses of Europeans against Natives [which] are alarmingly on the increase', and persons who 'rage in mad brutality against the Natives and who consider their white skin a charter of indemnity from punishment for the most brutal crimes'. The 'Natives might resort to self-help, that is, another native rising', he warned. There were to be no further risings. The wars that the Germans fought against the Herero and Nama tribes were the last of their kind in South West Africa – *and* the last that Germany won this century; her 'pacification' of the tribes left them scattered and weak for a new and different phase in the history of their subjection.

Part Three: The Lean Years of the Mandate

1. White Man's War

Between the suppression of the rebellions and the outbreak of the First World War, Germany had only seven clear years in South West Africa. Her wars against the Herero and Nama peoples cost her £30 million; and the Socialist opposition in the Reichstag at Berlin, querying the expense, the casualties, and the cruelty of the military expeditions, forced a new election. Nor did the end of the war mean an end as well to expense, for a strong military force had to be kept in South West Africa, with large sums voted annually by the Reichstag to keep it fed and ready.

Meanwhile the tribal lands of the Herero were expropriated, surveyed, and sold to farmers. Settlers began to emigrate in significant numbers, while former members of the *Schutztruppe* took off their uniforms at the end of their term of duty and began to farm in the land that they had helped to subdue. 'The whole country is open to cattle breeders,' wrote an enthusiastic German observer in 1914. 'Every blade of grass, every leaf, every shoot possesses unusual nourishing qualities.'

South West Africa now entered an era of profit more gratifying to Germany than that in any other of her colonies. The copper deposits north of Tsumeb were worked by the Otavi-Minen-und Eisenbahn-Gesellschaft, the harbour at Swakopmund was developed, and, with that lucky timing that marks mineral development in southern Africa, diamonds were discovered in the Luderitz district, and later in the Pomona area. In 1912 exports exceeded imports for the first time, as a consequence of diamond production. The report of the British Consul for 1913 revealed South West Africa in a thriving economic condition.

Colonies, it seemed to Germany at last, could be made to justify themselves. It was too late.

The world war that started with the shots at Sarajevo soon reached South West Africa, since the colony lay along the sea-route between Europe and the East. Britain looked to General Louis Botha, South Africa's first Prime Minister, to guarantee the defence of the Union, so that imperial troops could sail unhampered for other fronts. But Botha had troubles at home. Men who had fought in the Boer War as commandos against the British regarded Smuts and Botha as traitors for signing away Boer independence. Among them talk of neutrality in 'Britain's war' developed into hopes of a clean break with the British Empire, and even plans for a rebellion to achieve independence. A German patrol that violated the South African border tipped the parliamentary scales in Botha's favour, and the first vote, to maintain troops for six months, was passed. But even as parliament rose, a group of rebellious generals acted.

The conspiracy misfired. One of the generals, driving towards a defence force camp, was mistaken for a car thief and shot; a second, who thought better of open rebellion, called on the government instead to withdraw its troops from the German border and tried to work up a national demonstration against the war; while the third and boldest, General Maritz – having in his possession a treaty with the German governor promising aid, an independent South West Africa, and leave to annex Delagoa Bay in exchange for Walvis Bay – withdrew close to South West Africa and threatened to attack Upington in the Cape unless he was allowed to meet other leaders of the rebellion. His actions, together with a bold rebel assault on the Orange Free State, precipitated martial law in the country, the arrest and court martialling of the leaders, and the execution of one. The rebellion was crushed, but its legacy of bitterness provided part of the capital which put the Nationalist Party under Hertzog into office after the war.

It was eight months before Botha could turn his attention to South West Africa. The White miners' strike of 1913 and the general strike of the following year had been 'blessings in disguise', wrote a member of Botha's staff, Colonel Trew, who had fought against Botha in the Boer War but campaigned under him in South West.

The commandos had been called out for the first time since the Boer War, had been armed and fully tested, and so were fit to take the field. Botha struck at South West Africa from three points: one column under General Smuts moved up from the south across the Orange River, and two others attacked eastwards from the ports. The troops marched night after night through the Namib desert, while German engineers reversed sign posts on the roads, laid land mines, and poisoned water wells (of which they sometimes warned in advance). The German forces, greatly outnumbered, fought delaying actions in the knowledge that the decisive battlefields were on far-off fronts. But the campaign was soon over, with the three South African columns racing across country in untiring commando style and the greatest test being one of stamina in the heat, dryness, and spread of the land.

General Botha won the capital within weeks of going to war (his car embarrassingly stuck in the dry river bed of the Swakop River as he was on his way to accept the surrender of the town). His batman wired Mrs Botha: 'Me and the General took Windhoek today. The General is quite well.' In the fourth month of war, the General forced the surrender of the main body of German troops near Tsumeb in the north. The Germans had some 9,000 troops in the field, the South Africans a force of 50,000; but water and supply difficulties were such that there was never more than one in seven in contact with the enemy. South African casualties in the whole campaign totalled 113 killed and 311 wounded. It was a war without any real battle. Grootfontein, in the north-east, had been left in the charge of a German professor of chemistry, and he, over-anxious, surrendered not once but twice to Botha's scouts. During the surrender talks, General Botha communicated with two of his generals on the German field telephone, but in Zulu, so that Germans who might be tapping the line, would not understand the surrender terms too soon!

Not that Africans or Coloured men speaking Zulu or anything

else were allowed to approach the war too closely. Some, like Morris of the Bondelswarts (and his name, if forgotten after his war service, had good cause to be remembered by General Smuts in the twenties, for he was to play the central role in the Bondelswarts tragedy), were attached to the invading army as scouts. But, for the most part, they were ignored as though they had nothing to do with South West Africa and its future. From the start, the South African generals, politicians, and people displayed a singular disinclination, even inability, to understand the facts of South West African history and life. It is doubtful if they ever gave a thought to those who had been defeated by German troops only eight years before and who now, with suddenly awakened hope, watched their conquerors defeated in turn.

Early in the war the Germans had demanded conscripts from the Rehoboth community. Though they agreed to supply stretcher bearers and guards for war prisoners, the Rehobothers refused to fire on the South Africans. They themselves, they said, had come originally from South Africa, and in any event their treaty stipulated that they should not take part in a war of Whites against Whites. This time, they argued, they wished to remain neutral. The Germans issued an ultimatum. A group of Rehoboth leaders slipped secretly behind the German lines and crossed the desert to offer their help to General Botha. But the Commander-in-Chief rejected so compromising an alliance. This, he said firmly, was a White man's war, and did not concern the Rehobothers. 'The Coloured people have nothing to do with the war between the Germans and us, and it was my express desire that the Coloured people should not become involved in it', the general wrote – in a letter dated 28 April 1915 – to Rehobother Cornelius van Wyk. General Botha made a second declaration. Shown the Charter of Independence between the Rehoboth Gebied and the Kaiser, he is said to have tapped the document and said, 'All this gives you, that, at the least, you shall keep.' The Rehoboth deputation noted every word.

The Rehoboth community became involved in the war nonetheless. When once again it refused to put its men into German uniform, the Germans turned their guns on it. The Rehobothers now in battle, found cover for their women and children in a cave, and repelled the attack with two cannon and three machine-guns, after heavy losses on both sides. The letter from Cornelius van Wyk, Dirk von Wyk, and S. Beukes to General Botha reported: 'By order of the Commander-in-Chief we did not pursue the enemy. . . .'

Politicians and generals saw the short South West African skirmish as merely one more engagement in the struggle among the great powers for payable and strategic territories. The Herero, still a shattered people, the Nama, now calamitously reduced in resources and numbers, the Rehobothers, smarting under their recent war losses, were rather less worldly-wise; they actually believed the politicians and generals who cried that the war was aimed at restoring liberty and justice. The Allied denunciations of the German colonial system rang true; the indigenous peoples of South West Africa had experienced the horrors themselves. They saw victory, in their innocence, as a release. The German occupiers had stolen their lands, and then themselves been displaced by armies fighting under the banners of justice. It seemed to the non-Whites of South West Africa only just that their release from German rule should mean the restoration of the independence that they had enjoyed in pre-German times. The South African forces had invaded the country as liberators: who were to be liberated if not the Herero, the Nama, all those in bondage?

The atmosphere, too, seemed right for retribution. As soon as the peace settlement for South West Africa was concluded, the new administration, ruling under a state of martial law from 1915 to 1920, began a post mortem on German rule. Special criminal courts tried cases of brutal treatment and killings by Whites of Africans. In passing sentence, they took cognizance of, but also railed vigorously in judgement against, the former practice of *Zuchtligungsrecht* – the right of any German master to punish any servant. A Special Commission of Inquiry was appointed to gather and examine accounts of conditions under German rule. Herero Chiefs and Nama spokesmen, prisoners of war from Shark Island, Rehobothers who had served as transport drivers under the Germans, filed through the Commission hearings to detail the horrors of those years. In one volume the story of the German military operations against the tribes was published, with pictures of the crude executions, neck chains, leg and arm fetters, the flayed backs of women prisoners, the Herero refugees returning starved from the desert. The Report of the Commission – the Blue book produced at Windhoek in 1918 – set out to convince the world how unsuitable the Germans were to govern 'natives', and an accomplished job it did.

The German record in South West Africa was indefensible: it was one of insatiable plunder first, and then, when stung beyond endurance the tribes rebelled, of ruthless, wild repression in a fury of revenge and fear. Yet this was not a colonial record exclusive to Germany. The pacification of Algeria by the French, the rule of King Leopold's rubber régime in the Congo, the exploitation by the Portuguese, English, and Dutch of the slave-trade on the west coast of Africa, were all no less ugly. But by the twentieth century, they could be relegated to the history books. Germany as a colonial power suffered from two substantial handicaps. First, she had started late, and though her methods of penetration and rule had been employed on a larger scale and over a longer period of time by other colonial powers, this had been in the dark early days of colonization. Then, much that had happened in the village or the bush had never reached the telex operator or daily newspaper. What cruelties came to light had been excused as natural, the inevitable accompaniments of conquest and control. When all colonial powers behaved alike, who was there, but the colonized themselves, to accuse? In time, however, the anti-slavery agitation, the reports of the reformers, missionaries, and consuls who had collected information on the spot, had begun to stir the conscience of those who had set out to 'civilize the savage' and were well on the way to destroying him instead. As the nineteenth century drew to a close, the natural cruelties of colonization had come under increasing attack, with public indignation high in the colonizing countries themselves. But by then the scramble for Africa had almost ended. And it was just then that Germany had entered the race, in the last stages of colonization, at a time when international morality had at last opened its eyes. What others had done before her, in secret or silence, she could not do without discovery and assault.

Her second handicap was simply that she suffered defeat. The victor nations of the First World War had much to gain from Germany's decline and from as devastating a moral attack as could be mustered against her.

When Britain and South Africa put on display the results of Germany's colonial policy, it was not because they wanted to champion the African cause, but because they wanted to discredit the German one.

2. Sacred Trust

The war had been fought professedly for idealist purposes, and the annexation of colonies was not included amongst these. Lloyd George was to write in his memoirs that as late as 1916 the Allies had made no mention of their intentions towards Germany's colonies.

No country was prepared to perpetuate the horrors of such a war for the sake of wresting the German colonies from German control. Had Germany and her allies accepted in substance our terms, peace could have been established in the month of January 1917 instead of November 1918, without the surrender by Germany of one of her overseas possessions.

Yet Lloyd George was to mention a memorandum on war aims by General Smuts, dated 29 April 1917, which shows that Smuts for one was very much concerned with colonies. It stressed the need for defining Britain's war aims, and proposed above all else the destruction of the German colonial system, with a view to the future security of all communications vital to the British Empire. 'This has already been done – an achievement of enormous value which ought not be endangered at the peace negotiations.'

Secret agreements for the appropriation of German territories had been entered into by the Allied powers during the war. In 1916 France and England, for example, had exchanged notes on the annexation of the former German colonies in Africa. But as the war drew to a close, a suspiciously virtuous note began to creep into the declarations of statesmen. Lord Balfour spoke in 1918 of the 'God-willed capture of the German colonies', while Lord Robert Cecil said that Germany had 'no moral right to colonies'. President Wilson himself observed: 'The colonies should be taken from Germany because she uses them as objects of exploitation.'

There were strategic reasons why German colonies should be appropriated; but in the prevailing popular mood of enthusiasm for a new world, such reasons would not have sounded well. Power-political moves had to be cloaked as moral ones, for open annexation was recognized as popularly unacceptable. President Wilson's famous Fourteen Points stipulated:

A free, open-minded, and absolutely impartial adjustment of all colonial claims, based upon a strict observance of the principle that in determining all such questions of sovereignty the interests of the populations concerned must have equal weight with the equitable claims of the government whose title is to be determined.

Statesmen found the declaration capable of widely various interpretations; but, ambiguity notwithstanding, it became the basis of the armistice. At the Versailles Peace Conference, the mandate system was improvised – as an advance in colonial administration, some said, as a device, said others, to conceal the fact that a few powers, all of them hardened imperialists, were seizing the colonies of another power as the prize of victory.

General Smuts is sometimes credited with having improvised the whole system of international mandates, but the idea had been long canvassed by British and American liberals and social-ists, and had been discussed in print in good time for General Smuts to have read of it. In the '*League of Nations: A Practical System*', published in 1918, he dealt with the disposal of the Austrian, Hungarian, Russian, and Turkish empires and wrote: 'The mandatory state should look upon its position as a great trust and honour, not as an office of profit or a position of private advantage for it or its nationals.' The basis of the mandate system was to be that 'the well-being and development of primitive peoples form a sacred trust of civilization'.

It seemed a promising enough start. But General Smuts, for one, never intended the mandate system to be applied to the German colonies in Africa and the Pacific. Such places, he considered, were 'inhabited by barbarians who not only cannot

95

possibly govern themselves but to whom it would be impracticable to apply any idea of political self-determination in the European sense'.

South West Africa had been conquered by the troops of Botha and Smuts, and annexation would have seemed natural enough but for President Wilson's Fourteen Points and the climate of public opinion. Even in those early days, South Africa's policies had generated resentment and distrust. The outcry over the South African 1913 Land Act, which limited the acquisition of land for African occupation, had not yet been forgotten. Indeed, an African National Congress deputation was busy lobbying for a hearing at the Versailles Peace Conference. And South Africa's own constitution, not yet a decade old, had a colour bar at its base. An open annexation of South West Africa by General Smuts, himself part author of the mandate system, would hardly have gone uncontested. So South Africa had to submit to having her newly conquered domain placed under her control but subject to the supervision of the League of Nations.

The bestowal of a mandate did not confer full sovereignty, but only the responsibility of administering it, in conformity with the principles of the whole mandatory system, in trust for its inhabitants.

German East Africa was mandated to Britain (Tanganyika) and Belgium (Ruandi-Urundi); the Cameroons were split between Britain and France, as was Togoland; German New Guinea went to Australia; the Samoan Islands were handed in trust to New Zealand, the Pacific Islands to Japan; and South West Africa was mandated to South Africa.

The mandates themselves were classified into three types: 'A', 'B', and 'C'. The 'C' mandates, owing to sparseness of population, small size, remoteness from the centres of civilization, geographical contiguity to the mandatory itself, or other pertinent circumstances, could best be administered – held Article 22 in the Covenant of the League of Nations – as integral portions of the territory of the mandatory power, subject to safeguards in the interests of the indigenous population. General

Smuts successfully insisted that South West Africa be declared a 'C'-type mandate.

The Permanent Mandates Commission was set up by the League to examine reports on the various mandated territories as agent of the League Council. South African officials settled down in the *Tintenpalast* (The Palace of Ink, as it was called by the Germans) in Windhoek, to compile their first annual report on their new responsibility.

3. Punitive Expeditions

From the start South Africa had certain problems to tackle in South West Africa. So recently herself a colony, she had begun her international life as a new post-war Dominion by acquiring a colony herself. Now, governing the German conquest, she completed the job of stamping out tribal independence. Three punitive expeditions were launched, one in the first days of her occupation, before even the mandate system had been devised, and the other two afterwards, against the Bondelswarts tribe and the Rehoboth community. On these she was to be closely questioned by the Permanent Mandates Commission.

The Germans had scarcely surrendered to the South African forces before an expedition to announce the new rulers was sent to Ovamboland. As Major S. M. Pritchard, in charge of the expedition, made his way from Chief to Chief, messengers from farther north arrived with fervent appeals for help from a Chief Mandume, head of the Ukuanyama, the second largest tribe in Ovamboland, who had just been defeated in battle by the Portuguese. The Portuguese had mustered a force of 1,200 men, and suffered a hundred casualties. Between 4,000 and 5,000 Africans had been killed. The Portuguese announced that no prisoners had been taken during the action, that the bodies of the 'natives' which lay heaped before the trenches had been sprinkled with petrol and burned. (The Ukuanyama tribe, some 80,000 strong at that time, had accordingly lost about one in sixteen of their number.)

Soon the Chief himself, twenty-one years old, armed with a German mauser rifle and a Browning pistol, 'cruel and forbidding' in Major Pritchard's eyes, arrived to beg personally for protection. The South African official agreed to act as arbitrator and try to negotiate a termination of hostilities, for the Ukuanyama were fleeing across the border into South West Africa. The Portuguese Commander was emphatic: there were no hostilities between the Portuguese forces and the Chief, he said, it was a matter of pure rebellion. Major Pritchard lectured Chief Mandume on how the time had long passed since a tribe, however brave, could wipe out White troops in the field, and informed him that a large Portuguese army had freshly arrived in Angola. Still Mandume, with tears in his eyes, according to the official report, pleaded for protection, and at last he signed a declaration of allegiance to the new South African authority.

Armed with this, Major Pritchard asked the Portuguese to discuss the boundary between Angola and South West Africa, and meeting in the village of the defeated Mandume, the representatives of the two colonial powers drew a tentative border line. Chief Mandume was notified that he was to regard his tribespeople and stock on the Angola side of the border as lost, and the South African representatives warned him that if he tried to cross the frontier he would be left to his fate at the hands of the Portuguese.

The border ran through the tribal land of the Ukuanyama, leaving two-thirds of the tribe on the Portuguese side. It was not long before Mandume was charged with having violated the boundary line three times and was ordered to present himself to the Administrator in Windhoek to explain his actions. Tribal custom forbade any Chief to leave his domain, and Mandume's headmen vetoed his departure. 'The Chiefs in Ovamboland were now beginning to evince an interest in Mandume's affair, having closely followed his defiance and disregard of the instructions of government,' records the official report of the incident. A show of force was considered necessary.

From Lisbon the Portuguese government, dissatisfied with the way that he had escaped them eighteen months earlier, was pressing for the arrest of Mandume. The South African forces and the Portuguese met to discuss an operation against Mandume, and a military expedition into Ovamboland was authorized by General Botha on the telephone from Pretoria. The Portuguese assembled their forces on their own side of the border, ready to intervene if required; the Portuguese Commander placed his field guns at the disposal of the South Africans. In command of the South African forces was Lieutenant Hahn, to become the first Commissioner in Ovamboland and the official who handled the government's 1946 referendum on incorporation. Ordered by Hahn to surrender, Mandume sent a message: 'If the English want me, I am here and they can come and fetch me. I will fight till my last bullet is spent.'

In the ensuing battle nine were killed and thirteen wounded on the South African side, and a hundred killed and wounded of Mandume's forces, among them the young Chief himself, struck down by maxim-gun fire. His body was found in the scrub after the fighting.

The country is now entirely tranquil [reported the Administrator]. Our representatives in Ovamboland will continue to watch the situation closely and do all in their power to induce the able-bodied men of the different tribes to go south to engage themselves as labourers on the railways, mines and farms of the Protectorate. The supply from the Ukuanyama tribe has been much interrupted of late owing to Mandume's actions, but I am hopeful that it will soon be restored.

One further show of force was needed in Ovamboland. In 1932 the South African Air Force flew over the kraal of Chief Ipumbu of the Ukuambi tribe, showering leaflets, and Ipumbu himself was deposed and exiled from his people. The official reports talked of the Ipumbu affair as 'personal', but in the 1922 Report of the Administrator he had already been described as showing 'a certain reluctance to submit to the authority of the Commissioner'. It looked very much as though the authorities had bided their time for a convenient pretext on which to remove a recalcitrant Chief. The 1932 show of force was relatively painless – except that the tribe lost its Chief. Ipumbu was spirited away, and the tribe disarmed in a rapid action. The government then announced itself ready to 'negotiate'.

Bombing of the Bondelswarts

The Bondelswarts shooting was the Sharpeville of the 1920s. Central character was Abraham Morris, the outstanding Bondelswarts fighting leader in the second Nama war against the Germans, who had escaped to the Cape after his people's defeat, together with their hereditary captain, Jacobus Christian, and lived there with a German price on his head. He had taken service with Botha's Intelligence services as a guide, and now, hopeful of a new deal with the defeat of the Germans, he returned home, in his hand the rifle he had been given by the South African government as a reward for his loyalty, but no permit for entry to South West Africa.

If Morris himself was the central character, and his return from exile the catalyst, there were other elements composing the tragedy of his people. The Bondelswarts were one of the Nama groups that had migrated from the Cape into the Warmbad district towards the end of the eighteenth century, and had taken part in the 1896 Witbooi war against the Germans. Despite their decisive defeat, with its many casualties, they had risen again, in 1906, to be crushed once more. The treaty with the Germans which had concluded hostilities had greatly reduced the land of the Bondelswarts. They were no longer allowed to elect a 'captain', and were compelled to provide labour for public works and private employers.

The South African conquest of South West Africa, if anything, made their struggle for survival even more difficult. They did not get back their land, for the new government confirmed the German treaty; Timothy Beukes, the headman imposed upon them, commanded no respect; the cattle-branding regulations were irksome; and though their work for the White farmers was supposed to be paid at the rate of ten to fifteen shillings a month, together with food, in practice the cash wages were often withheld. The last straw was the dog tax, first levied by the Germans but quadrupled by the South African administration. The Bondels, who needed dogs for hunting, tried to raise the tax by selling their stock, carting wood, and burning lime, but, living on the extreme edge of destitution (the official report), were hard pressed to find the money. Between September 1921 and January 1922, no less than 140 cases for failure to pay the tax were taken before the magistrate, and one hundred men were convicted and sentenced to fines of £2 or fourteen days' imprisonment.

It was at this time that Morris, Christian, and a handful of followers decided to return home, although they had been denied official permission. The arrival of a party of fifty men with women and children produced a White panic that 3,000 Nama were gathering to attack, and the police were alerted.

From this point onwards, the accounts diverge bewilderingly. A police sergeant, Van Niekerk, who intercepted Morris at Haib, commended him for handing over his rifle cartridges and Union permit, and suggested that he would get no more than a small fine for having entered South West Africa with a gun and his cattle but without permission. A priest who witnessed the interview later claimed that Van Niekerk had promised, if Morris would only go to Warmbad, that everything would be forgotten and forgiven. Suddenly the Bondels were ordered to hand Morris over to the police. When they demurred, the police spokesman threatened: 'The lead of the government will now melt upon you.' The Bondels took this to be a declaration of war and asked Morris to lead them.

The police were the worst possible agents to negotiate for the government in what was then still a mild misunderstanding. All trouble might have been avoided had the Administrator shed a little of his dignity and gone to see Morris himself, the Permanent Mandates Commission later suggested. When the Commission reviewed the episode, it complained of having received four different versions of the incident. It would most readily have accepted the majority report of the South African government's commission of inquiry into the events had Major Herbst, who appeared before the Permanent Mandates Commission to explain his government's actions, not condemned the report as coming from persons 'ignorant of local conditions' – the very men whom the government itself had appointed to investigate!

The Administrator G. R. Hofmeyr, far from hastening to mediate, was already in the saddle. He took personal command and led into action a makeshift force of policemen, farmers, and Civil Servants. The *Windhoek Advertiser* of the day poked fun at the self-appointed Commander-in-Chief. It was possible, the paper held, that he possessed the military qualities of a Napoleon, but he had reached middle-age without giving proof of his capacities in that direction. A communiqué from the front announced: 'Bondelswarts completely crushed in operations lasting five days.'

The government had sent an air detachment, which had dropped sixteen bombs, not only on the Bondels in the field but also where the women and children had taken refuge. One hundred men, women, and children were killed in the campaign, among them Morris; their Captain, Jacobus Christian, and 150 of his followers were taken prisoner. When the large number of Bondelswart dead was unfavourably commented upon at Geneva, Major Herbst told the League that anyone acquainted with the conditions of South African warfare, with the skill of the average farm lad in the use of the rifle and natural cover, would not marvel at it. 'There is no such thing as volley firing. Each individual selects his mark, aims at it and seldom misses.' Hardly an occasion for praise of South African marksmanship. . . .

The Permanent Mandates Commission, faced with a jumble of conflicting facts and interpretations, was restrained from remonstrating with the South African government by the protective intervention of the Portuguese representative, but it could not hide the astonishment with which it learned of subsequent developments.

Beukes, the puppet chief, was given a government job as a gaol warder, but soon dismissed for unsatisfactory service. Jacobus Christian, whom the Bondels considered their headman, was found guilty of sedition, but amnestied during a Royal Visit, and when released was officially recognized as headman – sixteen bombs and one hundred corpses too late.

The Permanent Mandates Commission asked whether the Administration had done anything to restore the economic life of the tribe. Nothing special, Major Herbst replied. The men were merely encouraged to find work. In the Major's pocket was a telegram from the local magistrate informing him that the men had been offered jobs on the railways but had refused to leave the district; the wages would have been one shilling a day.

A police officer commented: 'The effect of the lesson taught in this short campaign will leave an indelible impression not only on the minds of those who resorted to the use of arms in defiance of lawful authority, but on other native tribes in this territory as well.'

Trouble in Rehoboth

South Africa's ears were stinging, if her heart was not contrite, by the time that the League and the world's Press had done with the Bondelswart affair. When next a force was dispatched to a recalcitrant area, it was not the Administrator who rode at its head.

The Rehobothers emerged confident from the First World War, for they had defended their territory by force of arms, and General Botha himself had seemed to accept their charter of independence. They sent a batch of petitions to Lloyd George and to Smuts, asking that they be permitted to retain their status 'as an independent people under the Union Jack'. And they became avid petitioners to the League, irritatingly irrelevant at times, but anticipating the later Trusteeship Council in their requests for personal appearances by their spokesmen before the Permanent Mandates Commission. They even found their Michael Scott, in the person of a White South African, Dewdney Drew, who became a vigorous champion of their cause and advised them to petition Britain for the establishment of a separate Rehoboth territory, in status like the three Protectorates.

In 1923 the South African government offered the Rehobothers an agreement which would give their traditional Council or *Raad* official recognition as one of its own administrative organs in South West Africa. Though the members of the Council signed the agreement, the majority of the Rehobothers were incensed, opted for complete independence, and constituted a new Council. A prolonged and rancorous dispute ensued. The Administration recognized that the new Council was by far the more representative, but declared its election void. Fresh elections were proclaimed, but the new Council refused to participate. The old Council was the *de jure* government, but altogether powerless. The new Council represented the majority, but was snubbed by the Administration. After a year of deadlock, the Administrator suspended the 1923 agreement, transferred by proclamation the powers of the Council to a magistrate, and demanded as a token of submission that the community observe the Administration's cattle-branding regulations.

The leader of the new Council did not brand his cattle. When the police summonsed him, all his followers demanded to be taken into custody as well. The Defence Force was called up, martial law declared in Rehoboth, and three aeroplanes dispatched. The Rehoboth village was surrounded one daybreak, and an ultimatum to surrender or face assault delivered. Taken prisoner were 638 men: 289 Rehobothers, 75 Namas, 56 Berg-Damaras, and 218 Herero. To the Administration the presence of the Herero was the most ominous feature of the incident. The Herero themselves, grazing their cattle in Rehoboth territory because they had lost their own lands, seemed surprised that they were suspected of any involvement.

The Rehoboth Council was now stripped of virtually all its powers, except its right to talk, and talk it did. The South African High Commissioner in London complained to the League that the Rehobothers had a circular mind: they could think of nothing but independence.

On the Permanent Mandates Commission Lord Lugard observed that the grant of complete independence to a particular people would be incompatible with the terms of the mandate, but a large measure of independence could certainly be given. The Administration replied that the Rehobothers were not qualified for this.

4. Land Rush

In 1920, when the Permanent Mandates Commission first went to work, General Smuts, though familiar with the wording of Article 22 in the League Covenant, could have had little intention of observing its spirit. Still firmly fixed in his mind were all the arguments for regarding South West Africa as a mere extension of South Africa, despite any sacred trust for the territory's indigenous inhabitants that he had assumed. He approached the problems of the mandate as an exercise in veiled annexation.

The policies that he initiated then are those for which South Africa is today still having to account before the world. The foundations of African poverty and of White supremacy were laid in those lean years. For Smuts to have built any differently in South West Africa from the prevailing pattern in South Africa, he would first have had to put his own régime in South Africa to the test, and to have found it wanting. He and his government saw South West Africa simply as a country suitable for White settlement, ready for parcelling into White men's farms. *South Africa had acquired a colony*. If the African was to survive, he would have to adapt himself to South Africa's traditional system, entering the White man's service in a permanently subordinate position.

To the eye of the enthusiastic settler, South West Africa's vast stretches lay unoccupied, unclaimed. Under the Germans the largest tracts of land had been owned by the government and large concession companies like the Deutsche Kolonial gesellschaft. The South African government expropriated the land of the concession companies and declared all unallocated areas to be Crown land.

When South Africa took over the administration of South West Africa, there were 1,138 farms in White use, totalling 11,490,000 hectares. She immediately applied her own land-settlement legislation to the territory. A Land Board was set up to allocate farms to new White settlers, and the land rush began. The Board was besieged by applicants pressing their claims. For the first seventy-six farms advertised, there were between 800 and 900 applications. By the end of the first year of the mandate (1920), 169 holdings had been allocated to 203 settlers; by the end of 1925, 880 holdings to 1,106 settlers. By 1926 the White population had swollen to almost double that of 1914, despite the repatriation of some 6,000 Germans. In six energetic years of land settlement, the 'sacred trust' had been secured as a White man's country.

The government could not do enough for the new farmers. It gave them generous loan terms, granted them remissions on rent arrears, built dams, bored for water, advanced capital for stock. Vast loan amounts were never recovered and were cheerfully discounted. Land-hungry South Africans, spilling across the border, were allocated huge farms, virtually for the asking, that were then petted and pampered into eventual solvency. Expense seemed no consideration. Even during the years of gloomy Land Bank reports on drought and the shrinking markets for cattle, the settler schemes continued.

The South African government, against the wishes of the South West Legislative Assembly and the Administrator, even set up a special fund of £500,000 to coax into the territory the families of 301 professional trekkers – the Angola Boers. These were people who had turned their back on the Transvaal Republic in 1874, drifted through South West Africa and Angola, and were now once again on the move. Each family was guaranteed a farm and cattle, together with a handsome cash advance. The majority of them, reported the inspector in charge of the Angola scheme, would make a success of farming given 'a reasonable chance', but with some 'trekking had become second nature'.

The settlement schemes and especially the Angola Boer project went sour during the years of drought and depression, when critics charged that the farming crisis was due as much to the poor type of settler as to the drought. South Africa, the critics accused, had failed to investigate sources of revenue before fixing the scale of expenditure. She had poured hundreds of thousands of pounds into projects which had failed and could be saved from complete disaster only by pouring many more hundreds of thousands of pounds into them. By the 1930s, South West Africa was bonded head and shoulders to the mandatory. Much of the capital invested in farming turned out to a waste of resources, and the more land that was allocated to new settlers, the heavier became the territorial commitment to continuing subsidy.

White settlement was halted during the critical depression years of 1930–3, but begun again straight afterwards. By 1937 the Annual Report confessed that land suitable for settlement was fast running out; the Administrator was purchasing unused land from private farmers and handing it over to newcomers instead. And from 1946 onwards, the Administration used its powers under the land-settlement law to purchase individual farms for settlers (who had to pay only one-tenth of the value at once, and the balance over thirty years).

Lardner Burke, Member of the South West Legislative Assembly, told a 1935 government Commission:

The settler farmer is an earnest and frugal man, anxious to make a success of his farming. A large number are, however, ill-informed, obstinately conservative, self-opinionated, ignorant of finance except in its very simplest forms, with their sense of obligation to the State distorted and spoiled by the ease with which they have secured financial assistance for almost everything they require. Deferred to by politicians and accustomed to being described as the backbone of the country, they have cultivated the conviction that if they fall, the State must fall and that, in consequence, the State must come to their aid whenever necessary. There are 1,519 settlers in this country, the majority of whom are probably true to type.

In just over a decade the 1,519 had become ensconced in one-sixth of the territory's farming land, and some of the most fertile at that; they were absorbing the greater part of the country's capital outlay; and they had an administration deluded into believing that it was the duty of the State to help them at any cost. The newest arrivals in the country, they had become the masters of it.

5. The Tribes Retreat

The tribes looked on in stupefaction. The First World War had thrown the country into confusion. Africans wandered with their herds, awaiting the conquerors in the hope that they would have their lands restored. They had memorized the promises made at meetings in all the important centres by the Governor-General of the Union, Lord Buxton (it was his ancestor, Thomas Fowell Buxton, who had coined the phrase 'a sacred trust of civilization', at the time when the British slaves had been emancipated). On each occasion Lord Buxton had promised the Herero their 'old freedom', along with great possessions of land and unlimited herds of cattle.

That was all they longed for [wrote Vedder*]. They laid down their work on many farms in order to make sure of being in time when South West Africa should be partitioned . . . But the partitioning of the country was not effected in the way the Hereros expected . . . The Reserves set aside for the aged and those incapacitated for work were not as extensive as had been expected. The farmers, moreover, remained on their farms, and many other farmers arrived.

Some unoccupied lands were allocated to the Herero by the military administration, but the government that succeeded it regarded these as 'black islands' of a temporary nature. Africans who had thought themselves settled were required suddenly to move – despite the cynical self-congratulation in the Administrator's Report of 1921.

The temporary arrangements made during the military occupation were appreciated by the Natives, and healthy, well-nourished children

* op. cit.

born during that time are now observed there, representing potential labourers of the future.

In 1922, after very speedy work, the government reported that 'the areas (for African Reserves) have *been selected with every care and consideration,* so as to obviate, as far as human agency can prevent, the occupants from being disturbed even in times of the most severe drought'. Another page of the same Report, however, confessed that land recommended by the Commission had been found by the searching drought to be unsuitable, 'and we have found better and more suitable land by patient investigation'. '*Selected with every care and consideration*' – perhaps, but only so as to obviate any conflict with the expansion of White settlement.

The new Reserves comprised large areas of sand-veld, where grazing lacked phosphate constituents and *gallamsiekte* was rife, where underground water supplies were very deep or unfavourably situated. In Epikuro Reserve a well had to be driven 800 feet before water was found. The average depth for all wells drilled that year (1925) was 241 feet. Well drilling in areas allocated to the tribes often achieved nothing at all. (Of thirteen wells completed in the Reserves, only six yielded usable water.)

The Herero have recounted themselves in an early document prepared for the U.N.* how they were driven 'from fertile valleys to the sandy regions'; how they wandered – or were driven – over the years from places first granted to them, and then coveted by Whites.

HEADMAN FESTUS KANDJO: In 1913 the Germans promised that we should be given land that we could develop for ourselves at Orumbo and elsewhere. [The Germans had begun, in the last years of their régime, to earmark land for African Reserves; but by the time that the First World War broke out, the Reserves had not been surveyed or formally proclaimed.]

The war broke out in 1914, and nothing came of this promise. So in 1917 we left for Orumbo from Windhoek. While we were at Windhoek, a certain Englishman got hold of the German book in which it

* U.N. doc. A/c 4/L. 66, pp. 19–23.

was written that Orumbo and other places were reserved for the Natives. He then approached the Herero people and told them that they have been given those places and that it was high time they left Windhoek for Orumbo and all the places round about – Okatumba, Seeis, Okaruikakao, Otjinunaua, Okamuraere, Oputae, Orutekava-hona. After we had been at those places for four years, we were given additional lands.

When we were given these additional places there was no open water. So boreholes were put down for which we paid with Trust money [tribal money], and we put up windmills. ... We only stayed three years in these new places. After that we were chased away.

We were told that the grass was finished at Orumbo and that we should now move on to the new places. When all the cattle had been removed to the new places, the government put a fence between the new places and Orumbo. Then they told us not to return to Orumbo as Orumbo was to be given to White farmers. We wanted to know why we were being chased away from the places where there was water in the river beds or not far below the surface. We were told that the White farmers are always complaining to the government that we Africans steal their cattle. We told them that if we steal cattle there are policemen there, and there is the welfare officer who brands all the cattle. No cattle are branded without producing a certificate. We were then ordered to remove all our belongings from Orumbo to the new places where our cattle were, and never to dream of Orum-bo again. In this way Orumbo became the land of the White man's farms.

The people at first refused to leave Orumbo, but then they came from Windhoek and set our houses and gardens on fire. Although the houses were burned, we remained at Orumbo for some time. But most of our cattle were on the other side of the fence and they were not allowed to return to Orumbo. So in this way, in the end, we were obliged to leave.

We stayed for two years at the new places. Towards the end of the second year we were told that the government was going to look for a big and fertile place and that this place was to the north-east of Gobabis – what is called Ovitore. The government told Chief Hosea and Chief Nicanor that they should go to Ovitore with twelve men and see if it is a good country. The twelve men were chosen. ...

CHIEF HOSEA KUTAKO: When they [the twelve] came back, they told us the country is good country and worth living in. I and Nicanor went down to Windhoek and told Mr Smit, the Secretary for South West Africa, that the country is a good country and worth living in, and that we should like to go there and live there as a nation undivided. There were no people there. It was a wild country. We were then told that the government would inform the magistrate at Gobabis that from Ovitore up to Epikuro will become the Herero land and will be given to the Herero. This took place in 1924.

One other official, after hearing this, told the Secretary for South West Africa that the country is the best in South West Africa and should not be given to any Natives. Then the Secretary told us that the official had said that that part of the country is good and is wanted by the White people. We were then told to go and explore north-east of Gobabis toward Epikuro.

FESTUS KANDJO: In 1924 Chief Frederick Maharero, Chief Hosea and all the leading Herero set out for Epikuro. Epikuro itself was a Roman Catholic mission and we thought we were meant to go there. But when we arrived at Epikuro, we found there a man who had been specifically sent by the government. He said – 'No, you are not to stay here but to go farther east. That is your country which has been set aside for you.' On their passes, though, was written Epikuro, so they took their passes and said – 'There is no Epikuro farther to the east. Where are you now sending us?' They said – 'Go to the east. What is meant is the District of Epikuro.' From Epikuro we travelled for about thirty miles. On our arrival we found a borehole dug by the government in the desert country.

CHIEF HOSEA: We slept there. The following morning I and Chief Frederick and Mr Cope went out to see the place and travelled over the whole country which is now the Reserve. We came back at night and slept there. The following morning they pumped out water from the borehole. We were then told this is only the first borehole. Others will be dug and this will become your country.

Chief Frederick was then on a visit from Bechuanaland, and Mr Cope said to him – 'I know your people want you back here. What do you think of this country?' Chief Frederick replied – 'I have nothing to say. I am only a visitor. My Uncle Hosea will tell you what is his opinion.' I then told Mr Cope – 'We are a big nation and as such we shall not develop in country like this where there is only deep borehole water. In fact it is a desert where no human being ever lived before. It is a country only good for wild beasts. On top of that it is not healthy for the people or the cattle. Only one farm can depend upon borehole water. It is no use for a whole nation.'

We told Mr Cope – 'We are the original inhabitants of South West Africa and we know the best and worst of the whole country. We know the parts which are good for cattle. We know the parts which are good for wild beasts. We are human beings and we do not want to be changed into wild beasts. Only wild beasts can live without water. We spent a lot of money on boreholes at Okamuraere and the places where we went before. When one windmill was broken at one place we used to get water from another, but here, when a windmill is broken where shall we get water . . .?'

Mr Cope was dissatisfied with this. He left us there and went back to Windhoek in his car. We travelled from Epikuro to Windhoek on horseback.

I told the Secretary that that part of the country had no water. Nothing can be grown there. It is unhealthy. Once the windmill is broken it is very difficult to get parts. So please give us a place where there is more open water.

I told Mr Smit – 'How is it that when we inhabited South West Africa, and the Coloured people [Rehobothers] were wanting land and came to Chief Samuel Maharero, he gave them a country to live in which had open water. Now you want to drive us to places where there is no water. When the Coloured people came they were only a handful, but because they had a land given them by us they are becoming a big people. Why do you not do for us what Chief Samuel Maharero did for them?'

Mr Smit said – 'Why are you so obstinate? If you speak like that we will give your land back to the Germans and you can then go and ask for it from the Germans.'

Years later the South African government was called to account for its land policy. Was it a fact, the Trusteeship Council asked in 1948 – the sole occasion on which South Africa submitted a report to the U.N. on its mandate – that the Herero had been split up into eight Reserves, and their lands never returned to them?

The Herero, replied South Africa, had been ousted from their land not by the Union government but by Germany, and the efforts by the Union government to resettle them were naturally limited by the extent to which land alienations had '*in the meantime*' taken place.

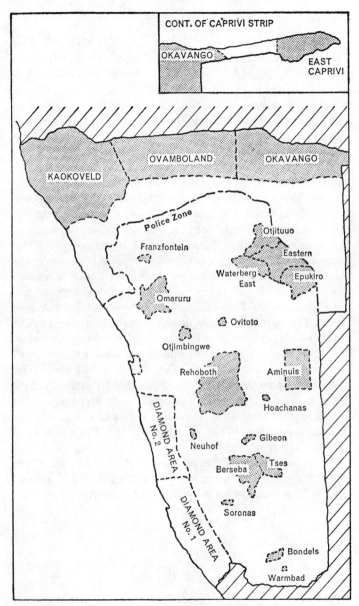

The present-day land position in South West Africa.

The tribes had asked for the restoration of their old tribal lands at a time when just over ten million hectares of the country had been in White use. The South African government had never displayed the slightest intention of conceding any African claim to their land. It had initiated instead White settlement with feverish speed, contrived the submission of the tribes with one makeshift after the other, and meanwhile manipulated the alienation of their land.

It was not a shortage of land that restricted African occupation, but a matter of policy, the traditional South African policy of rigid race rule. Throughout the history of its control over South West Africa, the South African government has always found enough land – and the best land – for White farmers, and never enough for the African tribes. Only the code of White supremacy can account for the double entries in the books of the Administration. In 1922 it was an 'utter impossibility' to restore the tribes to their former lands. In 1928 the Administration had huge areas at its disposal for the settlement of the Angola Boers. The 1937 Report complained in one paragraph that there was 'so little land available for allotment', and in another paragraph announced that 'over 21 million hectares are unallocated'.

White settlement in South West Africa is still expanding; the Herero were dismissed to the arid Kalahari sandveld in the twenties. Segregation policies initiated in the first years of the mandate entrenched for all the future of South Africa's administration a system of White privilege and non-White subjection in every sphere of life.

They were years of abundant opportunity for the White settlers, but lean and hungry years for the tribes. The state of South West Africa today is the legacy of those years.

Part Four: The Score—
In Black and White

Black and White

South Africa's administration of South West Africa has not changed much in the forty-odd years since she took possession of the mandate. Migrant labour remains the cornerstone of policy. The crowding of Africans into small Reserves has undermined their subsistence economy, while taxes have increased only their impoverishment. Labour regulations decree that a tribesman may enter a labour area and earn a cash wage, to pay his tax and tide his family over a short period in their rural slum, but that he must return home at the end of his labour contract. In this way, land and labour are inextricably linked in the mechanics of South West African society; and administrative policy has given the force of law to the silent inducements pushing tribesmen out of the Reserves to work in White-dominated South West.

1. The Wrong Side of the Line

The Red Line stretching across the map of South West Africa to demarcate the Police Zone marks the divide between progress, planned for and by Whites in the south, and careful stagnation in the northern African part of the territory. Few South West Whites know what goes on across the Line, and fewer care, as long as the people and the problems there are contained by it. In the Police Zone itself, a small minority of White voters, pampered by the South African Administration, run a world which Africans share only as unskilled labourers; beyond the Line four all-powerful White officials rule the lives of the remaining quarter of a million. White control, reared on Black-bogey stories, feels safer with the population ratio in the Police Zone at just over two Africans to every White (170,000 Africans to 73,000 Whites); the Line and the Law keep all other Africans, more than half the territory's total population, in political quarantine.

The Administration likes the Line as well, since it seals off, physically, the bulk of the African people and makes them easier to control; it keeps the most pressing problems comfortingly remote. The farther away from sight and hearing that the majority of Africans are, the longer they can be neglected. The Line is inviolate; should any African want to cross it freely, by his own decision, and not as a 'labour unit' contracted for a prescribed period by the recruiting body, he faces criminal prosecution; but the Line itself has often enough been known to move. Several times in recent years it has shifted northwards, to give the Whites more land; but, once extended, its control mechanism has snapped back into place, rigid as ever.

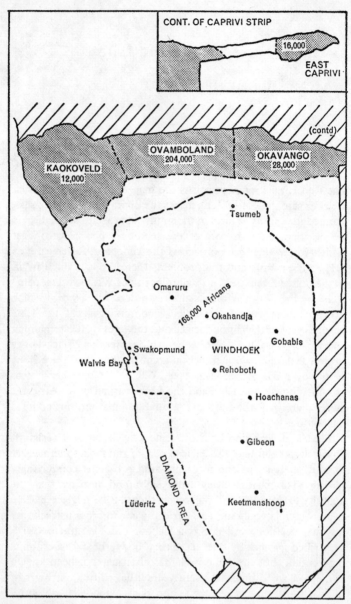

The distribution of African populations throughout South West Africa. In the country as a whole there are 428,000 Africans, 73,200 Whites, and 23,900 Coloureds and Rehobothers.

The Administrator and 30,000 Voters

For most of its existence under the mandate, South West Africa has been run by a Civil Servant, the Administrator – whose powers and capacities make him a combined Governor, Prime Minister, the ambassador of a neighbouring government, and Paramount Chief of all the Africans – together with some 30,000 White voters, who (as a Nama petition to the United Nations complained) 'have monopolized all the elements of superiority'.

Administration itself is a tangle of divided authority. The South African parliament and its successive governments have annexed extensive fields of legislation, in general those which are integrated with South Africa's own administration – 'Native affairs', defence and external affairs, railways, customs and immigration, police and the Civil Service, the courts, currency, and banking. The territorial Legislative Assembly is left to handle 'Coloured affairs', education, and health services, public works, agriculture, and mining; and it remains master of its own budget (the South African parliament may pass no law imposing tax burdens on the territory).

Newest field reserved for the South African government is the vastest and most important of all – 'Native' or 'Bantu' affairs, run since 1955 from Pretoria, though the costs are still met by South West Africa. As a result, eighty-four per cent of the mandate's population has been integrated with South Africa's own system of African administration, while twenty-four per cent of the land in South West Africa (all the Reserves) has been vested in a South African agency, the Bantu Trust. While African policy is decided in Pretoria, the chief authority on the spot remains the Administrator, who receives his power as fifth member of the South African Bantu Affairs Commission, from South Africa's own Minister of Bantu Affairs. One curious consequence is that the Administrator has refused to answer questions on Reserves or other aspects of African administration in the South West Legislative Assembly, but has told interested members that they may visit him in his office where, as a member of the South African Bantu Affairs Commission, he can provide

the information required! Apart from his dual role in the territory as chief executive officer of the Legislative Assembly, and
principal agent of the South African parliament, the Administrator sits atop a pyramid of Bantu Affairs Commissioners,
superintendents, and welfare officers in the Reserves, and, under
them, government-recognized Chiefs and headmen: a perfect
system for a sternly disciplined – and parsimonious – boarding
school.

The eighteen-member Legislative Assembly passes expenditure each year (including meagre amounts for African services).
But the budget debate apart, its proceedings are routine and
humdrum. Its ordinances are the stuff of day-to-day administration: town planning, game preservation, soil conservation,
stamp duties, supervision of the dairy industry, teachers' pensions. Policy remains in the hands of the South African government, legislation is debated not in Windhoek but in Cape Town,
and with few exceptions South African laws are applied to the
territory.

The South West Africa Affairs Amendment Act of 1949 gave
the Whites representation in the South African parliament – out
of all proportion to their numbers, because the Nationalist
Party was intent on increasing its majority – and so the territory
sends six members to the Assembly (among them the most
virulent anti-Semite in the House) and four to the Senate. Two
Senators are elected, and two nominated, one of the latter on the
grounds of his 'thorough acquaintance with the reasonable wants
and wishes of the coloured races of the territory'. Shrewdly, in
the interests of ruling White unity, the government has succes-
sively chosen as its Senatorial experts on the non-White peoples
of South West Africa two German settlers of long standing: Dr
H. Vedder, head of the Rhenish Mission Church, whom the
South African Minister of the Interior visited personally to
ensure his support for the Nationalist government after 1950;
and Dr Karl Frey, former war-time internee, who earned his
Senate seat by energetic campaigning for the Nationalists. In
one of his rare speeches in the Senate, Dr Vedder revealed the

ease with which he had slid from German to South African rule. South West Africa, he claimed, was the only country in the world where apartheid had been practised for fifty years.

Only Whites may vote or be consulted; Whites alone execute policy. The Civil Service is dominated by South Africans, mostly Afrikaners, who monopolize all the senior posts. Africans in the Civil Service fill the lower ranks; they are policemen (possessing no authority to deal with Whites), clerks in the Bantu Affairs Department, jail warders, and teachers (of Africans).

One of Chief Hosea Kutako's petitions to the U.N. stated: 'This is the country where no other races are allowed to rule except Europeans or people with white skins. All Europeans belong to a privileged group, they have the vote, they rule the country, they oppress the non-Europeans and they are free to go to the United Nations.' Even that last right, officially despised as it is, could hardly be allowed beyond White control.

Four Great White Fathers

In Ovamboland and the Okavango, government is of the people, by government officials, for the labour recruiter.

Administration has for forty years resided with successive Commissioners, who have energetically devoted themselves to improvising a form of indirect rule in the bush, with the object of ensuring a placid population and constant labour supply. White government is epitomized in the personal rule of these Bantu Affairs Commissioners: two in Ovamboland, at Ondongua and Oshikango; a third at Runtu, to run the Okavango and the western Caprivi Zipfel; and an officer-in-charge of Bantu Affairs at Ohopoho, to control the Kaokoveld.

Officialdom boasts that 'government is left entirely to the Natives'; that they run their own affairs under their traditional Chiefs or under Councils of Headmen. But if any question arises which Chief or Council cannot settle, the Administration – in the form of the all-powerful Commissioner – gives 'advice' and the necessary instructions. The tribe can govern by its own laws and customs, yet the Administration admits that 'laws and usages not in keeping with just rule and which retarded progress were by degrees eliminated'.*

Not only tribal usages, but tribal heads as well can be scrapped by the government. Of the seven Ovambo tribes, three are 'governed' by Chiefs, and four by Councils. There are few clues to the disappearance of those Chiefs replaced by Councils. Commissioner Hahn was asked in 1937 by the Permanent Mandates Commission to explain what the Portuguese representative called 'this small-scale revolution in the administration of Ovamboland'. Hahn volunteered the information that, in all, seven Ovambo tribes, or sub-tribes, had lost their Chiefs. How or why is difficult to discover. The conclusion, however, is certain. Customs and Chiefs remain secure for as long as they do not clash with the government's policy.

No South African government has ever wanted to hasten African advance, and encourage the development of democracy. The system of indirect rule has decided advantages. It is cheap. Petty Chiefs and headmen can be used to administer vast areas at rates of pay no White official would accept. Headmen in Police Zone Reserves, for example, are paid allowances as low as £24 a year. Above all, the system provides a much-needed safety valve. Responsibility for policies is deflected from government to Chiefs; and popular resentment is turned inwards, towards the organization of the tribe. Dissatisfaction with government policies is deflected into quarrels over succession, as happened most recently among the Ukualuthi tribe, where there were rumours of an 'underground movement' to dislodge the pro-government Chief.

The Chiefs are entrusted by the Administration with the unpleasant tasks of collecting taxes, conveying the orders of the Commissioner, and enforcing the law in times of trouble; they cushion the government from the demands and anger of their subjects. As applied in the northern territories of South West Africa, indirect rule assumes, despite all the evidence contained in most studies of these tribal societies, that the Chiefs were, by nature of their office, autocrats. The Chief is regarded as the sole

* Reports to the Permanent Mandates Commission of the League.

representative institution of the tribe, and the tribe itself as unaccustomed to any form of democratic consultation. Working on this theory, White government has enhanced the powers of the Chief at the expense of those very tribal institutions and customs which served as a check on his power. The old remedies of a tribe against a predatory Chief are no longer available, for the Chief is an employee of the government and no longer answerable to his tribe, but to a higher, intruding authority. Chiefs and senior headmen on the government payroll who fail to prove themselves sufficiently cooperative receive the treatment that any disobedient Civil Servant would get - the sack.

The Minister of Bantu Affairs has the power to appoint and dismiss Chiefs; to divide or amalgamate tribes; to levy annual amounts for reserve trust funds. Chiefs and headmen combine the roles of copper's nark and Civil Servant. They are obliged to carry out the orders of the White official placed in authority over them, comply with whatever is required of them by the Administration, and bring new laws and instructions to the notice of the people; inform on any strangers and fugitives in their areas; report all unlawful gatherings; supply labour for agriculture or any other purposes; and rigorously observe the prohibition against their becoming members of or taking part in the affairs of any political association whose objects are deemed subversive by the Administration. Chiefs bask in the honour, but the true rulers of the tribes are the officials who oversee them.

Even if the system were democratic, the development of effective tribal authorities would be rendered hopeless by the absence of so many of the men in employment outside the African Reserves. The greater the flow of men to the labour areas in the White south, the more tenuous becomes the authority of the Chief over the tribe. With every year of greater participation by the tribesmen in the territory's total economy, the system of indirect rule has less chance of working.

This is the weak joint not only of all tribal administration, but of the whole apartheid policy. Apartheid, as the physical segregation of Africans from the Whites, is more and more the pipe dream of an integrated economy. Every factory chimney, mine-shaft, and farm furrow bears the print of Africans drawn from their Reserves to work; and work in the industrial and labour centres has meant, in time, settlement too. Communities long urbanized, an integral part of the whole industrial pattern, are being told that their homelands are several hundred miles away in the kraal.

After the Transkei, Ovamboland is to be the site of the next well-published experiment in apartheid. Great Nationalist hopes are pinned to the project. Diligently the South African government is preparing plans for welding together into a so-called Bantustan the three areas of Ovamboland, the Okavango and the Kaokoveld. In South West Africa industrialization has barely begun; the Reserves outside the Police Zone are sealed off already by the Red Line. And the government is determined to keep it that way. South Africa's system of migrant labour provided the pattern for South West Africa, but now the pupil is to improve on the master. No permanent African settlement is to be permitted in the territory's urban areas, at *any* cost. The Red Line and the rigorous enforcement of the contract-labour system must ensure this. Nationalist planners even recognize that the population-carrying capacity of the African areas in the north must be improved if there is to be no uncontrollable overflow to the south, and an irrigation scheme is under way to make the region agriculturally more productive. More ambitious is a project to use the Ruacana Falls and the Kunene River for water and power supplies; but the Falls are on the Angola side of the border, and the project involves protracted negotiations with Portugal.

Apartheid may put its best foot forward in Ovamboland, but it will still trip over the ever present hurdle: the economy of the Police Zone would speedily disintegrate without labour from the northern territories (and Angola).

2. The Dignity of Labour

Men – and boys – at station sidings with labels tied round their necks: Thomas Abnael, looking about fifteen years old, and marked 'UNDER AGE' on the contract form he clutched; Shikingo Isaak, who had herded karakul sheep from before sunrise till after sunset for twelve months at a wage of 25s. a month and for the next six months at 35s., warned that if he lost a sheep he would have to pay for it: all are products of the huge labour-recruiting organization that covers South West Africa. Ovambos travel hundreds of miles, for days on end, clad in the regulation shorts and singlet, with one blanket (two for those exposed to the blistering winds on the Luderitz diamond fields), rationing themselves on a small store of mealie meal porridge, bewildered, bound for an unknown destination. The contract-labour system is known to the Ovambo as '*omtete uokaholo*': '*omtete*' means queue, and '*uokaholo*' is their word for the identity disc hung from the neck of the recruit.

If a Reserve does not supply enough labour [said one Ovambo], it is looked upon as a bad Reserve. A message comes from the Commissioner to the welfare officer. The welfare officer calls the headman and Reserve board members. The welfare officer reads the letter to the board members, and tells them that they want a certain number of labourers to work on the farms or on the roads, and this number must be supplied. If that number is not supplied, the headmen and board members are scolded. Then the Ovambo is sent off with a ticket. He does not know where he is going. The name of the master and the place are written on the label, and the people at the railway station send him where he has to go. After the station master has read the label, he rings up the police station to come and fetch this 'parcel', and he is taken to the police station, from where he is fetched by the farmer or taken by the police to the farmer. Sometimes men have to walk for fifty to sixty miles. They may just be shown the road and told to go.

The farmer dreads that the man on the road will never arrive, for drought and a labour shortage are the twin nightmares of White South West Africa.

Labour recruitment is a national institution. Grootfontein in the north-east is as much a nerve centre of the country as the capital, Windhoek, for here is sited the head office of the new South West African Native Labour Association, the efficient, semi-government monopoly whose only commodity is men. Grootfontein is in constant touch with the most remote employers. Every farmer's order for 'boys' is listed; every Ovambo labourer is card-indexed on a labour register; every movement of workers across the face of the country is charted. There is no national wage legislation, only the rate laid down by the recruiting monopoly and approved by the government. Ondangua in Ovamboland and Runtu in the Okavango are the administrative centres and the main labour depots. The Bantu Affairs Commissioners govern the tribes, and ensure that the supply of contract labour does not flag. The only government medical officers stationed in the area spend more than half their days examining and classifying recruits – into 'A', 'B', and 'C' types – those fit for underground work in the mines, for surface work on mines, and heavy farm work, or those fit only for light farm work as shepherds and cattle herders. Every employer of contract labour must pay a capitation fee of about £13 per recruit. No hours of work are specified in the printed contracts, only that 'the servant is required to render the master his service at all fair and reasonable times'.

At the beginning the government handled recruiting from the northern territories itself; the official sent north in 1915 to seek the cooperation of the Chiefs in encouraging their people to find employment on railways and farms, reported his confidence that, as the administration of Ovamboland developed, a valuable and permanent source of labour for the railways, mines and other industries could be secured. Labour remained perverse, however, 'happy and contented in their natural state', as the Administrator told the League of Nations in his 1926 Report. He gave four reasons for the discouraging position. The tribesmen were free of taxation (this was to be remedied soon enough); they had unlimited grazing; there were no traders' stores within European areas for which cash was needed; and the diet was 'different' in the labour centres. 'It is only', stated the Administrator, 'by close contact with the European races that in the hearts of these backward people will be bred that "divine discontent" which makes for progress, and although the efforts of the missionaries, who are so nobly working among them, will surely in time bring about an improvement, *the Administration is seriously considering other means of inducing labourers to come out.'*

There is a mixture of *naïveté* and candour in official admissions of the day, a refreshing directness – later to be submerged by evasions and deceit – in the way that the government set itself to do the will of the employers. The Luderitz Chamber of Mines asked for an official experienced in 'native administration' to help with recruiting operations in Ovamboland; the officer in charge of Native Affairs in Windhoek, Mr R. S. Cope, set off on his new mission, and by the following year recorded an increase of ten per cent in the labour recruitment figures. The government also sank boreholes in the dry stretch separating Okavango from the labour areas, to give migrant labourers a water supply on their journey to work; fines for breaches of contract were increased from £3 to £7, the equivalent of seven months' wages.

A sharp shock reverberated through the session of the Permanent Mandates Commission at Geneva when one of the South African government's annual reports in the twenties recorded that religious missions operating in Ovamboland were required to furnish a written undertaking to assist and support the policy of the administration, and *encourage all 'Natives' under their influence to seek employment in the Police Zone.* The Administrator, confronted with this, explained that the government had never contemplated turning the missions into labour agencies: it had intended only that they should 'inculcate into Natives the principle of the dignity of labour'. Once brought to light, this arrangement could not survive scrutiny. It was officially killed.

In 1925 the Administration called a conference of mining companies, and two recruiting associations were formed, one for the copper mines and northern farms, and the other for the diamond fields. Eighteen years later these bodies were replaced by the present-day South West African Native Labour Association, under whose more efficient régime recruiting figures have risen and generous savings effected in the *per capita* costs of recruitment.

By the middle forties, half the labour force on the sheep and cattle farms of the territory was recruited from regions outside the Police Zone. But drought and depression had been overtaken by the post-war boom, and the cry for labour had become more strident than ever. Even the spill-over of men from Angola (which persists to this day) did not help.

Farming interests pressed for an investigation, and for three years, from 1945 to 1948, the South West African Native Labour Commission probed. One widely held White myth it carefully contradicted – that Africans of employable age were lazy and idle, that thousands of the ungrateful creatures were lying about the Reserves and urban locations without work or the will to find any. The Commission dismissed such beliefs as unfounded in fact; in the Police Zone African men were fully employed, and many African women too, in part-time work.

Not only [observed the Commission] do the local Natives appear to be fully employed at present, but vital statistics indicate that the local population is not increasing to any marked extent, and that it would be more correct to describe it as just maintaining its present strength. That being so, there is but little prospect of increase of the local labour supply.

Employers were forced to look northwards in order to meet the annual shortfall of workers. There, however, farmers found that a more powerful competitor had preceded them. The trickle of men from the northern areas to the Witwatersrand gold mines had developed into a torrent, the Commission reported, 'draining away the labour supply which is so essential to the continued prosperity of the Territory, and creating a labour problem of very considerable urgency.'

The South West African Native Labour Association was learning fast, but it was still a novice at labour recruiting, at least in comparison with the vast Witwatersrand Native Labour Association, which had begun its operations in the 1890s. In Livingstone's day it was the Arab slave-trails which criss-crossed Africa; today, along the same routes and many new ones, the Witwatersrand Native Labour Association, with its various recruiting agencies, runs buses, trucks, and barges; flies plane-loads of recruits from swamp and bush to concrete compound. Recruiting posts connect remote geographical areas; top-secret labour treaties with other African territories make the W.N.L.A. more an empire than a mere labour agency.

In 1943 the W.N.L.A. had held discussions with the South West African authorities over the engagement of labour for the gold mines; two years later it had built rest camps at Runtu and Mohembo, cut a new road from Grootfontein to the Bechuanaland border, and received permission to recruit up to 3,000 men a year. The northern areas of South West Africa adjoin Angola, and the mines were thus sluicing off from the territory not only Ovambo and Okavango labour, but also the flow from the Portuguese reservoir. This interference, said farmers and the Commission, constituted a direct threat to the territory's economy. The Commission recommended that the contract with the W.N.L.A. should be ended, and that the South West African Native Labour Association should build its own recruiting posts and reroute labour to Grootfontein. In the tug-o'-war for labour between gold mines and farmers, the South West African Administration backed its own White voters.

The farmers evidently got their way, for the most part. The two recruiting monopolies of South West Africa and the Witwatersrand patched up a compromise division of the field. The South West African Native Labour Association has become a sub-agent of the larger recruiting organization, turning over to it such labour as is not required by employers in the territory. In 1961 over 27,000 Africans were recruited: some 14,500 from South West Africa's northern areas, and almost as many – 12,500 – from Angola. Of the total number of recruits, 8,658 were allocated to South West African farms; 9,559 to industries and public works; 6,703 to South West African mines; and 2,241 – about one in twelve – to the mines in South Africa. Of the latter total, only a few hundred were Ovambos: for almost all the men routed to the Witwatersrand mines are attested at Runtu in the Okavango and are drawn from Angola.

No fairy godmother could have been as indulgent to the labour needs of South West Africa's employers as the territory's Administration. It reconstituted by law the South West African Native Labour Association Board, and bought a seat on it for the Agricultural Union. It forks out subsidies for the transport of recruits, builds and guards rest camps along the labour route, and from public monies pays the tribal trust funds a capitation fee for each Ovambo or Okavango recruit who agrees to sign on for farm labour.

The farmers' government gained for farmers an entry into the recruiting monopoly; but with all the compulsions it could exert on labour, it could not overcome the reluctance of recruits to work on farms. The 1945–8 South West Africa Native Labour Commission had noticed and described this. At a parade in Ondangua, the Commission observed, some 500 recruits were seeking employment. Mine work was offered for less than a hundred 'boys'; but when the call came for farm volunteers, after the terms of employment had been announced, 'the only boys who stepped forward were about a dozen youths aged 14 or 15 years. An adult boy [sic] about to come forward was laughed at by his companions to such an extent that he shamefacedly retreated into the ranks'.

The Commission Report told the territory a few unpalatable truths about the labour shortage. Recruits travelled in *bambellos* – cattle trucks – standing all the way or sitting on the lurching floor with nothing to grasp. No water was provided, and sanitary arrangements were crude. Recruits having to find their own way to farms often arrived at their destination seven or ten days later, half-starved and exhausted.

The main complaint, after the low wages paid, reported the Commission, were the bad housing conditions, 'or more correctly stated – the absence of housing on farms'. White and African witnesses alike – and the Commission members confirmed this by their own observation – told of housing on farms that was primitive, unsatisfactory, and even nonexistent.

Unfortunately [stated the Commission] there are still farmers whose attitude towards natives' housing is that the natives in their natural state are accustomed to living under a bush and that accordingly they are not entitled to anything better from their employers. In point of fact this is erroneous. The huts in which the Extra-Territorial and Northern Natives reside in Ovamboland and the Okavango are well-constructed, well-ventilated, water-tight structures which are cool in summer and warm in winter. One of the most frequent complaints made by Extra-Territorial and Northern Natives to the Commission was that their employers never gave them time or the necessary materials with which to construct houses similar to those they occupied at home. They were told that they could construct a hut for themselves in their free time.

The Commission recommended, as did a Health Commission, that it should be made compulsory for every farmer to supply a certain minimum standard of housing. The recommendation was shelved. The Commission recommended a scale of rations. A Committee of the Legislative Assembly reported back in 1949 '... for obvious reasons [we are] not in favour of a prescribed ration scale'.

By the fifties and sixties, some but by no means all of the nastiest features of labour recruiting had been modified. Transport to the large labour centres is stream-lined today, but the life of the Ovambo shepherd, on whose vigilance and trustworthiness the costly karakul flock depends, is as wretched as ever.

With 25,000 labourers recruited each year and many of them extending their contracts, there must be between 40,000 and 45,000 contracted workers in the Police Zone at any one time:

men without families and, back home, wives without husbands, and children without fathers. Ovambo villages in Angola and South West Africa alike are drained of their young men. The social and human consequences are not contained in South West African or Witwaterstrand Native Labour Association reports. They cannot even be guessed.

Inside the Police Zone the contract labour system does not apply, but the Herero, Nama, and Berg-Damara are enclosed in an iron framework of laws, regulations, ordinances, proclamations, and official instructions.

Men are 'handcuffed' by slips of paper. They must have permits to seek work, permits to be in the area for any purpose other than to seek work, service contracts to prove that they are working, passes to prove that they are schoolboys and too young to carry passes, certificates of registration authorizing residence in the area, permits to travel, tax receipts, exemptions from night curfew. Passes and permits constitute their licence to live; they may move nowhere without joining the interminable queue at the government office for stamps of authority on their passes. No African in the Police Zone may buy a railway ticket without a pass issued by his employer or an authorized official. No African in a Reserve may leave it except by permit or in order to work for a White employer. Men have been reduced to mere labour units.

In a society where cheap African labour is so essential, any African's failure to work is a crime called vagrancy. This is defined as wandering abroad with no visible means, or 'insufficient lawful means' of support, and is an offence punishable by imprisonment. A first offender under the vagrancy law may, instead of going to jail, be placed in employment on public works or with a private employer, at a wage judged fair by the court.*

Rural areas of the Police Zone other than Reserves are considered White areas, regardless of how many Africans may live and work in them, and any African living on land allocated to a White settler must work for him, or leave the land. The number of Africans allowed into any urban area is based on the immediate

* 1920 Vagrancy Proclamation.

labour requirements of the area; 'surplus' Africans, even permanent residents, may be forced to leave. Any African living there must carry on his person a contract showing where he works, and if he should become unemployed, may be expelled after one month. Newcomers must acquire permits to seek work, and if they find no work within fourteen days, are ordered to leave.

Thus each Reserve, town, or farming area is an island surrounded by a sea of restrictions. Once a man is ordained to live and work in one area, there is little or nothing that he can do to change his situation. If he steps beyond the limits recorded in his passes, he risks arrest by the police, the detectives in plain clothes, the labour inspectors, who search everywhere for transgressors. The dragnet of the pass laws are inescapable. A young African political organizer in Windhoek spent some spare time sitting in court, listening to the endless petty infringements of the law: failure to produce a service contract pass on request – £1 or seven days' hard labour; failure to possess a travelling pass, entering the location without a permit, unlawful domicile (excluding Ovambos) – £3 or fifteen days' imprisonment; presence in the Police Zone without an exemption (this applies to Ovambos born outside the Zone) – £5 or thirty days' in jail with hard labour, and expulsion from the Zone; failure to pay the hut tax due before the fifteenth day of each month – 10s. fine or five days for each month unpaid; liquor offences (brewing liquor at home) – £1 a gallon for the first offence, but reaching £20 – £30 a four-gallon tin for an offender with previous convictions. Fines for contravening the labour regulations are out of all proportion to African incomes; innocent men find themselves helplessly behind bars or forced to join the convict gangs in red shirts on public works. If the incentives to work are not strong enough, men must be jailed into labour.

The legal code of the country has been shaped to overcome the labour shortage; but except in time of drought, when farmers need less labour, the shortage has become endemic. Compulsion, whether covert or open, has always been the accepted method of swelling the labour supply. Rational priorities, like raising wages and improving the conditions of work, are perpetually rejected. The only minimum wage proclamation prepared (in 1944) was announced but never enforced; wage increases recommended by the Native Labour Commission were implemented only in part. (At the time of the Commission the minimum wage for a shepherd was 9s. a month!) When the fishing industry proposed to the Wage Board an increase in the basic wage of the Ovambo labourer, the farming community, as usual, rose in strident opposition. Any step, but not wage increases!

The Administration has strenuously searched for new ways to solve the labour shortage: contractors engaged on large public works have been allowed to take their South African labour contingents into the territory; the railways have offered special incentives; labour has even been recruited inside South Africa and dispatched to farmers – at £3 10s. a month, considerably more than the Ovambo labourer earns – for Africans from across the border would clearly not enlist at South West African wage levels. The Administrator told a farmers' conference that, on a visit to the Okavango, he had met eighty-six women who had complained that their husbands were away from their homes for too long at a time; and the Chief Native Commissioner cajoled the Agricultural Union into opening negotiations with the South West African Native Labour Association over curtailing the contract period and raising the wage scale.

The 1962 wages and terms of work were outlined to me in a letter* from the Secretary of the South West African Native Labour Association. The maximum initial contract period for mines and industries is 309 shifts (working days), and twelve months for domestic service in the urban areas. Farm labourers are given the choice of signing a contract for twelve or for eighteen months. All contracts may, by mutual consent of the employer and employee, be extended up to twenty-four months for married men and thirty months for unmarried ones. The minimum wage laid down for contract labour in industry and mining is 1s. 9d. a shift for the first 155 shifts, 2s. for the next 77 shifts and 2s. 3d. for the last 77 shifts. In addition to the

* Dated 10 May 1962.

basic wage, many mines and industries pay allowances and proficiency bonuses to their labourers, depending on the quality of work performed. Farm wages fluctuate according to the medical classification of the labourer, from 25s. a month for inexperienced youngsters up to £4 for the more tried Class-'A' labourers. In practice, however, the farmers pay a higher wage than the minimum required. And here too, the proficiency of the 'boy' is taken into account.

I might mention that a shepherd earns a wage of 10s. a month more than the general farm labourer, and that natives taking on eighteen-month contracts initially earn a wage of 5s. a month more than the labourer taking a twelve-month contract on farms.

One year's work by a miner or industrial worker, at the highest South West African Native Labour Association rate paid, will earn £30. The man earning the minimum daily rate gets 35s. a month. Certainly some of the larger enterprises pay bonuses, but entirely at whim.

Wages rates in the farming areas are wretchedly low. In the urban areas they dip at least one-third lower than rates across the border in South Africa for building labourers, petrol pump attendants, delivery messengers.

POSTSCRIPT: Only the recent drought succeeded in dispelling for a while the constant scare of labour shortage. In 1962 the Administration was able for the first time to report an adequate labour supply. Farmers have been forced to reduce the numbers of workers they hire, while the parched land in the Reserves themselves has driven more Africans into the search for wage employment.

3. 'You are a Black Spot'

At Dar es Salaam in 1961, when the U.N. Committee on South West Africa heard evidence from petitioners who had fled the country, a former Windhoek social worker, Zedekia Ngavirue, criticized a U.N. report that had attributed the unequal distribution of wealth in South West Africa to the capital resources, education, skills, and experience of the White population, and to the superior assistance given them by the Administration. That was not the whole story, Ngavirue maintained. 'My great grandfather, the late Chief Kambazembi, had never been to school, but he had 25,000 cattle in 1903 before we were conquered. I have a college diploma but do not possess even a chicken.' African poverty, he claimed, was due to two main factors: expropriation of the land first by the German and then by the South African administrations; and the policy of economic apartheid pursued by the South African government, which 'serves to deprive the African people of the lands and other resources of the earth, and to reduce them to a state of servitude'.

The story of how the mandatory power plundered African land to encourage White settlement has already been told; the new South African régime took advantage of the tribal dispersions caused by the German conquest. A few of the old German treaties were respected; but most of the areas marked out by the German Administration for tribal use had not been proclaimed by the outbreak of the First World War. The South African government proclaimed some Reserves itself, but in the process dispossessed the Africans of better lands that the Germans had earmarked for African use. The area scheduled by the German Commander Oberleutnant Streitwold in 1902 for the people under the two Chiefs of Okahandja and Waterberg, for instance, was two and a half times larger – and in a far more fertile region – than the land which the people possess today.

If one knew nothing about the siting of the African Reserves, one could plot them on the map by tracing the least fertile areas. The only anomalies are the Rehoboth lands in the middle of the territory – a recognition of the community's special status half-way up the colour ladder between black and white – and the little Nama Reserves, recognized by German treaty, then expanded, and some of them tabbed 'black spots', which the South African Administration would undoubtedly have moved to make way for White farms had it not felt the hot breath of the U.N. on its neck.

The geography of this huge country is important, for desert and dryness set limits to where people can live and farm. The central ranching plateau lies in a strait-jacket of desert. Along the length of the western coast lies the Namib, barren in all but diamonds, which have been cornered by one of the two vast mining corporations that dominate the country. On the east stretches the semi-desert of the Kalahari, against which the main Herero Reserves have been ruthlessly pushed. The broad ranching corridor is arid in the south, but good for karakul sheep, the mainstay of agriculture. Rainfall increases, and so the prospects of cattle farming brighten, towards the north, where, too, great mineral wealth in copper, lead, and zinc lies buried.

The far north of the country is straddled by Ovamboland in the centre, the Kaokoveld to the west, and the Okavango in the east. Ovamboland, holding half the African population, experiences an annual flooding of the flat-as-a-plate countryside, and though the water irrigates it also submerges three-fifths of the whole region at times, so that the mound-and-furrow method of planting has to be used. Ovamboland is the only area where agriculture predominates, but even there the soil is no more than a thin layer stretched over salty deposits, sustaining so many people that the subsistence economy is always on the verge of collapse. The Kaokoveld is barren and mountainous, with a small sparse population who, in the best watered area of Zesfontein in the south, get a turn perhaps once a week to irrigate their land from the springs and water furrow. In the Okavango, most of the African settlement stretches along the river. The Caprivi strip, flung eastwards by the Germans to join their colonies on either side of the continent, leads into the Eastern Caprivi Zipfel, part of South West but administered as part of South Africa, which provides an important corridor for the transport of Central African recruited mine labour to the Witwatersrand.

Despite the drought, which comes with almost calendrical regularity, and the lack of any real industrial development, the country could sustain all its inhabitants, were it less mutilated by racial privilege.

Whites, though only one in seven of the total population, enjoy the exclusive use of two-thirds of the land. It has become an agricultural cliché that sheep farms in the south should have a minimum area of 10,000 hectares; cattle farms in the north, at least half that size. In 1952 the average White farmstead was 7,500 hectares or twenty-eight square miles in extent. Some farms today are as large as 20,000 and even 30,000 hectares. Such standards, of course, are rigidly racial. While 73,200 Whites (about 6,000 farmers) occupy and farm forty million hectares, 170,000 Africans inside the Police Zone are confined to 5.8 million hectares, and 261,000 Africans beyond the Red Line to sixteen million more. (Government statistics are elusive and, when found, usually approximate.)

Discrimination in land ownership and occupation is one of the pillars of White rule in South West Africa. The South African government claimed, when it condescended to take part in U.N. debates at all, that millions of hectares had been granted to the indigenous tribes. It has been an exercise in sleight of hand.

By the start of the Second World War, and the end to League of Nations supervision of the territory, proclaimed Reserves for African (and Rehoboth) occupation amounted to some 11·8 million hectares, with a further 4·2 million earmarked for extensions. From 1946 to 1962, the total area of non-White land increased from just over fifteen million to twenty-one million hectares. But of the 5.8 million hectares (scattered over seventeen different Reserves) allocated to Africans within the Police Zone, 2.3 million were theirs by German proclamation already.

New Reserves demarcated by 1947 amounted to some three million hectares in all. The largest were Epukiro, Aminuis, and Waterberg East – slices totalling less than two million hectares, compared with the whole of the central ranch-lands which the Herero had roamed before – and some extra Reserves like Tses and Gibeon for the Nama.

The only large additional allocation of land within the Zone has been the Eastern Reserve, of 1·2 million hectares, proclaimed in 1947.

The greater part (two-thirds) of the two million new hectares set aside for African use is beyond the Police Zone; the formal proclamation of Ovamboland, the Okavango, the Kaokoveld. and the Caprivi Zipfel as Reserves did not give Africans a single square yard of territory that was not already occupied by them. Some regions like the Kaokoveld are too barren and wild to be coveted by Whites. The whole area beyond the Police Zone has provided no new land for the tribes displaced by the wars with the Germans.

Land always occupied by Africans has been given the seal of proclamation not because it changes African land holding one jot, but because it makes the Administration's case seem a a little less shabby.

With few exceptions, the Reserves are situated in the driest and least productive regions of South West Africa, to support sparse and dwindling populations.

The conscientious investigations of the major Reserves of the Herero and Berg-Damara peoples, begun for the South African government by Gunter Wagner and revised by O. Kohler, describe, dispassionately, their drawbacks.

EPUKIRO, largest Reserve in the Police Zone, is totally un-inhabited in parts. Its endless dry river beds were the routes by which the Herero survivors of the Battle of the Waterberg tried to escape to Bechuanaland, and its water holes got their names from those days. 'There appear to be portions within the Reserve ... where boring holds virtually no promise. At some places the water is brackish.'

In the AMINUIS RESERVE, the water supplied by wells is 'good but insufficient in view of the steady increase in stock. After normal rainfall the grazing is good, but there are certain areas where the grass is hard and unsuitable'.

OTJITUUO RESERVE: 'The central portion of the Reserve is covered with sand dunes, water is scarce and the vegetation sparse. Covered mostly with sand, it is almost uninhabited.'

OTJIMBINGWE RESERVE: 'Only two-fifths of the Reserve can be grazed, as water is not well distributed over the whole Reserve. The area along the rivers is badly overgrazed and eroded. Of the four dams built, one had not had a drop of water in it for years. Boring has been done at spots selected by the government but most of them have yielded water which is not potable.'

OVITOTO RESERVE: 'The entire Reserve consists of hilly and in parts even mountainous country, with numerous deep and narrow valleys. The underground water supplies of the Reserve are very poor, so that only a few of the government's numerous attempts to secure water by boring have been successful.'

The OKOMBAHE RESERVE has 'relatively good grazing in the west, semi-Namib [desert] in the east. Boreholes have been dug, but the water is brackish here and there. At Kanian in the far south-west I found some Bergdama [Berg-Damara] who had made a fire under a drum filled with water. A long pipe sealed to the drum with clay led to a pail buried in the ground. In this way they were distilling the brackish water to get some water that they could drink. Dams have been built but these are only a limited success'.

WATERBERG EAST RESERVE: 'The sandveld is deficient in minerals. *Lamsiekte* is prevalent there. The centre of the Reserve is virtually waterless. Seventy per cent of the population is living along the dry river beds.' The Kalahari sand of this and other areas is chemically poor, with a low phosphate content which produces deficiency diseases in stock.

As dispersed as the Reserves are, they share several common features. Large portions cannot be inhabited, let alone farmed. The population (revealed in figures up to five years ago) has barely risen, and in some instances has dropped over the last two decades. Several age-groups are missing: the generations that were obliterated in the Herero war; and the young men, from fifteen to thirty-five years old, away working for White employers.

Of 171,787 non-Whites in the Police Zone at the time of the 1952 census, only 25,046 were living in the Reserves.

The Administration stated in its 1928 Report to the League of Nations:

> Men are not encouraged to remain idling in the Reserves. Only men who are physically unfit, or such as are necessarily required to look after the people in the Reserves and their stock and the stock of others who have gone out to work, are encouraged to remain there.

The Nama Reserves of the south were particularly hard hit by the 1959–62 drought. Families were scattered far and wide over the White farms in the area, trying to make a living as sheep shearers and herders and domestic servants. But even in better times – except for the minority of karakul sheep farmers in the Berseba, Gibeon, and Bondels Reserves – these Reserves are more the refuge of farm workers between spells of migrant labour, and the retreat of the aged, than the farming sites of the clans. The young men are away for half the year at least; many families own no more than a few goats; and poverty is so acute that some stock owners depend on the young men who work in the White labour areas to send home money for grazing fees.

Even since the U.N. began watching – from afar – every move of the South African government, the unfinished business of dispossessing Africans of their land has gone on unabated. White settlement has crept close to the Reserves, surrounded them, and then condemned them as 'Black spots'.

With the administration of all Africans in the territory

assumed by his Department, the South African Minister of Bantu Affairs affirmed that the removal of smaller Reserves was 'the subject of study ... It is our policy, with which everybody agrees, that the Natives should rather be placed on ground adjacent to the native areas.'*

Aukeigas lies at the heart of the territory, just north of the capital, an excellent farming area, with a good water supply as a result of the dams and wells left by its African inhabitants.

In the beginning, said Fritz Gariseb, a Berg-Damara spokesman, the people in Aukeigas were told to build their own dams and storage schemes.

The first dam was built by our people with the aid of the Boers and was Aukeigas dam, the second one was Autos, the third Kawabas. Here we lived until the South West African Administration deemed it fit to uproot the homes in the Reserve of Aukeigas without consulting the people and sent them by force to the present Damara Reserve of Okombahe in 1938. All the constructions in the Aukeigas Reserve were left behind. The second trek took place in 1941, also to Okombahe. The third and last lot trekked under very tragic conditions to Sorris-Sorris in 1958. We were promised a Canaan in our new homes, but even so this trek can be described as a national suicide. Thousands of their cattle died, and from the people who moved originally from Aukeigas only forty-six families remain. Today the Damara people are a fallen race in Sorris-Sorris and other Reserves. What happens in the Aukeigas district at the present moment? Two or three rich Whites have bought farms there and make use of the water storage left by the people. One of these rich people is D., the other is L. The other part of the Reserve was declared a game reserve. This means that even the animals have more state protection than human souls.

The home of 401 Africans, Aukeigas was divided into two White farms of 4,950 hectares each, with the rest turned into game reserve. The Berg-Damara were removed 250 miles north to land bordering on the Okombahe Reserve. The new area was slightly smaller than their Aukeigas home, but the size was not its main defect. In the judgement of the Agricultural Commission, a minimum of 10,000 hectares in the area was needed to provide a living for one farming family (White).

* Hansard, 1 August 1958, No. 4, Col. 1366.

The removal of the people of Hoachanas speedily became a *cause célèbre* in the committee rooms of the U.N.

We Perish ! ! ! ! ! ! [cried the petition from Hoachanas]
Most honourable members. How is it possible for a person to come from Union, England or elsewhere, and tell the one on whose place he came, and to situate around him, and become millionaire with his underpaid handwork, multiply your brethren round him, take away his land, deny him the privilege of education to keep him in eternal ignorance and servitude, take away all his rights and make him a blind, deaf-and-dumb voiceless creature, and afterwards tell him 'You did not originate here' and 'You are a black spot'? Our country has gone to strangers and they have become heirs and originals of it.

The headquarters of the Red Nation, the oldest Nama clan of South West Africa, had been encircled by White farmers, a list of whom was sent to the U.N. by the clan, and the people themselves ordered to remove to Itsawisis. 'We have inspected it', they said of the proposed new area, 'and found it useless land which is just good for a graveyard.' The Hoachanas preacher, the Reverend Marcus Kooper, became the subject of a test expulsion order from the Supreme Court, and one morning early in January 1959 police loaded him and a small party of his people, together with their belongings, into lorries. Today the Reverend Marcus Kooper is a petitioner at the U.N.; a handful of his people camp dispiritedly a half-mile from the Tses station (some of those removed have died); and the rest of the people of Hoachanas are still where they were, for the U.N. fuss over the proposed removal scared some of the aggression from the South West African Administration; Hoachanas remains listed as a 'temporary Reserve'.

The government had even less success with its Aminuis land-shuttle scheme. It proposed to take a slice from the west of this Herero Reserve and give in exchange the corridor of land between the Reserve and the Bechuanaland border. The Herero, however, proved competent adversaries in argument. And it helped enormously that the U.N. should have listened in so diligently to the debate. The corridor that they had been offered was theirs anyway, said the Herero. 'They took it away from us once, and now they are giving it back!' They proved right, too, for the Administration forgot that in 1933 it had told the League of Nations that the corridor was to be added to Aminuis. Hosea Kutako marshalled his other arguments.

The part of Aminuis Reserve which the government proposed to give to the White farmers is the best grazing area in that Native Reserve and there are five boreholes with strong water, and they are from 500 feet to 700 feet deep. In Kuridora which the government proposed to give to us in exchange for our land which is to be given to the White farmers, a kind of grass called *suurgras* grows in the largest area but only in the rainy season and lasts until the winter, i.e. from January to June, while Kuridora itself is in the Kalahari desert and is therefore subject to scanty rainfall, with the result that it is unsuitable for grazing. There are sixteen boreholes in Kuridora which are 1,200 feet and 1,500 feet deep. We have similar boreholes in some parts of Aminuis Reserve and the Lister engines which operate there are often broken, causing a shortage of water, while there is almost no water problem in our land which is going to be given to the White farmers.*

In 1962 at Windhoek, an official of the Department of Bantu Affairs freely admitted that the Aminuis removal scheme had fallen flat because the Herero would not agree to it. It must have been one of the very rare occasions when White farmers encountered any obstacle to expansion.

Since the end of the Second World War *new White settlement has absorbed ten million additional hectares* – an eighth of the territory. White settlement has advanced at a rate found disturbing even by government commissions, in 1948 and 1952, and the Land Bank. One commission reported that the resources of the territory had seriously deteriorated through erosion and overstocking in only two generations of White farming. The Agricultural Bank complained that some holdings should never have been granted, since the rainfall they enjoyed was too low, and that grazing reserved for difficult times had been allotted as farms.

The more farms there are in marginal areas, the heavier become the subsidies required from the state. In consequence,

* Petition to the U.N. dated 28 May 1957.

settlers have not only swallowed up vast vacant areas – many adjoining the present Reserves in the north-east and north-west which might otherwise have been used to extend African land holdings – but have inevitably, in doing so, placed an additional burden on state revenue. Farmers who got their land merely by asking for it have made fortunes; the government itself has taken the risks and provided the capital outlay. There can be few countries in the world where government expenditure per head of the farming community has been so heavy over so considerable a period. In the prosperous decade and a half since the end of the Second World War the debts of White farmers to the government and the banks have persistently mounted.

In 1950, the Land Bank extended loans and mortgages on 509 farms. In 1958, farm mortgages were six times that amount, or over £6 million. In 1950, 1,106 settlers owed the Administration an average of £1,086 each; in 1958, 1,575 settlers owed an average of £1,435*. By the end of 1961 White farmers owed the Land Bank over £10½ million, and this was by no means their only source of loans; they had borrowed, too, from private banks and special funds like the Farming Interests Board.

In drought years, generous grants become even more lavish. In 1959–60, White farmers received just over £1 million in urgent loans – more than the total budget for 'Native Affairs' during the same period. In 1960 alone, drought advances to 1,283 farmers totalled £750,960, while the Land Bank wrote back all arrear capital payments for five years. Rehoboth relief rations cost £500 in the same year – half the amount an individual White farmer could get for drought relief.

Only White farmers, of course, qualify for aid from the Land Bank. The Africans must survive drought as best they can. Within the Police Zone alone, during the drought of 1958–9, 50,000 cattle were estimated as lost. The Administration was asked in the Legislative Assembly what it had done to counteract African losses. It replied bluntly:

No special steps were taken to try to prevent stock losses in the Bantu areas and Reserves, except that for some Reserves lucerne had been

* Questions answered in the 1961 session of the South West Legislative Assembly.

ordered early. . . . Stock sales were held more frequently to allow the inhabitants to sell as much stock as possible. *No rehabilitation measures were considered as the end of the drought and its consequences are not nearly in sight yet.*

4. Wealth Accumulates, but Men Decay

South West Africa is on the lips of the politicians, in the hands of the farmers, and in the pocket of the great mining and finance corporations.*

Among the newer and smaller companies that jost e for position, prospecting rights, and new mineral finds, two giants stand pre-eminent, one South African and one American. Entangled with one another and with the economies of half a dozen countries in Southern and Central Africa, they lend massive economic backing to the political power of apartheid and give gilt-edged confidence to the South African government when it thumbs its nose at world opinion.

Consolidated Diamond Mines, of the vast De Beers–Anglo-American gold, copper, and diamond empire, makes an annual profit in South West Africa almost double the entire State budget.† The American company, Tsumeb Corporation, which operates in South West Africa, among much else, the largest lead mine on the continent, makes no bones about its attachment to the South African government. Parent company of Tsumeb is the Newmont Mining Corporation, which has been operating in South Africa for a quarter of a century. Said the Vice-President of Newmont, Mr M. D. Banghart, addressing the 1962 Annual Meeting of the American Institute of Mining, Metallurgical, and Petroleum Engineers: 'We know the people and the government [of South Africa] and we back our conviction with our reputation and our dollars.' Mr Banghart told the

---

* See Appendix, D.
† The budget for South West Africa in 1961 was £8,079,710. C.D.M. profits in the same year totalled £15,553,197.

meeting that American firms doing business in South Africa made an average profit of twenty-seven per cent on their investments. This was the decisive factor, he advised.

Consolidated Diamond Mines and Tsumeb dwarf all other companies in South West Africa, but there are others – though often merely associates or subsidiaries – in the field at one time or another. Many of the newer mining and concession interests are South African financed, but the Bethlem Steel Corporation (U.S.A.) has surveyed for oil; Rio Tinto, the mining-finance house, that through its Canadian and Australian operations competes with South Africa's uranium producers, has interests with Japanese capital in a copper project at Onganya; and the Etosha Petroleum Company (U.S.A.) has been searching for oil in Ovamboland and the Etosha Game Reserve.

Fishing is the assertive newcomer in the contest for South West Africa's wealth, and several Afrikaner companies have pushed their way across the South African border to the sea round South West Africa. The mandate has become a major outlet for Afrikaner capital. A few independent fishing companies apart, most fishing enterprises, fish meal, and fish oil factories, with the fast expanding canneries at Walvis Bay, are controlled by Federale Volksbeleggings, whose directors have connexions with I.S.C.O.R., South Africa's state-owned steel concern (that, incidentally, runs a tin mine at Uis, near the Namib desert in South West Africa), Afrikaner insurance houses and banks, and even the Nationalist Party Press.

The three pillars of South West Africa's wealth are mining, fishing, and agriculture. Together they support a highly specialized primary export economy, precariously dependent on the state of world markets and prices. In 1961, South West Africa's mineral output reached a record figure of £26½ million, produced by C.D.M. diamond sales of £18 million, and Tsumeb base metal exports of just under £7 million. Over the last two years, drought and foot-and-mouth disease have brought ruin to many cattle farmers and stagnation to the cattle towns of the north. But the rest of the territory is experiencing an unprecedented boom. Budgets are five times those of the immediate post-war years,* and thirty times those of the depression days. Taxes on diamond and base metal mining contribute two-thirds of total revenue. Only the hardships of farmers and the consequent decline in commerce provide a nagging reminder that the territory has known fluctuating fortunes in the past; that, because the economy is not diversified or developed enough, any serious slide in the world demand for primary products would be calamitous.

In the early days of the mandate, South Africa looked upon her ward as an expensive but strategically necessary stepchild. She assumed the deficits incurred during the martial law period of 1915–20, and with the tax payments of the diamond companies for the war years, put her Administration on its economic feet. The twenties were years of heavy expenditure on White settlement – criticized by many inside the country as reckless; and outside, by the League of Nations at Geneva, as consuming the substance of the non-White wards for the benefit of the guardians.

It is said that there is nothing of which one can be so sure in South West Africa as drought. When the world depression of the thirties hit the territory, it coincided with a disastrous drought. Revenue and expenditure slumped alarmingly. In the years from 1920 to 1940, ten budgets yielded small surpluses, while eleven showed deficits. South Africa advanced loans, allowing the mandate to pile up its debts, conscious that she was really assisting her own settlers and assuming in all probability that the mandate would soon be annexed and all indebtedness written off as a book entry. The Administration made no serious attempt to balance expenditure by revenue and propel the territory beyond dependence on loans. By 1937 annual revenue had dropped to £500,000, while the territory's total debt to South Africa stood at five times that amount. The economic activity on which the resources of the mandate were being spent – farming – brought no increase in revenue, except through the payment of

* Revenue figures: 1946–7, £2·9 million; 1956–7, £12 million; 1961–2, £15·7 million.

interest on monies advanced. The only substantial source of income remained mining, almost all of it from the diamond diggings, and the drop in diamond sales during the depression showed that this support, too, was precarious, and others needed to be developed.

In these tough years a small sheep came to the country's rescue, the karakul, affectionately known as the 'black diamond'. Under the German Governor Lindequist, ten karakul sheep had been imported from Russia, and they had flourished to form the basis of a vast new industry today. This eccentric animal thrives in the arid climate and on the poor grazing-ground of the south, even during drought. South West Africa has become the world's largest breeder of karakul, and the demands of fashionable women abroad now provide the mainstay of the mandate's agricultural community.

An auction sale at the end of the Second World War changed the economic face of the country once again. The Tsumeb Corporation bought the rights to the old German copper mine at Otavi from the Custodian of Enemy Property. Today Tsumeb is the world's sixth largest copper producer, operates the largest lead mine in Africa and the second in the southern hemisphere, produces zinc, silver, cadmium, vanadium, and, most valuable of all, germanium. The Corporation is opening a new mine at Kombat, and is in the process of constructing a copper and lead smelting plant. Ores formerly shipped to Belgium and Texas will now be processed on the spot by Ovambo labour (and White overseers).

The town of Tsumeb is in character and appearance the product of the Corporation. The main mining shaft dominates the main street, the new smelter works mark the town from the air; there is barely anyone in Tsumeb not on, or dependent upon, the company payroll. The Corporation runs the town: water supplies, street lighting, road tarring, the hospital, the airfield, the meat and milk supply, the vegetable farm, the cemetery. The second largest town in the whole territory has no council, but a Village Management Board, its powers limited to licences and permits, the abattoirs and rubbish removal ('though we pay for even that', said a spokesman of the Corporation), because the Corporation wants to run the show in its own un-interrupted way.

It is not unique in South West Africa. Far south, the other mining colossus, Consolidated Diamond Mines of South West Africa Ltd., runs Oranjemund. C.D.M., the Administrator told the Legislative Assembly gratefully, is South West Africa's fairy godmother. While karakul exports started the climb out of the depression years, and copper and lead boosted the economy further, diamond exports produced the greatest revenue. Between 1944 and 1960 the Treasury received more than £45 million from C.D.M. in income tax, diamond profits tax, and export duty.

You cannot simply walk along the desolate Atlantic coast and scuff diamonds, for they are buried beneath millions of tons of sand, hidden in the gravel of fossil marine beaches. Railway worker Zacharia Lewala found the first pebble which turned out to be a diamond, and handed it over in 1908 to the German rail-way gang foreman whose prospecting licences started the first diamond rush. In those days African workers were employed to crawl along the surface of the bleak, wind-blown desert to run the sand through their fingers and pick out the shiny stones. Sir Ernest Oppenheimer and an Anglo-American Corporation director who had been South African Minister of Finance negotiated the amalgamation of the mining companies along the coast, and in 1920 C.D.M. bought out the German properties for £3,500,000. The German companies of the *Sperregebiet* (for-bidden area) thought that the deposits showed signs of final exhaustion . . . but only a few hundred yards from the prospect-ing pits unsuccessfully dug in 1912, lay buried enormous quan-tities of exceptional gem stones, waiting to be mined. 'If faith moves mountains, so does the company mining the diamond coast,' says a glossy C.D.M. hand-out, describing the mechanical shovels, powered scrapers, rotary bucket excavators, the screen-ing, sweeping by broom, and all the other large-scale and pains-taking methods used in this huge earth-moving project.

Diamond security regulations govern the area. Free entry to or exit from the carefully patrolled area is prohibited, on pain of prosecution. Company employees – 600 Whites and 5,000 Ovambos flown to the desert diamond fields from S.W.A.N.L.A. headquarters at Grootfontein – are subject to X-ray examination as routine procedure. Regulations for employees have a Devil's Island isolation about them, though they, too, have become routine: no private cars are allowed in the town area, but must be kept in security-controlled garages on the northern bank of the river; radios, electrical equipment, and a long list of restricted items, must be lodged with the Company's security officer if they are to be reclaimed and taken out of the zone by their owners; families 'may spend Sundays at the river mouth and beach' if they catch the Company bus, states the C.D.M. handout. Still, somehow, despite the tightest possible security, ingenious operators pull off a diamond *coup* every now and then. Barmen, commercial travellers, and lawyers briefed in diamond cases, tell the best diamond stories, part of the folk-lore of a territory still steeped in the excitement of prospecting, ore rushes and the lucky finds of unexpected wealth.

Even Oranjemund's diamonds cannot last for ever, and expert estimates give these fields a further thirty years of life. Meanwhile, Anglo-American has a hand in the activities of the Marine Diamond Corporation – with a registered capital of £5 million – which hopes to extract diamonds from the bed of the sea by marine pumps lowered into the sand. This venture is backed as well by American capital, South Africa's General Mining and Finance Corporation, and a group of Afrikaner financiers including Captain J. H. F. Strydom and former Nationalist Cabinet Minister Van Rhijn.

So far, Afrikaner capital has had its best returns from South West Africa's fishing industry. Walvis Bay production is ninety per cent of the total in South West and South Africa combined. The best natural markets are in West Africa, but there the boycott of all South African goods has intruded. The industry is now strenuously searching for new markets. It is well organized and prosperous, and has coped well with competition, but the threat of bad seasons is always hanging over it. Meanwhile the industry is making the best of its hey-day. With its enormous volume of production, it employs a labour force of only 700 fishermen, with some 2,600 labourers in the canning factories, of whom about 2,000 are Ovambo working on contract.

Though agriculture represents the productive effort of by far the majority of the territory's people, its contribution to the national revenue, relative to that of mining and fishing, is negligible. White farming itself has been a heavy drain on government funds. The rearing of cattle and small stock, mostly for South Africa's meat markets, and the export of dairy products, have expanded rapidly since the end of the war. But the farmer finds himself stricken by recurring drought, which turns ranches into dust bowls dotted with shrivelled shrubs, and at the constant mercy of fluctuations in the South African beef market. South West African cattle export permits are restricted in good South African seasons, so as to prevent a drop in prices on the South African market. Cattle farming in the territory is thus held to ransom by the controlling power.

Though her economy has been diversified during the last decade, South West Africa remains dependent upon mining, fishing, and agriculture. Her main products are exported to a handful of markets. She has experienced little industrial development. She possesses still a colonial type of economy, with South Africa as the imperial power and a few international corporations sharing the spoils.

Over four decades large numbers of White South Africans have settled as farmers in the mandate. And South Africa now has her Sudetenland in South West Africa. Having established her nationals there, she uses them as her excuse for being unable to withdraw. For how may she leave them to the tender mercies of any other authority? The 'immigrant' picture at present is very different from what it was in the early period of the mandate. Then, many of the new settlers were poor and landless South Africans. But recent immigration has been nothing like the Angola Boer type. At the end of the Second World War, vast new stretches were opened and advertised for settlement by ex-servicemen. The Smuts government soon afterwards fell from office, but Nationalist farmers and politicians, with their sons, were not slow to take advantage of the project in order to add vast new acres to their family estates. Hemmed in by advancing Black Africa – Afrikaner farmers have been leaving Kenya and growing increasingly uneasy with developments in the Rhodesias – the trekking Boer has found that his *Lebensraum* has shrunk. South West Africa has seemed one of the last great empty – if you do not see the Africans – spaces. The 1951 census showed that fifty-five per cent of South West Africa's Whites had been born outside the territory, and of these, sixty-eight per cent had come from South Africa.

There has been heavy South African immigration not only to absorb large land holdings, but also to staff the Civil Service. And the 'colonist' not only runs South West Africa by virtue of his vote and influence with the government, but also sends his bloc of legislators into the South African parliament, to protect his interests there.

White Man Boss in South Africa has found a territory adjacent to his own in which to cement his political power, and in which as well to further his economic well-being. South Africa has used the mandate not only to settle her nationals, but also as an outlet for her industries and her capital. On her doorstep she has found a ready-made market for her products, and the territory makes a substantial contribution to the support of South African industries. It also swells its guardian's overseas trade. 1954 was the last year in which separate trade returns were registered for South West Africa, but then the territory's exports were ten per cent of South Africa's own (£31·9 million for South West Africa; £331 million for South Africa). Colonies *are* convenient! Afrikaner-financed companies, diligently fostered by the Nationalist Party's economic movement, the Reddingsdaadbond, entered commerce and industry late in South Africa, but found room to stretch in the domain that lay at South Africa's feet. The mandate has become a major foreign outlet for Afrikaner capital investment.

What does South Africa herself do for the mandate? The loans she gave during the depression years are being repaid. She provides subsidies to the mandate's uneconomic railways, and meets the cost of the police, as part of her own force. She bears, by her own decision, responsibility for South West Africa's 'Native Affairs', but the mandate itself pays in accordance with a formula based on past costs. It has happened more than once that the amounts voted for African affairs, meagre as they are, have not been fully spent in the period allotted, and the surplus has been credited to South African – rather than reverting to South West African – funds. This is one sphere in which South Africa should pay for progress. The Africans, after all, are supposed to constitute a sacred trust.

What of the Africans? Have they benefited at all from the strings of extra noughts added to the export, revenue, and profit figures by the territorial boom? The development of the South West economy has been altogether one-sided. The 1957 Report of the U.N. South West Africa Committee put it baldly:

The industries contributing to the relative prosperity of the territory are essentially 'European' owned and operated enterprises, in which the role of the Natives is generally limited to unskilled labour.... The greater part of the African population lives by subsistence agriculture and keeping of livestock far from the main areas of modern economic development. ... Their principal access to the monetary economy has been through the supply of their labour to the mines and 'European' farms in other parts of the territory. The Reserves are said to be the areas where they can farm on their own account. They are encouraged in theory to develop their areas, but the assistance they receive falls far short of the assistance given to European farmers. In the cattle areas separators have been supplied to groups of families, and transport provided to carry cream to the nearest creameries. The Administration stated that as a result of this scheme and from the proceeds of sales of cattle and hides, the producers in the Reserves received about £400,000 in 1955. The annual rates and other taxes paid ... supplemented by territorial funds amounting to £50,000 a year, are applied to the economic development of the Reserves. Drilling of wells and boreholes seems to be the principal new service provided by the Administration. It is difficult to measure the exact extent of assistance to African agriculture, or its results in terms of higher productivity and improved standards of living. Steps to encourage and stimulate productivity seem very limited. The same three subjects crop up every time government talks of improving the economic lot of the African: creameries, cattle sales, and water supplies. These – apart from recruitment into wage labour – remain the main ways in which African farmers can enter the money economy.

Certain statistical data is available which may give a general indication of the scale of administrative activity in Native areas by comparison with assistance given in European areas. ... From the Territorial Development and Reserve Fund, the primary source of funds for developing programmes, a total of £3·9 million was spent in 1955–6. One half (£1·6 million) was disbursed in the form of development loans to local authorities. Second largest item was government buildings (£873,000). Roads and telecommunications, primarily for Whites, took £736,000 and £359,000. The fostering of European land settlement and development cost £241,000, including recoverable advances, boring costs and survey fees. But under the heading 'Native areas' only £58,000 was expended – a sum smaller than, for example, a net loss of £79,000 which the Administration absorbed in writing off the cost of unsuccessful boreholes on European farms. ...

The primary role of the African population, determined by Administration policy and method, is to supply the labour without which the essentially European economy could not exist at all, and under conditions of cost and regulation without which it could not function as profitably as it does in the present forms.

Precious little of South West Africa's increased prosperity has been shared with Africans. The territory has no 'poor Whites' (except, perhaps, in times of extreme drought); but almost all Africans live below the bread – or mealie meal – line.

Research by Dr D. C. Krogh revealed that the *per capita* annual national income of South West Africa had increased from £59·6 in 1951, to £82·4 in 1956; *but, while the* per capita *income of residents within the Police Zone* (where White-controlled economic activity is centred) *was £176·1 – an average of high White and low African earnings – outside the Police Zone the figure was £8·5.* This last estimate covers not only employment income, but also the value of subsistence production. It must give Ovamboland and neighbouring areas beyond the Police Zone the lowest *per capita* income in Africa.

From 1920 to 1948 expenditure from general revenue on Africans in the mandate (over and above their own tax contributions, which are paid into Reserve Trust Funds) did not exceed seven per cent of total government expenditure. During depression years it fell to two and a half per cent. At some periods, less than 2s. a year was spent per head of the African population; rarely has more than 10s. per head a year been spent. And of the total amount, large sums went on purely administrative expenses, like salaries for officials.

The Administration has consistently held that Africans should pay their own way, for only if they did 'would they learn to stand on their own feet'. Too rapid a tempo of development would 'Europeanize' them, it was argued, though how the tempo could be too fast for water boring and the construction of hospitals, no one bothered to explain.

The sums now being spent on African services are considerably larger than the miserly expenditure of the drought and depression years, but they still constitute only a tiny part of territorial expenditure. In the main, the proportions spent on Whites and Africans remain the same. And expenditure on Africans has been pegged now and for the future in one particularly vital field: the economic development of their areas. From 1955, when the administration of 'Native Affairs' was switched from Windhoek to Pretoria, the South African government took direct control of the funds to be spent on Africans – apart from education and health, still part of the territory's Legislative Assembly budget. South West Africa is required to make certain annual payments to the mandatory: a sum equal to one-fortieth of its expenditure, other than from development funds, in the preceding year's budget; and a fixed sum of £50,000 for the ten years from 1955 onwards, to be entered in the South African Bantu Trust Fund to the South West Africa development account. The taxes paid by the Africans into tribal and trust funds are also vested in South African control. The provision for one-fortieth of annual expenditure was based on relevant statistics during the previous ten years, the Minister of Bantu Affairs hastened to assure the South African parliament, alarmed at the thought that, by assuming administrative control of the mandate's Africans, it might have to take money out of its own pocket. 'Year after year', said the Minister, 'expenditure has increased, and the ratio of expenditure on Natives to general expenditure has remained the same.'

In 1961 South West Africa paid over to the South African government the total sum of £225,000, which included the £50,000 for development.

In 1961 and 1962, the votes for African education and health services were higher than ever before, and an African hospital extension programme was initiated. Yet the sum of all expenditure on non-Whites was about £1,430,000, out of estimates totalling £17 million.

Any suggestion that the Administration should spend much more on the territory's Africans is usually met with the retort from White South West Africa: why should it? or how can it? Africans do not deserve more because they contribute so little.

Even within the muddled world of economic apartheid, this is a moot point. Income tax was introduced into South West Africa in 1942, and is still astonishingly low, though taxes were increased in 1962 and applied for the first time to lower White income groups. The new basic tax varies from £4 on £400 a year to £8 on £600 a year, for single persons; and £2 on £600 and £8 on £900 a year, for married persons. A White wage-earner with less than £35 a month pays no tax at all.

The non-Whites, of course, are almost all far too poor to fall under the income tax law; there are only between thirty and forty non-White tax-payers in the whole territory, most of them Coloured fishermen at Walvis Bay. African taxation takes the form of grazing fees, tribal and trust fund levies, dog tax (paid also by Whites), kraal fees, and school fees. A former Secretary for South West Africa and Chief Native Commissioner, Mr E. P. Courtney Clarke, said in 1937:

Under the system of grazing fees in operation in the Reserves, which in actual fact involves the payment of much heavier sums than under the Union taxation system, the Natives are compelled to obtain cash to meet the fees either by sale of their stock or by working or sending members of their families out to work.*

In the northern territories the compulsory tribal levy payable by all men over eighteen years, regardless of income, ranges from 10s. to £1 a year. In Ovamboland the tax may be paid in grain.

Monthly grazing fees, doubled in 1954, vary for some Reserves, but on the average amount to: 6d. per head for large stock and horses; 2d. for every five head of sheep or part thereof. From all but the very poorest, who own no stock at all, *the grazing fee system exacts a higher annual tax than that paid by the Whites*, and a tax higher than the poll tax paid by Africans in South Africa. The burden of taxation is far heavier on poor Africans than on poor Whites. In the Herero Reserves the average tribesman owns about ten head of large stock. His grazing fees alone accordingly amount to £3 a year; and to these must be added other levies. Grazing fees and tribal levies are paid into the Reserve and tribal trust funds, supposedly for services and development. Certainly, when the trust funds are exhausted, development comes to a standstill except for occasional grants from the Administration. Up to 1939 expenditure from all the funds did not exceed £15,000 in any one year. The monies may be spent on development of water supplies, and cattle improvement. But they are also used to defray half the cost of erecting fences to separate Reserves from adjacent White or government-owned lands, and to pay for the 'control and administration' of the people in the Reserves themselves.

The policy that the poor should pay for their own services means in effect that the poor have to do without them. Education and health services in South West Africa were until very recently left almost exclusively to the missionaries. Until the sixties, the sum of government involvement in schooling outside the Police Zone was the payment of small subsidies to the Church-run schools. The first government help to education in Ovamboland was extended eight years after the acquisition of the mandate, in 1928, when £100 was paid to a Finnish mission industrial school. Entire government expenditure on Ovamboland schools

---

* Memorandum quoted in the *Rhodesia Herald*, 3 September 1937.

reached only double that amount in 1935. The first government school for Africans inside the Police Zone was opened in the Aminuis Reserve in 1936, and then it was paid for not by the Administration, but out of the Reserve trust fund. 'I can't tax Europeans to provide schools for Natives,' the Administrator said.* Twenty years later this Reserve school boasted only four teachers, and sixty per cent of its pupils were in the sub-standards.

Today, where there are schools for Africans in South West, only two out of every ten African children of school-going age attend them, and very seldom for longer than two years. For many years the amount spent on African education in the territory averaged about one per cent of revenue. In 1962 the highest amount ever was budgeted for African education: £240,000. Even then, the figure comprised *one-eighth* of the territory's total education budget.

Without missionary efforts, African education would hardly exist. Finnish missionary work in Ovamboland is older than White settlement, though it has concentrated mainly on manual training. The Anglican Church in Ovamboland runs five accredited schools and fifty-five bush schools, the latter to give religious instruction. Half the classes in the accredited schools meet 'under a tree'. Many teachers have themselves not been educated beyond the sub-standards; by far the most have only attained Standard Four in the primary school; and the few who have advanced beyond that are shining rarities. Bush teachers and catechists in the Anglican schools report that students often stay for three years of religious instruction, as it is the only chance of learning that they have. *There are no more than three post-primary schools in the whole territory, two of them teacher training institutions as well.* In two successive years there have been only two African matriculants in South West Africa. Yet pupils are refused permission to cross into South Africa for high school and university education; and outside teachers are not permitted entry into South West Africa except to teach in White and Coloured schools.

* Permanent Mandates Commission, 16, p. 59.

164

In line with its policy of tightening State control, the South African government is taking over the mission schools in South West Africa, and introducing an Amended Syllabus – based on 'Bantu Education' – in the face of strong opposition from the Anglican (but not the Finnish) missions, Herero and Nama peoples, the A.M.E. Church which runs Nama schools in the south unassisted by the government, and the African teachers organized into the South West Africa Teachers' Association.

The Carpio U.N. mission was told very pointedly that Africans did not use the school facilities offered them. One reason may lie in the absence of school hostels. About half the White school-going children are accommodated in boarding schools. But the U.N. was told in 1958:

Within the Police Zone in all the Reserves there are only two government hostels to enable the children who have to come from such long distances to remain at the school. One of these hostels is at Aminuis and the other is at Waterberg. There are in all eight Herero Reserves. Only two of these eight have government schools with hostels attached. Six have no hostels but have schools for the children of the place where the school is. In distant parts there is no school for the children to attend. The Herero appealed to the government to build hostels in their Reserves. The government replied that the parents do not want to send their children away to school. But the parents naturally want to know that there is going to be a hostel along-side the school where the children will be looked after, before agreeing to send them so far to school. In our last meeting with the Chief Commissioner a certain Alfred Katjimuine requested the government to build a hostel in his Reserve. The meeting was in January 1958, and the reply he got was that the government is not prepared to build any more hostels. The people should rather build small huts in the Reserves, and then the government will provide them with a teacher and building materials, because they argue that the hostels are too costly to build and maintain. Many children of parents who are work-ing on European farms do not attend schools because there are no hostels in neighbouring towns where they can be looked after. Such children cannot be educated because they have no relatives and there are no hostels in the neighbouring towns. Thus it is that many of our children get no education and so are forced to become manual labourers on contract to White employers.

Plans to build the first government hospital in Ovamboland were only laid in 1962. Most of the mission hospitals are no more than first-aid stations. In the Police Zone a few Reserves are near to hospitals, but most only have clinics visited from time to time by a district surgeon. The Aminuis Reserve was at one time in the control of a former medical inspector of schools, who treated patients in between the monthly visit of the doctor. 'Our people die on the way to the hospitals,' Clement Kapuuo told me. 'Last year [1961] four babies died on the road between Aminuis and Gobabis [where there is a hospital].'

Following on the 1962 Carpio visit, Dr Verwoerd announced that he would personally supervise a five-year plan for the extension of African services. The South African government would be the last to admit it, but U.N. handling of the South West Africa issue has forced the Administration into greater expenditure on its wards.

Even with the extra allocations, however, the overall picture remains as starkly racial as before. The well-off Whites lean heavily on the Administration; the poverty-stricken Africans pay their own slow, hard way.

NOTE: The Minister of Bantu Administration and Development disclosed in the House in February 1963 that £20,000 was the amount spent from government funds on all the Africans in South West Africa for 1961-2. (see page 162).

Part Five: The World as Referee

I. The League of Nations: On The Geneva Carpet

At Geneva, year after year from 1920 onwards, the Permanent Mandates Commission, supervising the mandate system of the League of Nations, scrutinized the record of the mandatory powers in their trust territories. Composed of five members from non-mandate states and four from the mandatory states themselves, chosen not as national representatives but as experts on colonial matters, the Commission examined the annual reports which the mandatories were obliged to render and ferreted out volumes of information which the powers might have liked to keep concealed. The Commission showed no reluctance to criticize the mandatories.

South Africa was the most delinquent mandatory. She came in for more criticism than any other power. At times the members of the Mandates Commission grew quite testy. The early reports of the South African administration, they charged, were shoddy, incoherent, so fragmentary as to be worthless, even contradictory. (One report had two differing figures for that year's rainfall.) A procession of South African diplomats, South West African Administrators and senior officials passed before the Commission at Geneva. Mr Eric Louw on two occasions experienced a taste of the grilling he was to endure later at the United Nations. Gently the South African government spokesmen informed the Lord Lugards and the Lord Haileys that 'great harm was done to Natives through misguided efforts at kindness'.

Each Administrator proved more ingenious than the last in evolving those peculiarly South African explanations of 'how to treat the Native'. Administrator G. R. Hofmeyr answered a

Commission doubt that, under the system of segregation in the Reserves, the Africans would advance rapidly enough. The Reserves, said the Administrator, were not places where the 'Native' could pass his time in idleness, and so deteriorate. And he worked as well on the mines, railways, and government undertakings, so that he was constantly in contact with the Whites. There was therefore every hope of gradually civilizing him . . .! The High Commissioner for South West Africa, Mr Smit, had to explain why African convicts were hired out to private employers. The 'Native mind' was entirely different from the European's, he said. Jail was no disgrace to him, and he could not be put in a cell and then left idle. He would degenerate. He could not be used for skilled work. He was therefore employed on public works, under the supervision of a warder. The High Commissioner in London, Mr Charles Te Water, was asked to explain a paragraph in the Annual Report which quoted the Native Commissioner at Warmbad.

I regret to state that the handpumps supplied by the Administration last year have not proved welcome to the Hottentots, nor have they been a success for this reason: to start with, all work in the Reserves has to be done by the aged and infirm, as all able-bodied males go out to work. . . .

The Commissioner was really just making out a case for better pumps, said South Africa's representative, as he walked round this indictment of the Reserves as reservoirs of labour.

Some issues could not be evaded. The Mandates Commission would not let South Africa expropriate the South West African railway system; or hand over to British administration the Caprivi Zipfel. From both these infringements of the sovereignty of the mandate, South Africa had to retreat. Every South African politician's speech yearning for or prophesying the eventual incorporation of the mandate was produced before the South African representatives, who were then pressed for explanations. Tartly the Commission told South Africa: as long as South West Africa remained a mandate, it could not be incorporated. If incorporation took place, it would be subject to the grant of complete self-government and the surrender of the mandate, with the consent of the League. 'It is not for the White minority in a mandated territory to declare when the moment for independence has arrived,' observed Commission member Rappard.

After examining the reports on the territory for fourteen years, a Commission member said he could find no evidence of progress towards political self-administration. Of all the trusts that the Mandates Commission supervised, the African population in South West Africa seemed to be the most backward, its position static, and static at a deplorably low level. This was the only mandated area which was a White man's country, and the interests of White and Black were clearly in conflict.

During the years of the Mandates Commission, one central controversy dominated. Who in South West Africa was to pay for progress? At first South Africa hedged. Asked in 1925, when the water shortage in new African Reserves was critical, if the government could not meet the cost of more boreholes, its spokesman replied that it would be wrong to spend part of the country's general revenue on improving the *private property* of a particular tribe. For years the Commission urged the Administration to do more, to spend more on the Africans. The Administration laboured to turn every visible solution into a problem. Then in 1937 it threw a sudden fit of frankness. In the report for that year it pointed out that it had spent 'considerable sums' (not borne out by the record) in the early years of the mandate, but was not prepared to continue. The South African spokesman elaborated: the Administration did not wish to increase expenditure beyond the point at which the 'Natives' could appreciate what was being done for them. The Administration was opposed to making grants for speeding the development of the Reserves, as much in the interests of the 'Natives' themselves as of the European. It would certainly be unfair to burden the White section of the population with further taxes (they paid almost none at the time) for 'Native' development, where practically the whole of the African contribution to the revenue of the territory was handed out already to trust funds for expenditure on the Natives.

The Mandates Commission employed several arguments in

reply. South Africa had been entrusted with the mandate in the first place by reason of its resources, because it could help the territory to stand on its feet, because it was fitted – and willing – to undertake the responsibility. Minors always cost more than they could earn: this was the essence of the relationship between guardian and ward. The Whites in the territory were not entitled to favourable treatment because they paid more: they were not a sacred trust, and the Administration had no special obligation towards them. Secondly, it was not a question of trust alone. The South African government maintained that the Africans were entitled to the services they paid for, and that the Whites deserved more because they paid more. But the White population owed its superior standard of living to the Africans; it depended on them for labour. Low wages for Africans only meant higher White profits. African labour was itself a tax paid to the state by Africans. Thirdly, diamond royalties, which paid so much of the territory's way, could not be regarded as tax contributions paid by Whites. They were proceeds of the wealth that belonged to the original inhabitants of the territory.

The arguments are all minuted in the proceedings of the Permanent Mandates Commission. The debate was crucial to the policy pursued towards the mandate during the lean years, and it remained unresolved. The session at which the League and the government of South Africa had got to grips with it – verbally – was the last. The Second World War broke out, and supervision of the mandates by the League of Nations was suspended. The next spokesman for South Africa before a world body was General Smuts, who requested U.N. approval for the incorporation of the mandate.

The whole mandate system constituted a compromise between the open annexation of the colonies as envisaged in the secret treaties among the governments of the Allied Powers, and demands that the colonial territories be entrusted to international administration. It turned out to be a one-sided compromise, however, with the powers running the mandated territories virtually unfettered, except by occasional public scrutiny.

Although all nations voted in the League, the great powers decided. And while it may not have seemed so from the faces of the men round the Mandates Commission table, the great powers ran the Commission.

P.T. Moon (*Imperialism and World Politics*) described the weakness of the mandate system.

Charged with the responsibility of ensuring administration of the mandates in harmony with the humane principles of the Covenant [of the League of Nations], the League is nevertheless inadequately equipped with specific powers for the fulfilment of its task. It cannot, or does not, issue orders for the improvement of conditions, or injunctions to check objectionable practices.

The Mandates Commission, he added, felt that it could not consider petitions which questioned the terms of the mandate, for the terms could be modified only by the Council of the League. Since all the mandatories were represented on the Council, and since the Council's decisions had to be unanimous under the Covenant, a mandate could hardly be modified, therefore, without the consent of the mandatory itself (unless the matter became an international 'dispute likely to lead to rupture', in which case the interested parties would have no vote). It was even less probable that a mandatory power could be deprived of its mandate on account of misgovernment, since the mandatories were selected by the Allied Powers rather than by the League of Nations.

Throughout its life the League of Nations Mandates Commission was haunted by the ambiguity of Article 22 in the Covenant on the issue of ultimate authority. Whose was it? The mandatory government? The Allied Powers? The League? The Mandates Commission struggled with practical posers on nationality, the ownership of public lands, the guarantee of loans, and the investment of capital in mandated territories. The League, with its own limited powers, did not enjoy sovereignty itself. It was brought up short, in its supervision of the mandate system, by the knowledge that it had no power to bring an errant mandatory to book.

In its handling of the South West African mandate, the

Mandates Commission gives the impression of having tired towards the end. It continued its usual painstaking examination of every clause in every annual report, its courteous questioning of South African representatives, its periodic sharp probing. The Mandates Commission experts were well enough informed, but finally powerless. They could scrutinize policy, but they could not change it. The Commission could not even compile its own reports on the territories in its charge, or explore its own sources of information. It could send no investigating commissions to the spot; receive no petitioners at Geneva. The reports from the mandatory powers were partial and the Mandates Commission heard only one party to the clash of interests, the government's.

The mandate system lasted a quarter of a century until another world war, in 1939, interrupted this phase in the history of South West Africa and the other mandated territories. In between, the world was rent by one crisis after the other – the economic depressions of 1929 and 1932; the civil war in Spain (the Italian invasion of Ethiopia only very briefly); the *Anschluss*; Munich; and at last an end to appeasement, and the outbreak of war. The 'colonial problem' barely intruded. Little of what went on in the colonies or in the mandated territories ever reached the outside world. It was after the Second World War, when first Asia and then Africa strode to the centre of the world stage, that the problems of the colonies began at last to preoccupy not only colonial administrators, but all states and politicians. For, one after another, the colonies asserted their claims to independence and their seats among the established states of the world. What went on in a colony was no longer the private affair of the administering power. If universal declarations of human rights were to mean anything, they had to have meaning for all men.

2. The United Nations: Retreat from the Twentieth Century

If there was any one year which marked South Africa's retreat from the changing world of the twentieth century, it was 1945. General Smuts arrived at the San Francisco conference which brought the U.N. to life, with a proposal in his pocket for making his mandate an exception to any new international trusteeship system. 'We didn't want any United Nations trusteeship,' one of the members of Smuts's delegation told me in Windhoek. 'We didn't know what it was ... nor', he added bitterly, 'did the United Nations.'

The Smuts take-over bid was stopped at San Francisco, and all copies of the prospectus for it destroyed the day after its announcement. The moment for deciding the fate of the mandate and South Africa's annexationist ambitions had not yet arrived. The powers were engrossed with the future, in broad principle, of dependent non-self-governing territories; as a sign of the times the word 'colony' had fallen into disrepute. The mandate system was making way for a more flexible successor, international trusteeship. Not only was Smuts's proposal premature: it crossed the general grain.

The U.N. seemed a last prospect for peace among the powers after the most destructive war ever waged. Yet even as it planned to preserve the peace, the organization became the battleground, at one meeting after the other, between those trying still to retain their empires, and those who believed that there were no superior races anywhere destined to govern inferior races of men. The tussle had started some years before in San Francisco. President Roosevelt's advisory committee on post-war foreign policy, set up after Pearl Harbor, had sketched into its blueprint for a new world the concept of international supervision, not only of former mandates but *all* dependent territories. The committee had even agreed on the fixing of dates for independence. Within the United States government itself, however, the State Department was opposed by the War and Navy Departments, interested not only in colonies, but in what they called 'outposts' – the strategic, formerly mandated Japanese islands. So the concept was watered down long before the United States government representatives arrived at San Francisco; and even then it was hotly opposed by Britain, then still led by Winston Churchill, who observed tartly that he had not become the King's First Minister to preside over the liquidation of the British Empire. The newly emerged states of Africa and Asia, backed by the Communist world, held that it was no longer a question of how best to administer colonies, but how most quickly to set them on the road to full independence.

These sharply divergent views had to be reconciled before and at San Francisco, if a working system of trusteeship could be devised. Independence as the specific goal *was* at last written into Article 76 of the United Nations Charter. But the language is hesitant and hedged about with qualifications.

The aims of trusteeship are (1) to further international peace and security; (2) to promote the political, economic, social, and educational advancement of the inhabitants of the trust territories, and their progressive development towards self-government or independence as may be appropriate to the particular circumstances of each territory and its people, and the freely expressed wishes of the peoples concerned, and as may be provided by the terms of each trusteeship agreement; (3) to encourage respect for human rights and fundamental freedoms for all and to encourage recognition of the interdependence of the peoples of the world; and (4) to ensure equal treatment in social, economic, and commercial matters for all members of the U.N. and their nationals, and equal treatment for the latter in the administration of justice, provided this does not conflict with the attainment of the other objectives of the trusteeship system.

If, says MacLaurin, we may permit ourselves to mix

metaphors, we can describe Article 76 as a blueprint well sup-plied with loopholes. An administering authority anxious to carry out the basic objectives of the trusteeship system will find the blueprint an excellent guide; an authority anxious to evade them and retain its colonial possessions will find the loopholes serviceable enough.

Trust territories, it might be said, are areas where the colonial powers could not be trusted to govern. Supervising are the Trusteeship Council, founded on compromise since it is com-posed in equal number of governments that hold trust territories and those that do not, always including the Big Five of the Security Council; and the General Assembly's Fourth, or Trusteeship Committee, which examines the Trusteeship Council's reports, keeps a general eye on progress, and recom-mends General Assembly resolutions. All states are represented in the Fourth Committee, whose resolutions must themselves then win support from two-thirds of those voting in the Assembly.

The acceptance of independence as the goal of trusteeship and the extension of U.N. supervision over all non-self-govern-ing territories represented a major victory for the smaller, newly independent states like India, Iraq, Egypt, and Syria, but they and the Communist countries which backed them were defeated on a number of other vital points. India wanted the administering authority to be the U.N. The Soviet Union attacked as a viola-tion of the Charter the way the trusteeship agreements were negotiated. Egypt, India, and Iraq tried to provide for consulta-tion with the peoples of the trust territories themselves, while the Soviet Union pressed unsuccessfully to have non-voting representatives of the trust peoples permitted to participate in Trusteeship Council discussions on their own future.

The 'colonial problem' has led to some of the 'most bitter debates and deepest divisions in the U.N. The Charter and the trusteeship system represent on paper the maximum agreement of many divergent interests. Disagreements over aims, over the speed of advancement, have therefore, inevitably, continued. Trusteeship achieves nothing by its intrinsic nature: it is a machine which can be well or badly used.

By the twelfth plenary meeting of the General Assembly in January 1946, the machine had been assembled and could be set to work. Britain announced that she would place Tanganyika, the Cameroons, and Togoland under the trusteeship system; New Zealand followed with a pledge to do the same for Western Samoa; Australia, the same for New Guinea and the island of Nauru; Belgium, the same for Ruandu Urundi; and France, the same for those parts of Togoland and the Cameroons under its mandate.

Only South Africa struck a jarring note. South West Africa was a special case, she pleaded. She felt it essential to consult the people of the mandated territory about the form which their own future government should take, and such a consultation was about to take place. She herself meanwhile gave her assurance that she would administer the mandate in the spirit of the Charter. ... It sounded promising enough. South Africa got the postponement that she requested.

By the end of the year General Smuts was ready. He addressed the Fourth Committee at length, building a case for what he termed South Africa's legitimate concern in annexing the territory. Geographically and strategically, the territory was part of South Africa; it was economically dependent; its tribes came from the same ethnological stem; two-thirds of its Whites were South African nationals; South Africa had introduced a 'progressive policy of native administration, and the native policy of South West should be aligned with that of South Africa'. Most of the arguments buttressed the *fait accompli* approach: the mandated territory was now so thoroughly integrated with South Africa that its formal incorporation was needed to remove doubts, attract capital, encourage individual initiative. *Integration would be a formal recognition of the unity that already existed.*

Smuts was prepared to admit the logical conclusion of his approach. The fundamental principle of the mandate system and its successor, trusteeship, was ultimate political self-government and separate statehood, but the low economic potentialities of the territory and the backwardness of the vast majority of its people rendered this impossible of achievement in South West

Africa. He himself could not envisage South West African self-government *ever*.

South Africa got a thorough drubbing. Delegates vied with each other in claiming that it would be a backward step to endorse annexation of a mandated territory. The trusteeship system should not be permitted to become a system of plunder.

General Smuts produced the results of his hasty South West referendum, taken especially for the benefit of the U.N. by commissioners who understood fully the 'native mind'. The Whites had always expressed themselves in favour of incorporation. A poll of the non-Whites had shown 208,850 votes for incorporation, 33,520 against, and 56,870 not consulted. The delegates were disinclined to take the results of the poll into serious consideration. They expressed doubt – all except the British delegate – that consultations conducted exclusively by an administering authority could constitute sound evidence of support for incorporation; they queried whether the people of South West had fully understood the consequences of their decision.

Britain spoke in defence of South Africa, but abstained in the voting. When a Fourth Committee resolution that the U.N. could not accede to the incorporation of the territory went to the General Assembly for approval, thirty-seven nations voted in favour, none against, and nine abstained. The U.N. invited the South African government to submit a trusteeship agreement.

A year passed. For the 1947 session of the U.N., South Africa produced no trusteeship agreement, but announced that she did not at that time contemplate incorporation. Delegates disputed the need for a ruling from the International Court of Justice. India argued that South Africa was under a legal as well as a moral obligation to submit to trusteeship; the United States denied any legal obligation, but maintained that the U.N. could exercise its moral power and might in the long run prevail on South Africa to submit a trusteeship agreement; France claimed that, even if the Court decided there was no legal obligation, South Africa should still submit a trusteeship agreement.

Differences arose not only over legal interpretations, but also over the strength of the resolution to be passed. One group of states wanted a fixed time-limit to be set, while others, reluctant to put on the pressure, were content that a trusteeship agreement should be submitted 'at an early date'. The weaker resolution won the day.

In an atmosphere of temporary truce, South Africa made one gesture of compromise. She submitted a report on her administration of South West Africa in 1946. The Trusteeship Council scrutinized the report, as it scrutinized reports on all the trust territories, and invited South Africa – a routine procedure – to send an accredited spokesman to provide supplementary information. South Africa refused. The Council formulated a set of questions for amplification. In May 1948 South Africa supplied answers, but accompanied them with a statement that they were given voluntarily, for the purpose of information alone, and should not be taken as any recognition by South Africa that she was obliged to transmit information to the world body. General Smuts was considering his next step.

In South Africa's House of Assembly, in 1947, a leading Nationalist rose to explain why it would be fatal for South Africa to submit reports on South West Africa or permit any U.N. supervision whatsoever. Unlike the old League of Nations, which, with some half a dozen exceptions, had consisted of white states, the U.N. was a menacing amalgam.

It consists of predominantly Coloured and Asiatic countries, and of countries whose inhabitants are of mixed blood. . . . A large number of the South American and Central American peoples are predominantly of mixed blood. . . . The U.N. should be afforded no opportunity, by the submission of reports, to interfere with our affairs or discuss our administration of South West Africa.

The speaker moved for the introduction of legislation to provide for the incorporation of South West Africa into South Africa 'by granting to it provincial status on conditions to be determined in consultation with South West Africa and without responsibility of any kind, so far as the administration of the territory is concerned, towards the U.N. or towards any other body'. The speaker was Mr Eric Louw. Soon afterwards, the Nationalist Party swept the Smuts administration from power. Before the end of 1948, Mr Louw officially represented his country at the U.N., face to face with delegates from the world's two-thirds whom he had already rejected because their pigment was darker than the off-white of South African rule.

Suddenly from a side-door, to speak lines never written in the South African script, there entered other characters in this drama. The curiosity of a *New York Times* correspondent, Mr Archimbault, had been aroused by the referendum conducted in South West Africa. The South African government had always held non-Whites incapable of political decision. Yet all at once, it seemed, they had became capable of consultation on the destiny of their country. The correspondent reported some misgivings by the Bishop of Damaraland: the referendum results showed that those non-Whites with experience of South African rule (those within the Police Zone and those who had some understanding of the matter at issue) had rejected South Africa; the chiefs who had polled in favour of incorporation were employees of the administration, susceptible to pressure and with little idea of what was meant by trusteeship under the U.N.

Dr A. B. Xuma, President-General of the African National Congress in South Africa, had in 1946 cabled the strong opposition of Africans in South Africa itself to any incorporation of South West Africa. 'We have long experience of South Africa's policies' – he detailed the experience – and 'would not like hundreds of thousands more innocent victims to be brought under South Africa's race and colour dominated policies.' The African National Congress took a closer look at the referendum figures. 'In a population of 300,000 odd, how could one get 280,000 votes for or against incorporation, unless we are dealing with male soldiers at the front line? Were children and infants also voting in South West Africa, a practice not permitted even among white South Africans, the most privileged of the privileged?' asked Dr Xuma, sarcastically. He followed the cable to the U.N. and lobbied on behalf of the South West Africans.

The issue swept across a second border, into Bechuanaland.

Would not the claim for annexation of South West Africa be the prelude to the expansion of South Africa into Bechuanaland and the other two British protectorates? Chief Tshekedi Khama of the Bamangwato and five other Bechuana chiefs submitted a memorandum to Britain. Would not the incorporation of the mandate place Bechuanaland's trade routes at the mercy of the South African government? Bechuanaland had a common boundary with South West Africa for hundreds of miles. And the government of South Africa was continually expressing its desire to incorporate the protectorates.

Living in Bamangwato country were thousands of displaced Herero, some driven out in German times, others in refuge from the mandate. To Chief Frederick Maharero, living near the Bamangwato Kgotla, had come an urgent cry from his people:

> The heritage of your father's orphans is about to be taken from them ... our heritage may fall to that side for which we have no liking. Let the Chief, despite pressing duties there, come with all haste to us, we pray you, sons of the chiefs, our fathers. Come, come, come. We are being asked that our land be joined to the Union, but we have refused. ...

Frederick Maharero re-entered South West Africa only to die there in his last ailing years and lie in the Herero ancestral burial grounds at Okahandja in 1952. But in his place, and briefed by him, went Michael Scott, the Anglican priest who made this mission the theme of his life from 1946 onwards. The first Scott memorandum, long, rambling, but vibrant with feeling, appeared in the U.N. official records of 1947. It transformed the South West African issue from a tedious, legal wrangle with a minor government into a crusade to save a people.

The Scott papers threw a new light on the South West African referendum. An Ovambo said that he had understood the Native Commissioner to say that if the U.N. took over the government of South West Africa it would mean that people from other countries, such as the Indians for example, who could live on the smell of oil on a rag – just the smell of oil, he had said, could make them live – would come to South West Africa and take away the trade and livelihood of the Europeans and Africans. Chief David Witbooi of the Nama had been offered money for the preservation of the Witbooi ancestral grave by the government official consulting him. Some chiefs understood that they were being asked if they wanted to fall under the British Crown. A missionary of nine years' experience in the country said: 'I don't think there is any need to talk about the referendum. It was an absolute farce. That is what even one of the Native Commissioners said about it.'

At the 1948 U.N. session in Paris, Mr Eric Louw was a voluble South African delegate, craftily side-stepping a Press report that his Prime Minister, Dr Malan – who had visited Windhoek, but refused to meet a Herero deputation – had said that South Africa would incorporate the mandate rather than submit it to trusteeship. The Prime Minister, he explained, had spoken in Afrikaans. . . . 'There must have been some error in translation.' The League of Nations had not made the U.N. its legatee for the mandated territory, argued Mr Louw. But, he added, South Africa would administer the territory 'in the spirit of the mandate'. France urged that South Africa be given time to fulfil her obligations; the General Assembly asked gently for annual information on the territory, till agreement was reached with the U.N.; and Mrs Pandit, for India, characterized the resolution which was passed, after vigorous debate, as *lifeless*.

In 1949, South Africa announced her inability to comply with the trusteeship resolution and her decision to submit no more reports or information. With these two challenges went a copy of the South West Africa Affairs Amendment Act of 1949, which gave South West Africa representation for the first time in the South African Parliament.

It was four months later that Michael Scott first addressed the Trusteeship Committee. The angry mutter of Africa had broken through the crust of the U.N., wrote the London *News Chronicle*. Something new and unique had happened to the parliament of the world. To some of the delegations – the British among them – a very dangerous precedent had been established. To others, the U.N. had found its soul at last. Every strategem known to diplomatic experts had been applied, unsuccessfully, to silence Scott.

Michael Scott's credentials – pathetic bits of paper signed by scattered tribal chiefs to whom he had journeyed tirelessly over thousands of miles under the eyes of hostile police – were challenged up to the last moment. . . . Dr Malan's delegate has been instructed to boycott the session, and Mr Scott indicts an empty chair. Trumpets should be sounding for Michael Scott today in the kraals, shanty slums, leaky huts and shabby little Negro churches, which sent him to the U.N.

Scott, it was reported, spoke in the quiet tones of a sermon preached in an English village church. The prayer he said was the one spoken by Hosea Kutako when Scott attended the annual ceremony at the Okahandja graves of the Herero chiefs: 'O Lord, help us who roam about. Help us who have been placed in Africa and have no home of our own. Give us back a dwelling place. . . .'

The admission of agitators of the Scott type to U.N. council chambers created a serious crisis, Dr Malan observed that November, attacking the 'interference mania' of the U.N. That year India suggested that a U.N. committee be sent to South West Africa: the proposal was rejected by one vote.

3. Points of Law

The world body resolved to ask the International Court of Justice for an opinion on the international status of South West, and on South Africa's international obligations.

In July 1950 the Court delivered the first of its three opinions (the others were to follow in 1955 and 1956). South West Africa *was* still a territory held under the international mandate assumed by South Africa in 1920, it found. The South African contention that the mandate had lapsed with the dissolution of the League was rejected. If the mandate had lapsed, so had the authority of the South African government. To retain the rights derived from the mandate and to deny the obligations could not be justified. The Court maintained that South Africa had an international obligation to transmit petitions from the mandate's inhabitants; and the U.N. had power to exercise supervisory functions and to receive annual reports and petitions. The degree of supervision, though, should not exceed that applied under the mandates system and should conform as far as possible to League procedure. Was South Africa legally *obliged* to submit the territory to trusteeship? Eight judges said no, and six said yes. Finally, the Court held that South Africa acting alone lacked competence to modify the international status of the territory. She could only do so with the consent of the U.N.

Dr Dönges represented South Africa at the 1950 session and announced that his government did not consider the International Court's judgement as binding.

Year after year points of law constituted South Africa's strongest defence. The 'C'-type mandate, South Africa insisted, conferred the special right on the mandatory power to administer its mandate as 'an integral part' of its own territory. Assiduously South Africa's representatives side-stepped the fact that the 'C'-type mandate merely indicated another form of administration designed to promote eventual self-government or independence, and had never conferred any right of annexation on the mandatory power.

Yet, year after year, in South Africa and in South West [wrote Advocate Goldblatt, a prominent Windhoek barrister, in a booklet on the subject] possibly for party political reasons or possibly from sheer ignorance, we have had the same argument repeated that power to administer South West Africa as an integral portion of the Union and the power to apply its laws to the territory in some way conferred independent rights upon the Union. Once and for all let that ghost be laid. The right to annex is an independent right in favour of and for the benefit of the country claiming that right. The power to administer South West Africa as an integral portion of the Union and the power to apply its laws are mere authorities granted to the mandatory power, in order to enable it to perform its duties, to wit, those accepted in terms of section 1 and 2 of Article 22 of the Covenant in the form of a tutelage of a country not yet able to stand by itself. The Permanent Mandates Commission consistently and persistently maintained this attitude, the trusteeship system adopted this attitude, and the United Nations General Assembly by an overwhelming majority and without a single opposing vote rejected the opposing view. *Not the dominant consideration, but the only consideration is the interests of the inhabitants of South West Africa. The interests of the Union play no part whatsoever.*

Year after year South Africa was insistent that her legal rights should not be invaded. But when the International Court had delivered its judgement, South Africa took shelter behind the opinion that there was no legal obligation on her to conclude a trusteeship agreement (any more than there had been a legal obligation on France, Britain, Japan, or Belgium to permit their territories to pass from the mandate into the trusteeship system), and announced that she rejected all the Court's other conclusions. 'It is a legal fact that the Court's opinion is purely advisory in nature.'

South Africa would not recognize the weight of international law. She rejected the majority opinion of the world assembly.

She would not submit even to negotiation, because she refused to acknowledge the authority of the U.N. Her isolationist stand blocked the efforts of every negotiating committee. She was concerned only to play for time.

Negotiation and Stalemate

The International Court had not only indicated South Africa's international obligations towards the mandate, but those of the U.N. as well. Some special kind of agreement and procedure, with the voluntary cooperation of South Africa, seemed necessary for the supervision of South West Africa by the world body. An Ad Hoc Committee of Five was set up to confer with South Africa on procedural matters; the Committee was to consider reports and petitions from the mandate. South Africa emerged with a novel plan: she would negotiate a new international instrument for the control of South West Africa, but only with the three remaining principal Allied and Associated Powers of the First World War – France, Britain, and the United States. These powers, she averred, on rather obscure legal grounds – for how ignore the other signatories to the League Covenant, and the fact that the United States had not even been a member of the League? – were those who had conferred the original mandate, and she would hold herself responsible to them, but not to the U.N.

The Ad Hoc Committee, composed of representatives from the United States, Denmark, Thailand, Syria, and Uruguay (Britain having refused to serve), pointed out that it was bound by its terms of reference, which reflected the Court opinion that U.N. supervision was necessary. The Committee then submitted a counter-scheme for supervision, modelled as nearly as possible on the mandate system – a special committee of fifteen members, including South Africa. South Africa rejected it. Negotiations between South Africa and the Ad Hoc Committee reached an impasse. The reported stalemate came before the Fourth Committee at the end of 1951, but before it could be discussed a new storm had broken. While South Africa was manoeuvring to keep the mandate beyond reach of the U.N., petitions from

South West Africa had been received by the Ad Hoc Committee and, in accordance with Fourth Committee procedure, been forwarded to South Africa for comment. What is more, the Fourth Committee had agreed to hear Herero and Nama Chiefs in person. Dr Ralph Bunche cabled the mortation to them.

This action was maladroit, vindictive, and unconstitutional, declared Dr Dönges. He demanded a reversal of the decision by the President of the General Assembly – which the latter found himself constitutionally unable to do – and South Africa withdrew in protest from the Fourth Committee. This boycott lasted two and a half months. The Herero and Nama chiefs were refused passports; the Fourth Committee voted to hear Michael Scott in their place. As Scott entered, Dr Dönges stormed out. Once again the U.N. enunciated its hope for a solution, its solemn appeal to South Africa to report on its trust and conclude a trusteeship agreement within the framework of the International Court decision. The Ad Hoc Committee was reconstituted to negotiate further. The talks lasted five days and disintegrated. South Africa was prepared to make no concessions. She rejected the Court opinion.

The following year, the South West African item was crowded off the agenda. Then, in 1953 – in terms of the International Court opinion that the U.N. should ascertain whether the mandate was being administered in accordance with the terms of the trust – the semi-permanent Committee on South West Africa was established to exercise supervision over the territory and to negotiate with South Africa. In effect, this Committee was to fulfil the role of the Permanent Mandates Commission of the League, and it quickly became the eyes and ears of the U.N. on South West Africa. In the face of South Africa's blank boycott, it compiled its own informative annual reports, based on every scrap of information available, and these – allowing for some minor faults and gaps, and the occasionally fanciful version of events in the territory given by some of the petitioners - soon exceeded in scope and detail any public report previously compiled by the U.N. or South Africa herself.

In 1954, for the first time in seven years, procedural wrangles did not exhaust all the time of the Fourth Committee. The diligent report of the Committee on South West Africa, compiled from a list of mainly official publications, covered land and education, taxation and political rights. The South African delegate had to listen to a debate on a matter which he claimed to be nobody's concern but South Africa's. It was difficult for outsiders to assess the truth, he insisted. The representative of Uruguay replied pointedly that for this South Africa had only herself to blame; the omission could easily be remedied if South Africa would only admit U.N. observers.

Another legal storm broke that year over whether voting on the issue of South West Africa in the General Assembly had to be unanimous (as in the days of the League) or by a two-thirds majority, the strongest vote required at the U.N. The International Court of Justice, once again asked to adjudicate, upheld the majority decision of the Fourth Committee that a two-thirds majority vote was sufficient. The United States had withdrawn from the Committee on South West Africa during the bitter debate over the rules of procedure; now she returned. South Africa announced that she did not accept the opinion of the Court.

Suddenly, in 1955, South Africa announced that she was withdrawing her delegation, and closing down her permanent office at the U.N., not, this time, because of the South West African issue, but out of protest that the General Assembly had once again placed on its agenda the Question of Race Conflict in South Africa, resulting from the policy of apartheid.

The Fourth Committee soon afterwards dealt with another request for a hearing from Michael Scott. For two days the delegates deliberated, and then again tripped over a point of law: was it legally competent for the Committee to hear oral evidence? The International Court of Justice was consulted, and ruled 'yes'. The delegate of Uruguay, Professor Fabregat (later chairman of the Committee on South West Africa), observed that

the admissibility of requests for hearing was bound up with problems raised by the negative attitude of the Union of South Africa. In view of the Union's refusal to supply information on the territory, there was no way the General Assembly could be informed of the situation other than by granting the Committee on South West Africa the right to hear persons who were prepared to give it information.

As well as Scott appeared Mburumba Kerina Getzen, the first African petitioner from South West Africa – then a student in the United States – to appear at the U.N. Two White South Africans who asked by letter to be heard were invited to come and testify, but they never appeared. Since 1951 the suggestion had been made in petitions – by Scott – that U.N. members who had belonged to the League should ask for the compulsory jurisdiction of the International Court on South Africa's handling of the mandate. At its 1956 session, the General Assembly 'noted with concern' its Committee's conclusion that conditions in South West Africa were for the most part, and particularly for the 'Native' majority, still far from meeting in a reasonable way the standards implicit in the purposes of the 'mandate system. It drew the attention of the government of South Africa to the Committee's recommendations for the representation of all inhabitants in the territorial legislature, the revision of land settlement policy, the basing of public employment on qualifications other than race, and the elimination of race discrimination in education. It also asked the Committee on South West Africa to examine

what legal action is open to the organs of the United Nations, or to the members of the United Nations, acting either individually or jointly, to ensure that South Africa fulfils the obligations assumed by it under the mandate, pending the placing of the territory of South West Africa under the trusteeship system?

Partition ?

Suddenly, in the midst of the twelfth session (1957), Thonat Khoman of Thailand, speaking from the chair of the Fourth Committee, intervened with a surprise proposal that a Good Offices Committee be appointed of representatives from Britain, the United States, and one other member nation to be nominated by the General Assembly (Brazil got the seat), to negotiate with South Africa 'a basis for an agreement which would continue to accord to the territory an international status'. This was a carefully contrived behind-the-scenes manoeuvre. The Thailand delegate let it be known that the draft was acceptable to South Africa; the British delegate said that acceptance was conditional on no amendments being made to the text. Many delegates had misgivings. Years of cajoling and reprimand, backed by International Court decisions, had not moved South Africa. Would the appointment of a Good Offices Committee not merely defer the issue for another year?

The Good Offices Committee surfaced in 1958 with a scheme which the government of South Africa had proposed. South Africa would enter into an agreement with Britain, France, and the United States, proclaiming, vaguely, the 'international character' of the mandate. The U.N. had rejected it repeatedly before as untenable in the light of the 1950 Court opinion. The Committee also produced a partition plan: the territory might be split into a southern sector, to be incorporated in South Africa, and a northern sector, which South Africa would administer under a trust agreement concluded with the U.N. This misguided compromise (which had emanated in the deadlocked days of 1950 from Britain's Anti-Slavery Society, in the hope that at least part of South West Africa would be rescued for trusteeship in this way) had found top-level sponsorship at last.

It was small wonder that Mr Louw was partial to the plan. Granting even a part of South West Africa to South Africa would undermine the very basis of the U.N. claim that the whole was international territory. And the partition plan itself would involve the annexation by South Africa of the profitable areas, the good ranching land and developed mineral wealth of the country. The Africans in the north, placed under trusteeship, would not only be left the poorest part, but would in consequence continue to be governed by apartheid, since they would be compelled by their subsistence economy to seek work as migrant labourers in areas under complete South African jurisdiction.

Scenting defeat for the partition scheme, Mr Louw seemed

touchier than ever during the session. When the Fourth Committee granted Scott and Kerina hearings, he withdrew precipitately before the debate opened on the report of the Good Offices Committee, though his own government had devoted a year of negotiations to it.

Fifty-six delegates spoke on the partition proposal, and all of them opposed it, most taking the view that it was merely a disguised plan for annexation. The Committee was finally authorized to continue its efforts at negotiating with South Africa, but not to entertain any plan for the partition of South West.

Fourteen years of dispute over South West Africa had now gone by, fourteen years of earnest, repetitive speeches; plaintive appeals to conscience; fruitless resolutions; patient, but always abortive negotiation. The issue had been handled gently, as one incalculably fragile, and Fourth Committee speakers had congratulated themselves when negotiations solved nothing but had at least been conducted without angry recrimination. The U.N. tone had been temperate, in the hope of getting South Africa to conform. But South Africa had proved bluntly uncompromising, and the world body was left holding a handsome collection of platitudes. No grave legal problems or questions of U.N. competence remained unresolved, yet the world body appeared unable to act.

The Fourth Committee, it had been observed from the earliest days, was split into three parties: South Africa on her own; the conservatives from the colonial powers, side-stepping to avoid treading on South Africa's toes; and the rest – Asia, the Arab states, Latin America, Africa, and the Communist countries, joined in later years by the Scandinavian states, often Canada, the United States, and, occasionally, the Netherlands. Within this group, the Soviet Union and other nations objected that the Fourth Committee was going too far in its search for compromise solutions. The Soviet view of the legal issue was that there were only two courses open to the mandatory power, to bring the territory under the trusteeship system, or grant it independence. The Special Committee on South West Africa should not have been established at all, for it was a means of circumventing the Charter and the whole trusteeship system.

South Africa's struggle to defend her untenable position was based on threadbare legal arguments. Her tactics had been inept and clumsy. Far from evading scrutiny by refusing U.N. trusteeship, she had drawn more and more fire onto herself. Mr Louw, sulky, truculent, the wrongdoer acting wronged, had perfected jack-in-the-box blackmail diplomacy: first he would talk in debate, then stage a walk-out, and then return, only to leave again with another protest against 'interference'. South Africa, employing attack as the most effective form of defence, accused the U.N. of exceeding its powers. She seized on the hearings given to petitioners, on a few inaccuracies in reports on conditions in South West Africa, on attacks made against her policy in debate, as malignant acts that undermined all negotiation, whereas in fact she herself refused to move an inch towards any solution. The conservative group within the Fourth Committee and General Assembly was as protective towards South Africa as possible, proposing milder, more conciliatory resolutions, urging caution, pressing for less peremptory language, less speed, abstaining in votes on any resolutions which tried to go a little further or faster than the resolution of the year before. There had been fourteen years of debate and indecision. And after fourteen years it looked as though the South West African issue had been flogged to death. What point was there in continuing to flog it any further? What could it conceivably accomplish?

Only in the presence of the petitioners did something human flow through the dry and dreary debates. During the empty years it was these men who helped to keep the issue alive. It was easier to consider the plight of flesh-and-blood people than of imaginary ones. For many years Michael Scott had been the lonely but relentless lobbyist of a cause that seemed hopeless to all but the visionary. Then gradually he was joined by other petitioners. For two years, Mburumba Kerina, who had in 1952 wangled a passport to leave his home in South West Africa and study at Lincoln University, battled to give oral evidence before the Fourth

Committee. He was heard at last in 1957. A petition on tape arrived in New York smuggled out by an enterprising young Ovambo leader, Toivo ja Toivo: the tape was hidden in a book, appropriately, a copy of *Gulliver's Travels*. Three young Americans paid a visit to South West Africa, ostensibly to examine the flowers and wild-life. They smuggled out Hans Beukes, a young Rehobother who had won a scholarship to Oslo, but had had his passport confiscated, and they themselves reported on their clandestine meetings with Africans in the territory. Mr Louw attacked the characters of the three, Allard Lowenstein, Sherman Bull, and Emory Bundy. They in turn mustered Mrs Eleanor Roosevelt, Mr Adlai Stevenson, and Senator Humphrey to testify for them (on paper).

The 1959 meetings of the Committee on South West Africa were enlivened by the testimony of a new witness, Jariretundu Kozonguizi, chosen by the Herero through the Chief's Council, to be spokesman alongside Michael Scott, and the first South West African to leave his country specifically for the purpose of testifying at the U.N. as a petitioner. Showing impressive political ability, Kozonguizi dealt with the forcible removal by police of the Reverend Marcus Kooper of Hoachanas; the exile of Toivo ja Toivo to the north; the explosive situation in the Windhoek Location, where the residents refused to be removed from their homes to the apartheid location farther from the town. Hans Beukes himself appeared as a petitioner.

Fresh witnesses arrived: the Reverend Marcus Kooper, taken in a police lorry from Hoachanas to Itsawisis, had somehow managed to escape through Bechuanaland to New York; Jacob Kuhangua, whom the South West African government had tried to deport to Angola on three occasions, but who had been handed back by the Portuguese and placed under house arrest; Sam Nujoma and Louis Nelengani, who had fled to escape banishment to Ovamboland; Ismail Fortune, who had left with a passport ostensibly on a visit to Mecca; Oliver Tambo, impressive Deputy President-General of the African National Congress of South Africa, who had been sent abroad by his Executive just before the 1960 State of Emergency and who now, as key man on A.N.C. missions to numerous countries, lobbied with the South West Africans to prise the grip of the South African government loose at last.

In 1946 there had been a solitary petition in the form of a cable from the Herero and Nama Chiefs; in 1960, 120 petitions were directed at the United Nations Fourth Committee. Political organization was stirring in South West Africa.

4. How the People Organized

At first the tribal chiefs monopolized the political scene – ranging from Chief Hosea Kutako, whose leadership of the Herero has been a continuous inspiration ever since the 1904 Herero-German war; to the late Chief Johannes Kambonde of the On donga, through whom the government time and again silenced opposition among his people; and the malleable Ushona Shimi, head of the Ongandjera, doing the bidding, without question, of government officials. Political organization, such as it was during the early years, took a tribal form, and the only outlet for dissatisfaction was the chief's conclave with officials of the Bantu Affairs Department.

Michael Scott's arrival as courier from exiled Chief Frederick Maharero to Hosea Kutako initiated the phase of petitioning to the U.N. All the African groups joined, with the exception of the Ovambo, who only associated themselves some years later, but throughout the Herero led, as the most vociferous tribe.

In the 1950s, two sets of South African influences jerked African politics to life. Enterprising organizers of the Cape Town-based Food and Canning Workers Union took trade-unionism into Luderitz Bay, the fish canning centre of South West Africa. The union president, Frank Marquard, set to work there in 1949, and he was followed by Ray Alexander in 1952. Hours of work, rates of pay, and industrial legislation were probed. The union began pressing the Administration and the Legislative Assembly for laws to protect labour. Marquard supervised the enrolling of the first union members in 1949 and the first union general meeting. African contract workers from

Ovamboland formed a union too. Then, after Ray Alexander's trip, communications between the union branch at Luderitz Bay and the head office in Cape Town were abruptly cut. Police questioned and intimidated the union officials in Luderitz. The Suppression of Communism Act, in terms of which the Minister of Justice prohibited Ray Alexander from attending all gatherings and ordered her to resign at once from her trade union, stopped her activity in the field. Connexion with the South West African members became tenuous and intermittent. Trade unionism was being throttled in South West Africa, but not before two large strikes of Ovambo contract workers, in 1952 and 1953, had taken place. The police opened fire during the second strike and killed three workers. But union organizing bore a little fruit: in 1953 a factories, machinery, and building work ordinance was promulgated, reducing working hours from sixty to forty-six a week.

In the years since then, there have been no unions, but a few sporadic and spontaneous strikes have testified to labour unrest. There was one on a mine in the Namib desert, to break which armed police were summoned. There was another of Herero and Berg-Damara women in a small Windhoek laundry. There was yet another, of several hundred Ovambo contract workers, who struck at Walvis Bay in June 1962. Fifty-five workers were arrested, and fifty-four sentenced to a fine of £30 each (the total earnings in one *year* of a contract worker), or ninety days' imprisonment. The fifty-fifth accused was found not guilty and discharged because he had been given permission to go off duty; but he refused to leave the court and tried to join his fellow-workers on their way to jail. A court orderly had to lead him away.

The early fifties found the few African students from South West Africa at schools and colleges in South Africa stirred by the Defiance Campaign of the African National and South African Indian Congresses, when over 8,000 men and women courted imprisonment as a protest against 'unjust laws'. The South West African Student Body was formed. Elected to its executive were three men destined to be moving spirits in all subsequent political organization: Jariretundu Kozonguizi, now President of the South West African National Union (S.W.A.N.U.); Mburumba Kerina, also known as Erich Getzen and Chairman of the South West African Peoples' Organization (S.W.A.P.O.); and Zedekia Ngavirue, adviser to S.W.A.N.U.'s national executive. Kerina left South West Africa soon afterwards, on a passport under the name of Getzen, to seek a scholarship in the United States. Kozonguizi and Ngavirue were victimized for their student politics: Kozonguizi's bursary to Fort Hare University College was withdrawn by the South West African administration, and Ngavirue was expelled from the Okahandja Training College.

At the end of 1954 Kozonguizi was invited to join the Chief's Council of Hosea Kutako, at the request, he was told, of Michael Scott, who had urged the coordination of approaches to the U.N. Kozonguizi accepted, hoping to bridge the gap between the elders, who worked by petitions and deputations to the authorities, and the younger generation in the student body, growing impatient of debating-society politics, and anxious to replace tribal divisions with an aggressive and popular nationalism. Kozonguizi preached this new gospel to the elders, and at the same time helped draft the petitions to the U.N. The young men started the South West African Progressive Association led by Uatja Kaukuetu, now S.W.A.N.U.'s Vice-President, and in the meetings of this group the idea was born of a national political movement to lead the struggle for freedom and independence. Kozonguizi canvassed the scheme with the elders, and they approved.

Planning for the new movement went on desultorily over the years. Kozonguizi had again become a student, at South Africa's Fort Hare, where he served 'for experience' on the executive of the African National Congress student branch; and in Cape Town, where he met Toivo ja Toivo. Toivo himself is a redoubtable Ovambo, who had gone from Finnish mission industrial school in Ovamboland, into service with the Native Military Corps of the South African army during the Second World War. Emerging as a corporal, he had returned to school, entering Standard One at the age of twenty-three, and then taken work on the Witwatersrand gold mines. After a spell as clerk on a manganese mine, and brief training and duty as a railway policeman in South Africa, he had finally found a job in Cape Town, and had proceeded to organize a group of other Ovambo expatriates who had managed to get work permits and jobs there. He had then started up a correspondence with Kerina, who was studying at Lincoln University in the United States and who had offered his services as U.N. representative to the organization being planned at home. Toivo's tape-recorded petition, smuggled out in a book, created a sensation at the U.N., but also set the Special Branch on his trail, and he was given seventy-two hours to leave Cape Town for South West Africa.

It was on the eve of Toivo's enforced departure that Kozonguizi addressed the Ovambos organized around Toivo on plans to integrate the emergent Ovamboland Peoples' Organization into a South West African national congress, based on regional congresses in Namaland (the south), Damaraland (the central area), and Ovamboland.

With the police order hanging over Toivo's head and discussions on future action still incomplete, Toivo and Kozonguizi left for South West Africa together, stopping off at Keetmanshoop in the south to throw the political police off their scent and discuss with local Nama leaders the proposed national organization. Arriving in Windhoek, they talked with Hosea Kutako, Clement Kapuuo, and others. It was agreed that Kozonguizi would organize from the capital, and Toivo from Ovamboland.

Toivo was, of course, the one Ovambo whom the government was anxious to keep out of Ovamboland, but he brushed aside the Bantu Affairs Department suggestion that he remain in Windhoek, and journeyed northwards. Christmas Day of that year, 1958, he spent in jail for having entered the Tsumeb mine compound without a permit; then he was taken to Ovamboland under police escort, to be placed under house arrest and the watchful eye of Chief Kambonde. Spells of detention at the chief's kraal ceased only with the death of Kambonde himself, whose successor proved a less vigilant policeman of the government and allowed Toivo to move about more freely. Nowadays, not a single government official tries to hold a meeting in Ovamboland but Toivo or one of his lieutenants attends to attack government policy, demand U.N. intervention, and show how firmly political organization has taken root among the Ovambo.

Back in the Police Zone in January 1959, at a conference held in Aminuis Reserve, the Herero tribe debated an urgent request from Michael Scott for an African fresh from South West Africa to join him as a petitioner at the U.N. Since 1956, Kerina had been authorized to petition on credentials signed initially by Kozonguizi for the South West African student body, and later by Hosea Kutako for the Herero tribe. But Scott, and the tribe itself, felt that the U.N. front needed full-time attention from someone recently in touch with local conditions. The Chief's Council chose Kozonguizi. He packed his bags and escaped, through Bechuanaland, a month after the tribal meeting.

Shortly afterwards, in April 1959, Sam Nujoma and Jacob Kahangua organized the Ovamboland Peoples' Organization (O.P.O.) in Windhoek. The following month the South West African National Union, known as the 'First S.W.A.N.U.', was established with Uatja Kaukuetu as President and several members of the Chief's Council on the executive.

New elections in September broadened the leadership, for Nujoma and his O.P.O. members participated, as well as members of the Chief's Council. Kozonguizi was elected President, and Kaukuetu, Uaseta Mbuha, Nelengani, Appolus, Nujoma, and Mbaeva to official positions.

The organizations had risen to their feet, but only to find themselves faced with the two problems that have bedevilled the South West African political scene ever since: the relationship between the political bodies and the Chief's Council, and rivalry amongst the various bodies. Influential men on the Council seemed to want S.W.A.N.U. run by the Chief and his advisers, and real cooperation between the contending groups was restored only with the government threat forcibly to move Africans from their homes in the old location of Windhoek to the new distant Katutura township. S.W.A.N.U. and O.P.O. held joint protest meetings and decided to join in boycotting the buses and municipal beerhall. After the police shootings of December 1959 in the Windhoek old location, S.W.A.N.U. and O.P.O. officials gave joint evidence with Chief Kutako to the Hall Commission of Inquiry.

But fresh complications were looming. Kerina had written from New York to Sam Nujoma, O.P.O. President and executive member of S.W.A.N.U. urging the expansion of O.P.O. into a national organization for all the population groups. S.W.A.N.U., however, already claiming national support, condemned this proposal as leading to division. Meanwhile, the Herero tribe, urged by advisers abroad, was considering the election of a deputy to the ageing Chief Kutako, lest Kutako's death provide the Bantu Affairs Department with an excuse to choose a successor of its liking. Scattered over eleven separate Reserves, the Herero could not meet together, and delegated the choice of a successor to that section of the tribe living in the Aminuis Reserve. Clement Kapuuo was the chief candidate, but among Herero members of S.W.A.N.U. there was wide opposition to him, since in his evidence before the Hall Commission he had seemed to shrug off responsibility for letters to Kutako found in his home, and had disowned any association with S.W.A.N.U. (Kapuuo is a teacher in government service; his caution was not inexplicable.) Fighting a nomination battle, Kapuuo's supporters on the Chief's Council accused S.W.A.N.U. of opposing chieftainship as such, and set on a path of dividing the Herero. A letter from the Chief's Council urged Kozonguizi to resign the S.W.A.N.U. Presidency.

While visiting Monrovia on a tour of independent African states, Kozonguizi met Nujoma, who had left after the December disturbances in Windhoek to escape victimization. The two sat down to thrash out the muddle. It was surely difficult, argued Kozonguizi, to justify the existence of two national bodies (for the O.P.O. was about to be converted into a rival to S.W.A.N.U.). Could they not merge? Nujoma was concerned that the Ovambo, the largest tribal group in South West Africa, should not feel themselves submerged by the other tribes if the name O.P.O. disappeared, so Kozonguizi offered to recommend that S.W.A.N.U. itself change its name to facilitate unity. Nujoma and Kozonguizi jointly signed a letter home urging a merger between the two bodies and, if necessary, a change of name. But the merger struck opposition in Windhoek, where S.W.A.N.U. was in bad odour with the Herero Chief's Council; and from Kerina, who wrote pressingly from New York for the expansion of the O.P.O. into a South West African People's Organization. Finally, this new body was formed in June 1960.

Since then S.W.A.N.U. and S.W.A.P.O. have organized side by side. There is friction at the top-level, though not among all the leaders, since Kozonguizi and Nujoma, for example, remain on good terms; and there has been some quarrelling in little duplicated bulletins and in the South African political Press. But rank-and-filers seem to have little notion of the policy differences between the two bodies. At the United Nations the S.W.A.P.O. executive – its five key officials are all abroad – functions round the assertive personality of Kerina. At home S.W.A.P.O. leans heavily on the Chief's Council, Herero dominance in U.N. petitioning, and on Toivo's adroit organizing in Ovamboland. Chief Witbooi of the Nama takes a seat on the Chief's Council, and petitions appear over the name of Kutako, Witbooi, and S.W.A.P.O.; but Witbooi also retains amicable working relations with S.W.A.N.U. The Reverend Marcus Kooper at U.N. has likewise remained neutral and works with all the petitioners.

S.W.A.N.U. itself musters branches of lively young men dedicated to political struggle, some showing promise of considerable ability and leadership. But its development as a modern political movement and its attempts to build unity with S.W.A.P.O. have been bedevilled by the criss-crossing of political and tribal attitudes. The Herero are the fathers of the whole protest period, and they have made their impressive impact as a group because of their tight internal tribal discipline.

But the habit of dominance dies hard, and the two roles of the Chief's Council – as a tribal authority and a body coordinating Herero and other petitioning to the U.N. – have become confused.

S.W.A.N.U. opened itself to attack from the influential Chief's Council not only by the opposition of many of its leaders to Kapuuo's election as deputy chief, but also over its stand on the complex Herero–Mbanderu dispute. The Mbanderu, the eastern Herero, assert their right to their own chief, Munjuku II, who returned from exile at Lake Ngami in Bechuanaland a few years ago and was officially installed by the government. The rest of the Herero, however, citing a different interpretation of tribal tradition, deny that the Mbanderu are entitled to their own chief independent of the Maharero dynasty, as a member of which Hosea Kutako himself now rules. They fear that a separate Mbanderu chieftainship will be used to divide and weaken the tribe's political role, and this fear was fortified by government recognition of Munjuku II and the delight with which the White-owned Press in Windhoek seized upon the signs of tension and dispute. Munjuku II certainly soiled his political character by declarations of gratitude to the government at his installation ceremony, but his statements have since been revised or disowned in the Press by some of his more politically alert councillors. S.W.A.N.U.'s constitution forbids participation in tribal activities, but the organization has among its members some Mbanderu supporters of Chief Munjuku II, and this has brought the wrath of the Herero Chief's Council about its head. Trying to wean political organization and thought from the influence of tribal elders, S.W.A.N.U. has nevertheless found itself involved in tribal disputes. It will need to exercise some shrewd diplomacy if it is to extricate itself without damage.

S.W.A.N.U. spokesmen say that their main criticism of S.W.A.P.O., so closely allied in South West Africa to the Herero Chief's Council, is that it 'makes a career out of petitioning'. S.W.A.N.U. itself has more and more taken to emphasizing on public platforms and in published propaganda that the main effort for freedom must come from the people in South West

Africa. Werner Mamugwe, acting S.W.A.N.U. Chairman, told me in Windhoek: 'What is done by the outside world must be only supplementary to what is done here. The other policy spreads an illusion that we will get freedom from abroad. United Nations promises cool the courage and spirit of the people, and they do not realize that *they* must do something themselves to attain their freedom.' Sixteen years of petitioning the outside world for deliverance from South Africa have bred dependence among the older-type spokesmen. They display a reluctance to face the painful fact – and speak it out aloud to their followers – that the main burden of their deliverence rests upon their own shoulders, and that U.N. intervention is likely to help only those who help themselves.

This is one of the chief differences between S.W.A.N.U. on the one hand and S.W.A.P.O. and the Chief's Council on the other. S.W.A.N.U. rejects what Kozonguizi terms

the reformist approach in the struggle for liberation . . . reformism has had its time – 15 years of petitioning, of 'Native conferences' with Native Commissioners, of deputations to the Secretary of South West Africa, of appeals to Macmillan . . . We also reject the idea that our deliverance should rest entirely with the Big Powers. We appeal to all the states of the U.N. and particularly our brother states in Africa to *act* against South Africa but the right to *decide* remains vested in the people of South West Africa. It is for us to find the most effective methods to liberate ourselves.

Nevertheless, with the need to unite the forces for change of South West Africa, the two organizations cooperate through their petitioners at the U.N. and have lately moved closer in coordinating their efforts and contemplating a merger.

Both organizations expounded plans for a South West Africa wrenched free of South African control before the recent sessions in Africa of the U.N. Committee. Both agreed that the removal of South African authority was essential to the exercise of any real self-determination.

The S.W.A.P.O. representative asked for action to:

Terminate the mandate immediately, and entrust the temporary administration of the country to a United Nations Commission composed of African States, to arrange for free general elections immediately, to make possible the conditions for South West Africa to accede to: (1) self-government now, through the establishment of a democratic African government based on the principle of one man, one vote; (2) independence not later than 1963.

Establish a United Nations police force to facilitate the work of the administrative Commission of African States; to maintain law and order; to disarm all organized and individual civilian elements; to assist in the restoration of peace and security; to protect the lives of all the inhabitants, to free all political detainees and imprisoned leaders and members of S.W.A.P.O. and other groups; to disarm all South African military and para-military personnel and to arrange for their immediate repatriation to South Africa.

The S.W.A.N.U. spokesman stated that there could never be peace in South West Africa 'until the White settlers from the Republic of South Africa, who are determined to die fighting against the United Nations or any other administration in South West Africa' had been removed from the territory. If there was a way which could guarantee that their presence would not constitute a danger to the peace and security of South West Africa, they would always be welcome. In further explanation of S.W.A.N.U.'s position, Kozonguizi informed the Committee 'that the term "settlers" did not include South West African persons born in the territory who, in the opinion of his organization, had the same rights as all other South West Africans'.

S.W.A.N.U. insisted on speedy independence for South West Africa, and submitted an arrangement for the first stage of self-determination:

Acceptance of the principle that political decisions should be taken by the people of South West Africa themselves. For this purpose representatives of the various regions should be selected to participate in a constitutional convention, to be held under the auspices of the United Nations, which would provide advisers on problems of a technical nature. The convention would decide on the following questions:

(a) Political arrangements in the country, i.e. the form of government and its constitution; the Legislative Assembly representation.

(b) Administration: The United Nations to man the administrative section of the government, subject to the proviso that all South Africans who were supporters of the South African government be excluded.

(c) Maintenance of peace and security in the territory. That United Nations troops police the territory with troops drawn from Afro-Asian and other uncommitted countries, the right being reserved to the people of South West Africa to determine which countries they consider uncommitted.

(d) Technical Assistance: the principles of how the resources of the country could best be exploited; how the desired wealth could reach all the people; and how the people themselves could best take part in the development of the country.

(e) The United Nations and its specialized agencies. The United Nations might appoint a Committee of African States to advise the government and administration of the territory.

The programmes of the two organizations clearly differ in detail. S.W.A.P.O. has pinned its independence date to the fortunes of Africa in 1963, influenced possibly by the Pan-Africanist Congress cry in South Africa for independence by 1963. S.W.A.N.U.'s plan proceeds from a country-wide South West African popular consultation on forms of government; S.W.A.P.O. from U.N.-organized elections. S.W.A.N.U. has drawn lessons from the U.N. operation in the Congo and wants to reserve its rights on the extent and nature of participation by member states. But both bodies speak with one voice on the revocation of the mandate and agree over many of the steps necessary before independence. Spurred to united and coordinated action on the home front, they would probably find much else to unite them.

The leadership quarrels, reflecting some differences in policy, remain. Kozonguizi, disillusioned with the U.N.'s dilatory handling of the South West African issue, expressed his disappointment over Peking radio while on a visit to China. This exposed S.W.A.N.U. to criticisms of abandoning the West and seeking an alignment with the Communist world. S.W.A.N.U. leaders replied by attacking S.W.A.P.O. for its close connexions with the American Metal Climax Corporation, which has allo-

cated bursaries to S.W.A.P.O. members abroad and has sub-
stantial economic interests in South West Africa through the
Tsumeb mines. S.W.A.P.O. leaders objected to Kozonguizi's Pek-
ing speech because it was strongly anti-imperialist in tone, and
delivered before a Communist audience. They claim that any
South West African identification with the Communist countries
would damage the South West African cause throughout the
West. Kozonguizi, on the other hand, argues that South West
Africans must seek aid wherever they can find it, and that the
Western powers were shaken into a more progressive stand on
South West Africa after his Peking speech, because they
realized that their policy had to stand comparison with the
strong support for South West African independence shown by
the Communist states.

At home in South West Africa the differences between the two
movements, however, are more apparent than real, for
S.W.A.N.U. and S.W.A.P.O., at work have far more uniting
than dividing them. Prospects for unity have been clouded by
recrimination and counter-recrimination, much of it trivial, and
arising from personal differences among the top, influential
leaders. But in both organizations the realization has grown that
rivalry is wasteful of political energies abroad, and that in South
West Africa itself the people can little afford the luxury of internal dissension.

Both political movements are very young – not yet three years
old. They are still too largely the surface growth of politicians,
with much spade-work to be done if roots are to be sent down
deep among the people themselves. The need to fight the South
West African independence struggle on two fronts – at the U.N.
and at home – has been a source both of strength and of weakness. The petitioners at work abroad in the committee rooms
and lobbies of the U.N. can look back on several years of
outstanding effort by which the South African government has
been beaten even more on to the defensive. But through the
absence of the petitioners abroad, the people at home have been
deprived of their most experienced and able leadership. There
has inevitably been some loss of contact between home and

abroad, some distortion of perspective by petitioners cut off from daily participation in the struggle of the people they represent. Policies that should be reached after prolonged discussion and debate in Windhoek and Keetmanshoop, Ondangua and Tsumeb, are formulated in New York and air-freighted home. Local grievances, local conditions assume slightly different shapes abroad; at times their remoteness from the scene has led the petitioners to overstress some facts and underplay others. The two fronts of political organization are deeply dependent on one another, but physically separated by thousands of miles and acute communication difficulties.

Yet, with all the problems and weaknesses of young political movements, S.W.A.N.U. and S.W.A.P.O., together with their allies on the Herero Chief's Council, among the Nama chiefs and within the Rehoboth community, nurture the future leaders of South West Africa.

Membership figures and accurate assessments of their strength are difficult to obtain, for neither of the bodies yet boasts the working machinery to translate into membership its areas of support and even wider potential following. Political organization in South West Africa was born late, but it is rapidly coming of age.

5. Sharpeville and the Sixties

The 1959 session of the U.N. Fourth Committee had drifted into the usual impasse on South West Africa – member states had decided that the welfare of the people demanded a change in the administration of the territory 'without undue delay', and their attention had been drawn to the conclusions of the sub-committee on possible new legal action – when on 11 December, the day before the General Assembly was scheduled to adjourn, the Fourth Committee was asked to hear the South West African petitioners again as the result of tragic new developments in the territory. Eleven Africans, including a brother of petitioner Mburumba Kerina, had been killed, and forty-four wounded, when police opened fire on a crowd in the Windhoek old location. The petitioners presented the Committee with information they had received by cable and trans-Atlantic telephone that afternoon. The victims of police fire were the very Africans whose removal to a new apartheid township the Trusteeship Council and the General Assembly had condemned earlier in the session. And the shooting itself had taken place, with terrible irony, on Human Rights Day, 10 December.

The new township had been called Katutura: officialdom appeared not to know until the name had been gazetted that this was Herero for 'we have no permanent abode'. Objections to the removal had simmered among the people from 1958, perhaps earlier, but the African advisory board could not summon up the courage to say so, and when resistance at last rose to the surface, the aggressive paternalistic Mayor dismissed it. In September 1959, outspoken Zedekia Ngavirue, social worker, leading

S.W.A.N.U. member, and founder-editor of the first African-run newspaper in the territory, suggested privately to the superintendent of the old location that he meet the true leaders of the people. The superintendent agreed, but first held informal talks with three politicals, Ngavirue, Mbaeva, and Tjingaete. 'He boiled at one point,' recalled Ngavirue, 'but then calmed down and started learning.' The superintendent then invited top municipal and administrative officials to meet S.W.A.N.U. and O.P.O. men. Their attack was so strong that the official interpreter 'started shivering' – to continue Ngavirue's account – 'and even tried to modify some of the statements. But the people shouted, "Talk, Talk." The people chose their own interpreter and continued their attacks.'

An open-air meeting of location inhabitants was summoned and asked to appoint a property valuator, to join those selected by the administration and the town council, but the meeting refused to do so. Meanwhile, Ngavirue himself had conducted a house-to-house survey in a section of the location and revealed how desperate was the poverty of the people. The rents in the new township were to be £2 a month, compared to the charge of 3s. 6d. for stands in the old location. But there were other African objections to the move: Katutura was farther from the town, and bus fares to work would be high; there would be no freehold ownership; screening would weed out those judged not 'fit and proper'; the municipal regulations promised to be unbearably irksome; above all, the removal was clearly part of the whole apartheid scheme to segregate Africans, control their every movement, shift them 'from place to place at the whim of the White administration'.

When their objections were ignored and enforced valuations of their homes relentlessly pursued, the inhabitants of the old location organized a boycott of the bus service, the municipal beer-halls, and the cinema. Officials dug in their heels, called a meeting in the location, and demanded an end to all boycott by the following day; when an advisory board member tried to speak, the officials told him that they had come not for discussions, but to warn the people. The arrest of three pickets outside the beer-hall drew a large crowd, which the S.W.A.N.U. Vice-President, Kaukuetu, tried to disperse. He told the police officer in command that the crowd would not leave until the police themselves had withdrawn from the location. That, said the major, was impossible, for the police had come to keep order. Meanwhile, the police had acquired sten-guns. (The Mayor, who had gone for reinforcements, travelled back in the car with the guns, on his own admission.)

The police were ordered to fire. Later they claimed that this was retaliation for stone-throwing from the crowd; S.W.A.N.U. officials said that the stones were thrown in fury at the firing.

One month afterwards a one-man commission was appointed of Mr Justice Cyril Hall, then Judge-President of South West Africa. The inquiry lasted three days, and found the police shootings to have been justified. A substantial part of the report reproduced letters from petitioners abroad, Kerina mostly, to their colleagues at home. These, said Mr Justice Hall, 'prove that the opposition to the removal ... was organized to strengthen the hands of those endeavouring to achieve their political aims through the intervention of the United Nations'. On claims that the regulations at Katutura would be too strict, Mr Justice Hall pronounced, 'I am not in a position to judge ... the regulations were not put before the Commission. ...'

After the shooting two of the injured died, to bring the death-roll to thirteen; S.W.A.N.U. and O.P.O. members were ordered out of Windhoek within seventy-two hours – Kuhangua under escort to Angola, Nujoma to Ovamboland, and Mbaeva to the Epukiuro Reserve. Ngavirue was sacked as municipal social worker. Fourteen Africans were arrested and charged with public violence in the longest trial ever to have taken place in the territory. All were found not guilty and acquitted when the proceedings came to an end in December 1961. Some of the accused, it transpired, had been in their homes when the firing broke out.

Five months after the shooting in Windhoek, Saracen armoured cars and sten-guns were used against a peaceful, waiting crowd, killing sixty-eight and wounding over 200, at Sharpeville in the Vereeniging area, some forty miles from Johannesburg. If this was the way the guardian behaved in his own family, what could the stepchild ward reasonably expect? Sharpeville provided a tense and passionate background to the South West African issue in 1960; apartheid in both South Africa and South West Africa was claiming its casualties. The largest number of countries ever, forty in all, pressed for a motion of censure against South Africa to be placed on the agenda after Sharpeville.

During 1960, Africa swept into New York's East Forty-Second Street. Seventeen new member states were admitted to the U.N., sixteen of them African (two were former trust territories), to swell the African bloc from nine to twenty-five, and the Afro-Asian group to forty-six out of the total U.N. membership of ninety-nine. By July 1962, U.N. membership had risen to 106, with Sierra Leone, Mauritania, and Tanganyika joining the company of Mali, Senegal, Nigeria, the Congo Republic, and others. African emphasis on the one-ness of Africa, the summit conferences of African independent states and statesmen, charged old issues with new fury. The second conference of independent African states at Addis Ababa in June 1960 spurred Liberia and Ethiopia to institute a new action at the International Court at The Hague for a compulsory judgement on the mandate, and recommend U.N. action against South Africa under Chapter 41 of the Charter – sanctions.

From 1960 onwards, new member states, reinforcing the group of militants on colonial issues, brushed aside with impatience the old courtesies towards South Africa. A fresh wind blew through Assembly debates. Now pressure gathered from two sides: a changing and newly articulate South West Africa, a changed and urgent Africa.

During the 1960 and 1961 sessions, the new member states reminded the old that the path of polite persuasion had led nowhere. The increasingly negative reaction of the South African government indicated beyond any reasonable doubt that the solution of the South West African problem could not be made contingent upon the voluntary observance by South Africa of the General Assembly resolutions, said Mexico.

Norway's delegate said that she had studied the 1960 report of the U.N. South West Committee in the hope of finding some evidence, however slight, that South Africa was willing to fulfil the international obligations under the mandate. Once again she had been 'utterly disappointed'.

Even the United States delegate was sharp: the policy of the South African government, he said, was out of place in the modern world, where 'tensions are likely to give rise to a general catastrophe and where all people demand the freedom to which they are entitled'. United States policy on South West Africa had begun to change, imperceptibly at times, but basically for the better, during the late fifties, when attitudes to race and colonial issues had to be refurbished so as to build a firmer basis for relations with the growing number of independent African states. At one time the United States had sent to the Fourth Committee prominent and decorative amateurs like Irene Dunne; United States membership of the futile Good Offices Committee had dissuaded her from voting for a pious resolution that 'expressed deep concern' over conditions in South West Africa. In 1959 the United States representative was Mason Sears, an independent former Republican Party legislator from Massachusetts with a personal record of finding out about Africa at first hand, and he swung the United States delegation behind the strongest resolution on South West Africa to date. The U.S. vote, for once, was not in line with N.A.T.O. Afterwards, State Department policy suffered a relapse, and the United States joined the ranks of abstainers in South West African votes.

A colonial policy that will not estrange the African countries, but will make instead the United States seem preferable to her rivals for trade and influence on the continent, is still being sought by the United States Administration, but the quest runs aground in the East–West struggle. Free and sovereign states in Africa – suggested Winifred Courtney in an article for the journal *Africa South* on African issues and U.S. policy at the

1960 session of the U.N. – must be treated as free and sovereign states, not as trenches in the Cold War.

May one respectfully submit to the new United States Administration that 'We must stop the Communists at every point in Africa' is just no substitute for a sound African policy. The N.A.T.O. alliance must be seriously re-appraised. Is not the friendship and trust of all Africa, Asia, and South America the greater bulwark today? The most crucial foreign policy decision which the United States has now to make is to stand for what we claim so strenuously to believe; to offer the states of Africa – and Asia and South America – cooperation in their enormous social, economic, and political needs *as they see them*, not paranoiac pressures against an 'enemy' ideology; world-mindedness, not blind battle fever; the forces that build, not those which destroy.

The power behind conciliation of South Africa at the U.N. has been Britain, her delegation composed of smooth and persuasive lobbyists, her policy, ostensibly, cautious in the hope of achieving compromise. In recent years Britain's role has come under strong fire in open session. Britain, said Ceylon, talked of the need to reach an agreed solution. With whom could agreement be reached when for sixteen years South Africa had rejected every solution proposed, refused to negotiate, refused to recognize the authority of the Committee set up by the U.N., ignored the advisory opinion of the International Court, and flouted resolutions of the Assembly? Guinea charged aggressively that the reason why apartheid measures were increasing every day in severity was that South Africa believed she enjoyed the support of the great powers, on a policy that, in the common interest, there should be regular abstentions or negative votes against resolutions for action.

If United States policy has changed basically for the better since the late fifties, India's has grown more cautious. Once chief fire-eater on apartheid and the violation of the South West African mandate, India seems to have shifted her role to one midway between the conservative, colonial N.A.T.O. powers and the militant African states, in an attempt perhaps to win distinction as a mediator between the two groups.

The vastly increased African representation at the U.N. however, did not result merely in strong new votes being cast against South African intransigence, but in policy adjustments by the great powers, in a new temper during the debates and in the drafting committees. The shots at Sharpeville, 21 March 1960, echoed through the lobbies.

Liberia and Ethiopia took the new case against South Africa to the International Court of Justice on 4 November 1960, and Eric Louw tried to have all U.N. discussion of the mandate adjourned on the grounds that the matter was now *sub judice*. But this time passion triumphed over procedure. South Africa was roundly defeated in the Fourth Committee (sixty-seven votes against, eleven abstentions) and even more heavily in plenary session (eighty-two votes against, and nine abstentions, among them Britain). South Africa boycotted the debate after this defeat.

The conviction was spreading that South Africa could not be trusted, that all her stratagems were merely designed to gain time. During the 1961 proceedings of the Fourth Committee, South Africa, in an attempt to head off decisive action, again argued the *sub judice* procedural point, and the United States delegate put her suddenly to the test.

MR BINGHAM (United States of America) noted that the representative of the Union of South Africa had reaffirmed that the question of South West Africa was *sub judice* and had referred in respectful terms to the International Court of Justice. He then asked the following question: 'Does this indicate that the Union of South Africa is prepared to and would agree to accept the decisions of the International Court of Justice and to abide by them?'

MR FOURIE (Union of South Africa) made the following statement in reply:

We have all respect for the Court and for the principles – here, for one, the principle of the *sub judice* rules to which I have referred. It is a rule which, I quite accept, is not so strongly adhered to and accepted in the United States as, for instance, in my country, and that, I think, is one of the basic reasons for a fundamental difference in approach between our two delegations, and any aspect that is pending before the Court, would, in our opinion, be ruled by that rule, and therefore it would be out of place for me here to comment upon it.

MR CARPIO (Philippines) wondered whether the South African representative's reply to the question had been affirmative or negative, or whether he had not replied. He would be grateful to the South African representative if he would repeat his statement.

MR ZULOAGA (Venezuela) felt that the Committee should give the South African representative a second chance, for his first reply to the United States' representative's clear and categorical question had been too rapid, too confused, and too mysterious.

MR FOURIE (Union of South Africa) said that he had said what he had had to say and did not think he could improve on his first reply.

MR CHAIRMAN said that the United States representative's question and the South African representative's reply would be reproduced *in extenso* in the recording of the meeting.

November 1960 marked a turning-point in the long South West Africa story. From that date resolutions got tougher, the political organizations back home set their sights not at U.N. trusteeship, but at independence, and the petitioners cried, 'No more declarations – action!' Guinea and other African countries added a firm new element: the mandate should be surrendered to the U.N., and a Committee of independent African States set up to administer the territory on behalf of the U.N.

South Africa's refusal to commit herself on whether she would submit to a new ruling of the International Court played its part in deciding member states not to suspend action till the judgement was given. In any event, petitioners and delegates pointed out, the case could drag on for years; were the inhabitants of the territory meanwhile to be abandoned to their fate? Petitioners argued hotly that it would be a travesty of justice if the legal action designed to enforce rights already adjudicated by the

International Court should be used to defer General Assembly action. The petitioners requested the establishment of a special U.N. Commission, with authority to draft plans for an eventual transfer of South West Africa administration. While the petitioners recognized that the actual creation of an alternative administration would anticipate the judgement of the Court, 'preparations must be begun of measures necessary for the restoration of rights and for the most urgent tasks of social and economic reconstruction'. These measures should provide for the assembling of resources, the training and equipment of personnel from South West Africa, and the coordination of skills and apparatus through the special agencies of the U.N.

In 1960 the General Assembly did not go as far as the petitioners wanted, but instructed its Committee on South West Africa to investigate and propose 'conditions for restoring a climate of peace and security' and 'steps to enable the indigenous inhabitants of South West Africa to achieve a wide measure of internal self-government designed to lead them to complete independence as soon as possible'. Seventy-eight nations voted for, none against, and fifteen abstained, among them Britain, the United States, Canada, Ireland, and Portugal. South Africa did not vote. The Committee on South West Africa was also instructed to investigate the mandated territory, with the cooperation of the South African government if possible, and 'without it if necessary'.

For the first time since it had been constituted in 1954, the Committee left its offices and went to Africa. It requested visas for an on-the-spot investigation of South West Africa and talks with the South African government. The South African government refused. But Ghana notified the Committee that there were South West Africans in Accra waiting to give evidence, and the Committee resolved to visit Ghana, then travel to Bechuanaland, where the British government was arranging for the Committee to interview Hereros at Maun and Ghanzi, and from there, it hoped, South West Africa. On the return trip, it planned to visit Tanganyika and the United Arab Republic, where more South West Africans were waiting to give evidence.

As the Committee started to move south down Africa, Eric Louw issued threats. An attempt to cross the South West African border illegally, with or without the help of dissident elements, he said, would be prevented; it would involve the U.N. in an act of aggression. The Press reported Mr Louw as having threatened the arrest of the Committee; the Minister said he had not used that word, but another. In South West Africa itself, meanwhile, South African police and army units patrolled the roads and helicopters watched the border. At Maun in Bechuanaland I watched District and Regional Commissioners supply tents and trucks, itineraries and facilities for the press to report the meetings of the Committee with those Herero living in the territory and any others that succeeded in filtering over the border from South West.

Suddenly Britain demanded an assurance from the U.N. Committee that it would not try to enter South West Africa without the permission of the South African government, and when no assurance was given, suspended the visas for the Committee to enter Bechuanaland altogether. Committee Chairman Fabregat later called this 'the most excruciating experience of the mission'.

By now the U.N. Committee had reached Salisbury, and there it was locked in conclave, trying to manoeuvre between the demands of South Africa and Britain. The Assembly resolution had instructed the Committee to investigate South West Africa, with or without the cooperation of the South African government. But, Britain argued, she herself had abstained on that particular paragraph, and consequently felt in no way bound by it.

In Maun a petitioner arrived by road after days of travelling a circuitous route, only to hear the news over the radio that the Committee had had to abandon its mission in both Bechuanaland and South West Africa, and was therefore flying homewards.

By its sixteenth session in 1961, the U.N. temper was hotter than ever before. The reports of the Committee on South West Africa contained testimony, taken in Accra, Cairo, and Dar-es-

Salaam, from Zedekia Ngavirue and Nathaniel Mbaeva, who had left South Africa hurriedly in May 1961 to meet the Committee a month or so later; Charles Kauraisa, a former teacher, and Uatja Kaukuetu, S.W.A.N.U. Vice-President, both studying on scholarships in Sweden; Mrs Putuse Appolus, a S.W.A.P.O. member and nurse, together with a host of others.

The Committee's report minced no words. It considered the South African government unfit to administer the territory. It recommended that South African rule be terminated and that the U.N. assume, directly and indirectly, through a Special Committee, the administration of the territory. Specifically the report pressed for the Special Committee to organize a convention which would draft a constitution for an independent South West Africa and for the election of representatives to the Legislative Assembly on the basis of universal adult suffrage; an intensive fellowship programme to train the largest possible number of South West Africans in the techniques of administration, economics, and law; the training of a people's police force by the U.N.; the cessation of all organized immigration of Europeans, especially South Africans, into South West Africa. It called on the Security Council, with all other organs, and the member states of the U.N., urgently to consider 'all measures or courses of action for immediate institution of a United Nations presence in South West Africa'.

The proposals of the Committee having been tabled by Chairman Fabregat of Uruguay, they might have been expected to form the basis for debate. But South Africa proceeded to argue once more that South West Africa could not be discussed while the issue was before the International Court of Justice. Mr Louw announced that his government would *invite three former Presidents* of the General Assembly to visit South West Africa and submit a report, not to the U.N. but to the South African government itself – a crafty attempt at using U.N. prestige and testimony to present South Africa's evidence to court, while circumventing U.N. machinery. (Mr Louw's plan for a visit of three Presidents failed when he could not find a single one willing to make the trip.)

The better part of the debate centred around several draft resolutions which were more the outcome of the South African proposals than the recommendations of the Committee itself. Three different draft resolutions were tabled by Britain, Sweden, and six 'unaligned' states respectively. The British one virtually supported the South African position; it proposed a Special Commission to make a further study of the question taking into account the report of the U.N. Presidents invited by South Africa, and the judgement of the International Court. Sweden's resolution took a similar form, except that the activities of the past Presidents were to be brought indirectly under U.N. control through having them vetted by the current President. The resolution introduced jointly by Cuba, Guinea, Iraq, Mali, Morocco, and Tunisia urged members of the U.N. and 'any person connected with or delegated to the United Nations' to refrain from participation in studies or investigations decided upon unilaterally by the government of South Africa, and reminded South Africa herself that any attempt by her to disregard the U.N. would be considered null and void. The wide support that this seemed likely to achieve forced the withdrawal of the British resolution, after a long debate, while the Fourth Committee overwhelmingly rejected the Swedish formulation. The resolution sponsored by the 'unaligned' six was then withdrawn, in favour of an Afro-Asian one on the lines proposed by the Committee on South West Africa.

It was a compromise that was finally adopted as the main resolution on South West Africa. It proclaimed the 'inalienable right of the people of South West Africa to self-determination' and established a U.N. Special Committee of Seven to achieve, in consultation with South Africa, the mandatory power: a visit to South West Africa before 1 May 1962; evacuation of South West Africa by all military forces of the South African Republic; the release of political prisoners; the repeal of all laws or regulations confining the indigenous inhabitants to Reserves; the preparation of general elections to the Legislative Assembly, based on universal adult suffrage and held as soon as possible under the supervision of the U.N.; advice and assistance to the government resulting from the general elections, with a view to preparation of the territory for full independence; coordination of the economic and social assistance with which the specialized agencies of the U.N. will provide the people in order to promote their moral and material welfare; the return to the territory of indigenous inhabitants without risk of imprisonment, detention, or punishment of any kind because of their political activities in or outside the territory.

In the General Assembly, the resolution establishing the Special Committee of Seven to arrange for South West African independence won ninety votes. One country, Portugal, voted against, and four abstained. Britain continued to insist that any action should depend upon 'further study of the problem' and the judgement of the International Court, that nothing would be achieved without the cooperation of the South African government. The United States delegation condemned South Africa strongly in its speeches, was vague in its objections to the main resolution, tried several times to amend it, and voted in favour at the end.

A General Assembly resolution for world economic and diplomatic sanctions against South Africa failed by twelve votes to win a two-thirds majority (forty-eight votes for, thirty-one against, twenty-two abstentions). It was a beginning.

The Carpio Fiasco

The General Assembly adjourned, while the newly established Committee of Seven began work. Confidential negotiations took place in New York between the representatives of the South African government and the Chairman, Mr Carpio of the Philippines, and the Vice-Chairman of the Committee, Dr de Alva of Mexico. South Africa offered to invite the two U.N. emissaries to South West Africa in time for the Committee's deadline of 1 May 1962. But, stipulated Eric Louw, though he would cooperate over the visit, he was not prepared to discuss the other objects of the U.N. resolution: elections in South West Africa based on universal adult suffrage, preparations for full independence, economic and social assistance, the evacuation of

South African military forces. The ill-fated Carpio-de Alva mission flew into South Africa, held talks with the Prime Minister, Dr Verwoerd, in Pretoria, and agreed on a ten-day safari through South West Africa. It squeezed in a fifteen-minute meeting with South African Congress leaders, at which Carpio delivered an impassioned assurance that he could make no compromise with apartheid. But it soon seemed that Carpio formulated his assurances by reference to his audience of the moment. He was against apartheid, he thought it was an interesting experiment, he looked forward to watching its functioning in the future. These verbal caperings were then crowned by a joint communiqué, in which the U.N. mission and Dr Verwoerd agreed to place on record that there was no evidence of genocide in South West Africa, that there was no evidence of military installations in violation of the terms of the mandate, that there was no threat to international peace and security arising from South African administration of South West Africa.

The communiqué created a furore. Old Chiefs Hosea, Kutako and Witbooi said bluntly that they did not believe it. Carpio, ill in hospital during the last stages of the talks with the Prime Minister, said – but only three weeks after the issue of the communiqué – that he had had no hand in it. The charges and counter-charges became ludicrously bewildering. 'Carpio says South West is no Threat to Peace'; 'Carpio: South West Could be a Threat to Peace'; 'Carpio Denies a Denial', ran the newspaper headlines. With every Carpio statement to the Press, and later, before the U.N. Special Committee on South West Africa, the mystery of the joint communiqué deepened. Carpio himself proved an erratic and unreliable witness. The U.N. set up a special committee to investigate the part played in the drafting of the communiqué by the two members of the mission.

The South African government, of course, was jubilant at the Carpio confusion, and poured scorn not only on the ineptness of the U.N. mission, but by implication, on the whole world body. Carpio had opened his mouth too wide from the beginning, and Dr Verwoerd had neatly slipped a hook into it. The two men had accepted the visit to Pretoria and the terms of the mission –

in flat contradiction of the U.N. resolution, for the South African government had stipulated that the visit would not imply any admission of U.N. authority over South West Africa – in the hope, perhaps, that with two men through the door, the rest of their Committee might follow. They had agreed to make their report in the first place not to the U.N., but to the South African government. And by the time that the report came to be made, the South African government was shrewd enough to have inserted in the communiqué those aspects of the case against her which seemed the least capable of proof. (The communiqué ignored the major, unanswerable charges.)

Genocide, by definition of the Convention on Genocide, is not practised by the South African government in the sense of acts committed with intent to destroy a national group; though the social, economic, and health policies of the administration have been characterized by a ruthless neglect and callousness, and these policies *are* deliberate. On the issue of military installations in the mandate, South Africa has shrewdly made the utmost use of Walvis Bay, which is anomalously part of South Africa, not South West Africa, and the military build-up at this port has proceeded apace. A special troop-train from South Africa took 400 men to Walvis Bay in April 1962, for training in desert combat. It is one convenient site for building a military force that is not, technically, in defiance of the terms of the mandate. The South African government has created another in the Caprivi Strip, which is part of the mandate but is administered directly by South Africa. Here there have been numerous Defence Force exercises, and the South African government has negotiated with Britain, not apparently with success, to set up a training school for tropical warfare in the area. Carpio and de Alva saw no military exercises at the calm time of their visit; in 1961 the South African Minister of Defence said that his government would not hesitate to move troops northwards from Walvis Bay if it ever regarded the situation as threatening. In any event, South Africa's own massive military might is but a few hours' flying time from the territory. As for the charge that South West Africa is a threat to international peace and security, race discrimination practised on the scale and with the intensity of South Africa's record is an incitement to disturbance and bloodshed, and a threat to peace far beyond. The system outrages all Africa with especial force, and might well end in a racial eruption of the continent, if not immediately then in the not too far-off future.

The two-man U.N. mission had attempted a strategy of sweet agreement, in the hope that South Africa could be inveigled into cooperation. But South Africa had no wish to negotiate, to cooperate, even to talk, except on terms of her own. And this became manifest once more as the mists of the Carpio mission began to clear. South Africa had scored a tactical victory, but it was one of temporary duration. By the time Carpio had formally, before the Special U.N. Committee, denied any part in the Pretoria communiqué, no one was really interested in his individual role any longer. Both South Africa and the world body were back to where they had been before the mission – except that U.N. prestige in South West Africa and the rest of the continent had suffered a nasty jolt. The 1962 session would have to pick up the pieces of the South West African problem again.

The Maun affair demonstrated to the world how far South Africa – propped up by Britain – would go in defiance of the U.N.; the Carpio fiasco demonstrated the trivial concessions that South Africa was prepared to make for a reconciliation with the outside world. Henceforth, the world body could not reasonably entertain any illusion that compromise was possible if only an adequate courtesy were shown.

It remains to be seen whether anything effective will come of the General Assembly's resolution in 1962 – by ninety-six votes to none – requesting the Secretary General 'to take all necessary steps in order to establish an effective United Nations presence in South West Africa'.

Legal issues will for the moment loom large, as South Africa tries to parry the proceedings at The Hague. She has already failed in her argument that the International Court has no jurisdiction to deal with her administration of South West. In December 1962 the Court found by eight votes to seven that it has jurisdiction to try charges by the governments of Liberia and Ethiopa that in every important consideration South Africa has violated the terms and spirit of the mandate. Without the consent of the U.N., in a way inconsistent with the international character of the territory, South Africa has altered its status. She has failed to promote Article 2 of the mandate, which charged the mandatory power with the material well-being and social progress of the inhabitants. Specifically, she has introduced apartheid into South West Africa, and this alone, the Court will be asked to rule, is a violation of the mandate. The trend of administration, Ethiopia and Liberia will argue, must accord with current international standards, like the Universal Declaration of Human Rights (which South Africa has never signed), the advisory opinions of the International Court of Justice, and the resolutions of the General Assembly of the U.N. If the Court rules that violations of the mandate have occurred, then the continued disregard by South Africa of the judgement could lead to an attempt at legal revocation and transfer of the mandate to another authority.

Such a Court judgement will give international legal support to the political contention of the world's overwhelming majority: that the trust of the mandate has been betrayed, and that the territory must be taken from South Africa's grip in consequence and placed under the protection of the U.N.

The dossier on South Africa will be more damning than ever; the case for action more urgent. But it will still need U.N. *action*, as distinct from words and legal judgements, to change life in a mandated territory that could, like Tanganyika, be independent today, had South Africa not made of it a front line in her battle against progress.

Part Six: Next Round?

Next Round?

Dr Verwoerd is clearly a happy man these days, wrote Allister Sparks, the political correspondent of the Johannesburg *Rand Daily Mail* the week after the Carpio–de Alva visit.

There is a jaunty confidence about his step as he walks into the House and his benign smile has taken on a particularly paternal quality. Gone is the occasional worried frown which used to furrow his brow a year or so ago. Today his is the face of a man who has shed the last faintest feeling of suspicion that perhaps, somewhere, he may not be completely and utterly right. The reason for this is not far to seek, for recent events have convinced him that things are working out in complete accordance with his basic political theory – and even faster than he had hoped. From time to time Dr Verwoerd has allowed us a glimpse of this basic theory which accounts for his every act, from the swollen Defence Vote and the Sabotage Bill to the Transkei scheme and Mr Carpio's visit. Put in simple terms, it is the theory that South Africa is the victim of a temporary wave of world madness – and that the answer is to keep an iron grip on the country until the madness passes. Such temporary 'waves' crop up every few hundred years, Dr Verwoerd told us last year, as he recounted what must surely be his favourite historical story – the French Revolution, with its cry of 'liberty, fraternity and equality' – all followed by the great empire-building era and the unseemly scramble for Africa. The learned doctor has put the world on a couch and diagnosed a recurrence of the same mental ailment – a temporary wave of 'sickly humanism'. He feels, however, that while we wait for it to pass we should take some precautions, just in case the patient should break out of his padded cell before he is quite cured. That is why there was a 67·13 per cent increase in the Defence vote this year; that is why we have the Sabotage Bill now. ...

The politicians clustered around the Nationalist centres of

power believe not only that apartheid is the most profitable policy for South Africa to follow, and that the world opposes because it so sadly misunderstands, but that in time humanity will honour Dr Verwoerd as statesman and trail-blazer. The week following the near success of the first sanctions vote against South Africa at the U.N. a letter in a national newspaper compared apartheid with some of the greatest advances in history, made – like apartheid – in the teeth of mass opposition. This opposition, said the writer, should not be allowed to deter the protagonists of the theory. 'By the same reasoning Galileo should have forgotten his ideas and Pasteur his experiments. . . .' Galileo was executed for his conviction; the Nationalists will fight, they say, to the death for theirs. Cabinet Minister Paul Sauer told the South African parliament: 'There is only one way in which South Africa can be forced from the stand it has taken . . . by military intervention from outside.'

The Nationalist Press turned the 1961 U.N. visit into an invasion scare, warning every able-bodied man and woman that they might be called to the colours. A vague threat that Afro-Asian armies were mustering to the north provided the justification for the swollen 1962 Defence budget, though the Minister of Defence overplayed his hand so clumsily that even the Prime Minister joined in the general scepticism. The elusive 'red menace' hovers, for the government, always over the continent, and with it the threat of subversion from within – every African is seen as a potential guerrilla fighter ready to link himself with invading armies. Above all, South West Africa has been made the acid test of patriotism, and U.N. insistence that the territory be brought under international supervision has been used to foster the national war psychosis. From the permanent army to women's pistol clubs, White South Africa is being conditioned to a state of semi-permanent hostilities. The budget for guns, tanks, and soldiers has risen steadily since the Nationalist government came to power in 1948, and has tripled during the last two years alone. The arms budget totalled £10 million in 1948; in 1962–3 it is to be £60 million. (The figure for defence expenditure at the peak of the Second World War in 1944 was

£58 million.) The total bill for measures against those who disapprove of apartheid, both at home and abroad, is nearer the £80 million than the £60 million mark, for police (£20 million) and prison votes must be included. The vastly expanded permanent army is highly mobile and decentralized. By 1966 there will be 60,000 trained men – all White. Commandos or civilians are being organized on military lines, as an important auxiliary force. Paratroopers have been sent on training exercises to Moçambique; the Chief of Police inspected French methods in Algeria; the air force is being equipped with French Mirage jet fighters, while French armoured cars are being produced under licence in South Africa.

Why doesn't South Africa falter under criticism? Why doesn't the Nationalist Cabinet crack under the sustained pressure of world opinion? Why is there no sign of conciliation, compromise, or even a readiness to negotiate?

The South African government will not change the direction of its policy, indeed cannot change it, because its own survival depends on the subordination at every point of the interests of the Africans to those of Whites. The details of apartheid are well enough known, the multiple manifestations of its inhumanity. Race classification is supposed 'scientifically' to separate White from Black; 'scientifically' – by shades of colour – it splits families, wrenches children from parents, brother from brother. Blood transfusion regulations on the bottling of blood observe the skin colour of the donor no less strictly than his blood-group. Colour, not ability or hard work, is the criterion of success. The rate paid is not for the job but for the worker's parentage. Children are indoctrinated in their schools to believe that race marks the master and the servant. Men of colour must travel in separate buses and trains, live in separate townships, but labour within the home, factory, or workshop of the white man in subservient positions.

These are the effects of apartheid, but its inner nature, its motive force must also be measured. The race laws are merely outgrowths of an economic system which has certain unique features, and it is these that explain the back-to-the-wall defiance of three million Whites among twelve million African, Coloured, and Indian.

The colonial progression to independence, that has been so relatively swift and painless in West Africa, is proving slow and agonizing within the strongholds of White settlement in Southern Africa. In Ghana and almost all its neighbours, climate and the mosquito deterred any substantial White settlement, and colonial control consisted of an alien Civil Service with overseas investment in plantations and a few profitable mines. Colonial powers in wide areas of Africa rebuffed independence demands until it seemed preferable to surrender some control in order to save the rest; to cede formal independence in the hope that economic arrangements, mutual defence treaties, loaded constitutions, would leave economic spheres of interest intact. It has been tricky juggling, trying to maintain as much as possible of the economic, political, and strategic substance of colonialism while compromising on the form. It has called for nice timing and shrewd bargaining, and the best-laid plans of investors and colonial experts have often been upset by the force of African political struggle.

The farther south in Africa, the more extensive the strongholds of White investment and settlement, the sharper the conflict has been. Yet even in Northern Rhodesia, majority government cannot now be far away, and in Angola, the society so long stagnant, now gripped by war, Portuguese control is slowly slipping despite the sudden concessions – too few and too late.

Only in South Africa does government policy march steadily backwards into the past, offering tear gas instead of conciliation, entrenching itself in power with guns instead of votes, denying Africans the last shreds of their parliamentary representation and promoting despotic chiefs as their rulers instead, encouraging balkanization with dreams of small, separate tribal Bantustans.

It is cruelly ironic that the richest, most developed country in Africa should adhere to feudal labour relations and the most outworn of political ideas. A modern industrial state, it is built on the colonial subjugation not of a territory across the seas, as in the classic imperialist pattern, but one that exists everywhere within its own boundaries. In South Africa colonizers and colonized live side by side, and apartheid is the state machine which balances them in their uneasy relationship, close and mutually hostile.

The White South African colonizers operate giant mining, finance, and industrial concerns, thriving on an abnormally high rate of profit, enjoying inflated standards of living and, as its prerequisite, a monopoly of political control. Every White man is a 'boss', basking in the superior status and the material benefits of the colonizer. Every White artisan has a stake in the industrial colour bar, since it secures the skilled jobs and skilled rates – regardless of ability – for him. Every farmer is dependent on the traditional system of cheap migrant black labour, on the laws which decree that outside of his Reserves (twelve per cent of the country's land area) the African farmer is a labourer on a White-owned farm.

South African non-Whites bear many marks of the colonized. The Reserves are economic backwaters, where the African peasantry practises a below-subsistence agriculture; everywhere outside, African work is unskilled work, African wages a fraction of White ones. (In 1958, the average African wage was £13 a month: the average White wage, £57 16s. 7d.) Political rights, civil liberties, all forms of representative government, are denied.

Gold mining had much to do with the origins of this system, for though it no longer dominates the South African economy as once it did – secondary industry has for some years displaced it as the major source of national revenue – the labour practice of the mines early and ineffaceably stamped its character on the whole country, shaping the wage structure and most aspects of 'native policy'. Gold is found in a unique blanket formation of reefs and is extracted by a huge force (about 400,000 nowadays) of unskilled African labourers, recruited on short-term contracts from all corners of South Africa and half a dozen countries beyond. These labourers are untrained, unskilled, and, above all, cheap, on the excuse that they are really peasant farmers at home and have their plots of land as basic means of support. But to propel a peasantry from the land to the mines, successive South African governments have limited African land-holdings and trade rights, practised a rigid system of labour control, and increasingly pursued a policy of political repression. Cheap labour is, in consequence, all conveniently African. The White artisan class, British immigrants in the main, were given a stake in the system when it was decreed that skilled labour had to be White. Race has been made the outward sign of status, but the real dividing-line, covered over with colour, is economic.

The White South African, Afrikaans- or English-speaking, is no more racialist by nature than the Belgian or the Britisher. South Africa operates the most vicious race discrimination because every White man – and the country has the largest White population in Africa – has been turned into a colonist and given a stake in the survival of his racial rule.

In South Africa, this unique form of colonialism is defending itself by force from an independence revolution within. And the 'independence revolution' itself takes the form not of cries that the settlers go home – the three million Whites are not settlers in that sense – but of assaults on the colour bar, on job reservation, on the gates of parliament and all the citadels of White privilege.

The structure of apartheid is intricate and delicately balanced. Laws have to be rigid if they are to operate at all. Give Africans more land, and the pressures upon them to work on White farms or down White mines will inevitably ease. Give Africans higher wages in industry, and they will turn their backs on the mines and on the farms. Give them technical training, and they will disprove the myth of their inability. Above all, give them the vote, and they will spend money on their own technical training, legislate higher wages for themselves.

The workings of apartheid in South Africa are highly relevant to South West Africa too, because the mandate has been assiduously turned into a little South Africa, the ward into a copy of its guardian.

The reasons why the Verwoerd government will not compromise in Pretoria are the same as the reasons why it will not negotiate in Windhoek. South Africa cannot change its ways in South West Africa, and is terrified of letting anyone else try. Proper U.N. supervision would speedily enough abolish race discrimination. The whole structure of White privilege would disintegrate. With the exception of the three small British Protectorates, all vulnerable to her slightest economic pressure, South Africa is secured by hundreds of miles of friendly neighbouring White supremacy states. Only her South West African flank is exposed – in theory. The Nationalist nightmare is that the assault, and not necessarily a military one, on race rule in South Africa will be launched from there.

The first defeats inflicted on apartheid – as the South African government is quick to see – need not be in Johannesburg or Bloemfontein, but along the byways that lead from the Ovambo and Herero Reserves. Once South West Africa is thrown open to the influences of the world, once U.N. intervention, however limited, tumbles apartheid in South West Africa, the whole edifice of White rule in South Africa will be rocked to its foundations. Free elections among the Herero would be tantamount to giving the Africans of Johannesburg the right to help in choosing the mayor of their city and formulating its budget. If apartheid goes in South West Africa, with it will go as well the faith of White men that it is an eternity rooted in God's will; and African freedom movements in South Africa will receive their most powerful stimulus.

This is why South Africa clings so tightly to its mandate, and why the world has a chance to end apartheid not only there, but in South Africa too, before her conflicts develop into open and prolonged racial warfare.

There are other reasons, of course, for South Africa's refusal to compromise. Over the years South West Africa has been grafted onto South Africa's economy, to provide the mandatory with considerable economic advantage: South West Africa's diamond and karakul wealth helps to swell the exchequer in Pretoria. And, above all, South West Africa has immeasurable strategic importance, for it possesses a common border with South Africa for several hundred miles. South West Africa's coastline, her port at Walvis Bay (geographically part of the territory, but technically owned by South Africa), her frontier with war-torn Angola, are politically and strategically more vital to South Africa than ever Gibraltar and Cyprus were to Britain. The very mention of a U.N. trust territory or an independent, African-majority governed state on its border is enough to make the Nationalist Cabinet reach for its guns.

Verwoerd feels secure for some while to come because he is flanked by Salazar and Welensky, and all three have been supported by considerable capital investment from the great powers of the West. Total foreign investment in South Africa alone at the end of 1959 was officially announced as £1,528 million, of which £903 million (sixty per cent) came from Britain. The Export-Import Bank, a U.S. Federal Agency, has recently lent more than £33 million to South African gold-mining companies. Some £200 million of United States money is invested in the country, and there are also heavy French, Swiss, and West German capital commitments. The demands of justice, or even international law, have little chance in a struggle with such deep economic involvement.

Mary Benson related, in an article for the London *Observer*, how on a mission to South West Africa she had to tell Chief Hosea Kutako that Britain had voted with South Africa at the U.N. The interpreter turned to her with tears filling his eyes. 'I cannot tell the Chief that,' he said. By 1962 Chief Kutako was no longer so trustful, or naïve. 'I have struggled a lifetime,' he told me. 'Now I look to the United Nations.' And the same month he told a United States vice-consul, Mr J. C. Curran: 'If the United States had exerted the same pressure at the United Nations as the Afro-Asian bloc, South West Africa would have been free today.'

To the interlinking directorships of a dozen giant companies, state boundaries have become mere lines on the map, and political systems, provided that they remain securely profitable for investment, irrelevant. South Africa's large mining corporations and their subsidiaries made a profit of £99 million in 1958, and paid out dividends of £43 million to share-holders. One quarter of the capital in the seven dominant mining-finance houses is owned abroad by British and American investors. And the gold and diamond companies of South Africa are themselves the centre of a network of other companies which possess vast mining interests in Northern Rhodesia, Katanga and South West Africa, Angola and Tanganyika; and have huge stakes in real estate and industry and commerce throughout the sub-continent.

The Oppenheimer empire, Anglo-American, provides a spectacular example. Monopolizing world diamond production, one of the giants of gold mining in South Africa, it is connected with four of the seven companies mining copper in Northern Rhodesia, and with Tanganyika Concessions, which itself not only owns a large portion of shares in Union Minière, the dominant mining company of Katanga, but also controls the Benguela railway in Angola, built to transport Katanga minerals to the west coast. Both Anglo-American and its subsidiary, De Beers, are linked with the British South Africa Company in the Federation and Bechuanaland, the old instrument of Cecil John Rhodes (which pocketed £50 million from mining royalties in the five years to 1960 alone.) Anglo-American, through African Explosives and Chemical Industries Limited, is linked with I.C.I. and is building new armament factories for the Verwoerd government. All diamonds mined in Angola, about three-and-a-half per cent of Western production, are channelled through the Companhia de Diamantes de Angola, on whose board sit Messrs Oppenheimer and Joel of De Beers. The company recently lent the Portuguese government £1,250,000, at only one-per-cent interest, to help bail Angola out of its economic crisis.

These economic alliances between South Africa and its colony South West Africa, the Portuguese empire, and the Federation of Rhodesia and Nyasaland, have in turn been welded together by a common political outlook and mutual defence arrangements. South West Africa is a part of the Salazar-Verwoerd-Welensky jigsaw. All three politicians seize every opportunity to attack the interference of the U.N. A threat to one is a threat to all. They will muster support for one another and will defend their interests against the world . . . as long as they feel that they can rely on powerful states like Britain and the United States to back, or at least connive at them.

Every time they vote at the U.N., Britain, the United States, France, and Belgium have to consider their relationship with South Africa, with the most powerful single force south of the Sahara in economic, political, and military terms. But they have also to consider South Africa's own relationship with the rest of Africa, changing fast, embarrassingly fast. How much time has White rule left in Africa? The Federation of Rhodesia and Nyasaland, the great dyke in Central and Southern Africa against African self-government, has cracked under the strain of trying to keep first Nyasaland, then Northern Rhodesia under control. How long Portugal can hold on to Angola depends not only how soon the Angolans, now receiving training from the Algerian F.L.N., can pass to a new guerrilla offensive and so pin down even more than the 20,000 Portuguese soldiers already deployed in the colony, but also on how long Salazar can survive popular discontent within Portugal itself.

Angola is South West Africa's back door. Though it is doubtful whether significant African resistance has yet spread into the southern portions of the colony – where the Ovambo tribes of South West Africa have villages – this could happen. White South Africans know this, and formed in August 1961 the Freedom Fighters' Movement to rally recruits to the Portuguese Army. This was an unofficial move, of course, like the signing on for service in Katanga of South African mercenaries who, publicly at least, were an embarrassment to the South African government; on the official level, defence talks have taken place between South Africa and Portugal, and the governments can be depended upon to lean on one another. While any one of the states in the Welensky-Salazar-Verwoerd alliance has to defend itself under arms, there is a danger that the conflagration will spread.

The South African white garrison has not lacked skill in

suppressing the revolts of its non-white subjects. For ways of preserving rule have had to change. In 1904 the Germans hunted down like animals the Herero and Nama who dared to rise against them in revolt; British and Boer for their part had shown no quarter to resisting tribes. The Nationalists counted carefully the score of dead and injured at Sharpeville in 1960 and at Windhoek in December 1959, to argue passionately against exaggeration. And the picture has changed for the conquered too. German occupation forces in South West Africa were at one time in serious danger of being overrun. German detachments in the field had to postpone an offensive to await the arrival of reinforcements on the next troopship. The Herero had a short respite to rally fighting men, and they resisted final defeat for four years. The struggle does not reach the stage of open warfare any longer – or has not yet. The Africans are weaponless, policed and patrolled. Almost every White man is a potential defender in arms of the racial régime. Apartheid seals off physically black men from white, and has introduced refinements of control under the pass laws which tie Africans hand and foot to the employer, the township superintendent, the local police station. The government pursues a policy of mass indoctrination through the schools, the radio, and the Press. (Nationalist companies and politicians have even annexed a substantial stretch of African journalism.) Strenuously it wages psychological warfare against chiefs and traders and men elected to positions on advisory boards or appointed to chiefs' councils: those who want power or advancement get nowhere unless they gravitate towards the Nationalist orbit. The 'agitator' is arrested and jailed, or if a court trial secures no conviction, is banished and restricted or placed under house arrest. The misery and the resentment remain, and the will to resist, but methods have had to change. Africans in South Africa and South West face a modern state supported by a mechanized army, an air force, and armed, ubiquitous police. There are still the occasional collisions, the outbreaks of rioting and violence when the burden seems suddenly impossible to bear: Zeerust, Cato Manor, Langa, Mabieskraal, Harding, Windhoek. But for the most part, and in South

West Africa especially, the African struggle has gone on unseen: in dark huts, in the minds of men turned to modern-day politics, engrossed with the problem of building political parties, with programmes, conferences, and constitutions, training those who can organize beyond the scrutiny of the policeman and the police informer.

In South West Africa an awareness is spreading among Africans that the U.N. will act only for those who first act themselves. Sixteen years of debate and legal hair-splitting have raised a doubt that the world body can bring itself to turn resolutions into action. The ludicrous cavortings of the Carpio mission did more to shatter confidence in one month, probably, than throughout the sixteen years before. It is dawning on many Africans, who once placed blind confidence in the U.N. and the liberal role of Britain and the United States, that before the West will take or permit really effective steps to free the mandate from South African control, the walls of self-interest will have to tumble.

Many Africans now feel as well that it is too late for trusteeship. The petitioners and political organizations have dropped that demand for one of full independence. For if the self-interest of some great powers can block U.N. action, it can block too the transition from trusteeship to real independence.

There are still those in South West Africa who wait patiently for the U.N. to free them. But the young men have different ideas. They know that the struggle of the trust territories took place not so much at the U.N. as in Africa, in the trust territories themselves. Those who thought that the trusteeship system would have teeth in it were mistaken. The colonial powers got bitten, but not by trusteeship. The system merely helped to create a favourable climate for African advance. It put the colonial powers on the defensive and exerted moral pressure upon them.

The transition to independence was easy in Tanganyika because the political movement in the territory was powerful, united, and under a skilful and flexible, though determined, leadership. The attempt at transition in the Congo ended in disorder because Congolese independence was sabotaged by the

Belgians: over the years, by the colonial paternalism that stunted African development, and, at the hour of independence, by intervention and disruption of the new state.

In the main street of Windhoek I was stopped by an irate and nervous businessman. 'Do you want another Congo here?' he asked. Another Congo! Another Congo! It is echoed everywhere in South West Africa, and in South Africa, still.

The Congo, however, is the wrong analogy. Algeria would, unhappily, seem more like the right one. The parallels between southern Africa and that former French colony are urgent and real – both countries crushed under the weight of predatory white settlement, with frustration among the majority rising to resentment, despair, and at last rebellion. In South Africa political movements began to discuss 'new methods of struggle' after Sharpeville and the defeat of the May 1961 strike against the apartheid republic. Mass meetings and protests have been outlawed, but African nationalists are gathering their forces for struggle of a different kind. The first experimental sabotage operations have taken place. The Pondoland peasant resistance movement has survived two periods of martial law and remains uncrushed. Mass resistance could yet crash over the border into South West Africa, the responsibility of the U.N.

Can the world body intervene before it is too late? Intervention would send a shock shuddering through White-dominated Southern Africa, but it could prevent far greater tremors and loss of life in the years to come. The danger of the dislocation that intervention would cause is not as serious as the inevitably bloody consequences of non-intervention in the future. This is the hour before the battle. There is still time to stop it. Must blood flow before the world body will act? The powers, led by Britain, who caution against strong words and action against Verwoerd, argue that their policy is to relax tension, to prevent a flare-up, to damp race antagonisms in South Africa, to prevent the crisis of Verwoerd against the U.N. rising to a head. The effect of this policy of caution is to give Verwoerd his head. If he believes his apartheid fortress is impregnable he will launch one assault after another on the rights of his own subject peoples and the mandated territory. The apartheid system battens on the weakness or hesitation of its opponents.

It is too late to believe that the South African Government will strike any compromise over South West Africa. Her record shows that she is unfit to rule and cannot mend her ways. She may try, under pressure, to strike a deal, but it will be a dishonest deal, like all the phoney negotiations in the last sixteen years that circumvented the international authority of U.N. over the territory.

In South West Africa there have been no offers of concessions, no attempts to negotiate with the tribes that have not involved agreement with, or subservience to, apartheid. If South Africa wished to persuade the world that she can change, without pressure, she has had long years in which to offer Africans greater participation in government. Her argument is that Africans are unfit to rule, that premature self-government would create chaos. Unless one believes that the South West African tribes must eternally live in subjugation, government must lay some foundations for self-rule. Apartheid government cannot do this, for apartheid is a preparation for perpetual servitude. The system by its nature blocks African training in self-rule and independence. The longer apartheid retains its grip on South West Africa the greater the backlog of lopsided economic development, inexperience in government, and race tension that any future administration will inherit. It is South Africa that is trying to make another Congo of South West Africa by preventing any orderly transfer of power to the Africans.

The outside world could prise loose South Africa's grip on South West Africa, break the back of White Supremacy rule, and prevent the approaching clash in southern Africa. The motion for economic sanctions against South Africa in 1962 achieved the required two-thirds majority at the United Nations. South Africa's intransigence would be shaken if Britain and America *acted* on it and, together with the other member nations of the world body, showed that they are in dead earnest. South Africa will not be persuaded that the U.N. means business over South West Africa until the states of the West show that South

African and foreign economic and business interests can never be inviolate from reprisals as long as they prop up South Africa's defiance of the world in her handling of South West Africa. If the U.N. cannot or will not act as a body to discipline South Africa, she must accept the inevitability that states like the Afro-Asian powers which see this as a test case of U.N. efficacy might – in time – be driven to unilateral action.

The longer that intervention is delayed to stop the ravages of apartheid in South West Africa, the greater the chances of a conflagration. If the U.N. cannot act to make South West Africa a land fit for Hereros to live in, the Hereros and others will seek other ways.

One of these other ways must inevitably be a realization, on the part of African political movements in both South West Africa and South Africa, that the future of the two countries is intricately connected (though one of the first acts of an African majority government of South Africa would undoubtedly be to ensure South West Africa full and unfettered independence), and the struggle for rights and independence of the two peoples must be joined, the sooner the better. The Nationalist Government has entrenched itself in two countries (one of which is stolen), and the assault against it must, to be successful, be launched from both fronts. For the future and freedom of South West Africa cannot stand or fall by the debates and resolutions, even acts, of the U.N. alone. The main burden of the deliverance of the people of South West Africa rests upon themselves and the people of South Africa. Pressure from the outside world will help, but for some time to come it will still be only auxiliary to the main effort of the peoples living at the foot of the continent. Here tension and turmoil are bound to grow because South Africa's government policies are hide-bound and White supremacy knows no way to remove the suffocating pressures on the African people. The biggest world outcry over South West Africa followed the Windhoek shooting; the biggest outcry over South Africa was after Sharpeville. Further turmoil is inevitable and in a situation of turmoil the world body may act. Today South Africans and South West Africans are rapidly shedding any illusions that their salvation will come through outside intervention alone. But the U.N. and the world must also face the fact that it will be a travesty of the principles of the U.N. if this body acts not to prevent conflict but waits until it has already broken out.

Appendix A : What Is Protection?

Conversation between the Imperial German Commissioner
Göring and Chief Hendrik Witbooi: Hoornkrans, 9 June 1892.
(*Translated from the Dutch of Witbooi's Journal*)

COMMISSIONER: [I have] come to you as a friend with good
advice . . . Place yourself under German protection as other
Chiefs have done.

WITBOOI: What is protection and against what will we be
protected?

COMMISSIONER: Against the Boers and other strong nations
who want to force their way into the country without asking
the permission of the Chiefs.

WITBOOI: It seems strange to me and impossible and I cannot
understand it. The duty of an independent Chief who governs
his own people and country is to protect them personally
against any danger or disaster. For this reason the kingdoms
have been separated and each Chief has his own people and
land to govern. When one Chief is subordinate to another, the
former is not independent and master of himself or his people
and country because he is subordinate; all who are subordinate are merely subjects of the one who protects him, because
he holds the upper position, and he who holds the upper
position is the lord and master and chief of everything. I do
not therefore see how it can possibly be argued that the chief
who submits himself to another is an independent chief who can
do as he pleases. Africa is a country which belongs to our Red
Chiefs,* and when danger threatens a Chief and he feels he is

* The 'Red Nation' - one of the Nama clans.

not in a position to combat that danger single-handed, then he can call his fellow-brother, or brothers, the Red Chiefs, and say to them – come brother or brothers, let us defend our country, Africa, and ward off this danger which threatens to force itself into our country, because we are the same colour and characteristics. This Africa as a whole is the country of our Red Chiefs, and our different kingdoms are but a trifling sub-division of our Africa.

COMMISSIONER: You are not compelled to go in for this protection but take into account that, although you may have brave warriors, of what use can they be when you are not equipped with ammunition? When the other side is so equipped and shoots you with bullets, while your men take the rifle by the barrel and hit with the butt-end, that you surely cannot do.

> [*The Commissioner said the nations Germany, England, Russia, France, Italy, Spain had agreed that no more arms and ammunition would come into the country so war would stop.*]

WITBOOI: . . . It is on account of the stopping of your great men that the war has lasted such a long time.

Appendix B: Land Ownership

Total area of territory: 82,347,841 hectares (1,000 hectares = 3·86 square miles), comprising land set aside for White or non-White use; urban areas; game reserves; also desert land.

	1937	1948	1955	1962
Outside Police Zone	30,101,000	30,101,000	27,445,618	
Inside Police Zone – desert	7,164,860	7,164,860	7,564,971	
other	45,025,000	45,025,000	47,337,252	
White farm lands				
a. Farms in private ownership	14,708,692	23,749,778	25,828,653	
b. Government farms surveyed	8,828,187	7,052,200	261,594	
c. Farms leased to settlers		2,540,413	10,967,166	
d. Company (registered) farms	2,077,331	227,744	810,711	
TOTAL WHITE FARM LANDS	25,614,210	33,570,135	37,868,124	approx. 39,812,000*
Non-White (African and Coloured)				
a. Proclaimed Reserves (within and outside the Police Zone)	11,887,557	11,947,924	18,630,597	
b. Areas reserved for extension	4,225,800			
c. Set aside but not proclaimed	13,900	13,900	13,900	
d. Rehoboth Gebied	1,244,400	1,244,400	1,244,400	
TOTAL NON-WHITE LANDS	17,397,757	15,143,324	21,825,997	21,825,997

Sources: *South African Yearbook*, except for the figure * which was supplied by the Lands Branch of the South West African Administration.

247

Appendix C: White Settlement

Year	White population	Number of farms	Extent in hectares
1913	14,830	1,138	11,490,000
	(About 6,000 Germans had been deported by 1920.)		
1920–2	An additional 4,844,626 hectares allocated for White settlement in the first three years of the mandate.		
1935	31,800	3,255	25,467,628
1946	37,858	3,722	27,413,858
1955	49,930	5,050	37,868,124
1962	72,000	approx. 5,500	approx. 39,812,000*

*Approximate figure given by Lands Branch of the South West African Administration. The rest of the figures are taken from issues of the *South African Yearbook*.

Appendix D: Foreign Investment in South West Africa

The Giants

CONSOLIDATED DIAMOND MINES OF S.W.A. LTD, controlled by De Beers Consolidated Mines and part of the Anglo-American empire of Harry Oppenheimer. Anglo-American has concluded deals with the Engelhard group in the U.S.A., the British South Africa Company, the Deutsche Bank Aktiengesellschaft of Frankfurt, Germany; has bought shares in the Hudson Bay Mining and Smelting Co., a Canadian producer of copper and zinc. C.D.M. (De Beers) produce 99·6 per cent of S.W.A.'s diamonds, and 80·6 per cent of South Africa's. Anglo-American itself produced in 1957: 25 per cent of South Africa's gold, 24 per cent of her uranium, 43 per cent of her coal, 51 per cent of Northern Rhodesian copper, and 41 per cent of the value of total world diamond sales. The South African Government, the South West Africa Administration, and De Beers, each have a representative in the Diamond Producers' Association which controls the world diamond monopoly.

Capital: £5,240,000.

Dividends: 1946–9, 40 per cent and 10 per cent bonus each year; 1952–8, 150 per cent each year; 1959, 200 per cent; 1960, 200 per cent.

Profit for year ended December 1959: £15,553,197 (£4,784,732 was paid in taxation): for 1960: £15,186,657.

TSUMEB CORPORATION is a giant complex of American mining companies. Tsumeb Mines is their S.W.A.-registered company.

Newmont Mining Corporation and American Metal Climax hold equal interests (29 per cent) in the Tsumeb Corporation; and smaller interests are owned by Union Corporation (9 per cent), Selection Trust Co. (14 per cent), O'Okiep Copper Company (9 per cent – held in turn by Newmont and American Metal Climax), the South West Africa Company (7½ per cent), and De Beers (2½ per cent). The Chairman of the Board of Directors of Tsumeb is also Chairman of the Board of American Metal Climax. Tsumeb's managing director is manager of O'Okiep and vice-president of Newmont Mining Corporation. The directorships and presidencies of the companies go on doubling up on one another.

AMERICAN METAL CLIMAX controls mining, metallurgical, oil, and gas industries through subsidiary companies. Holds interests in Roan Antelope Copper Mines, Rhodesian Selection Trust, Bikita Minerals, San Francisco Mines of Mexico, O'Okiep mines in Namaqualand, also mines in Texas.

Profit for 1959: $30,832,879 (after allowing $15,510,229 on U.S. and foreign income taxes).

Capital: £1,050,000 (S.A.) in 4,200,000 shares of 5s. each. 4,000,000 shares are fully issued and paid: held 28·5 per cent by American Metal Climax; 28·5 per cent by Newmont Mining Corporation; 14·25 per cent by Selection Trust; 9·5 per cent by O'Okiep Copper; 2·37 per cent by South West Africa Co.; and 16·88 per cent by Union Corporation Ltd and others.

Dividends (per share): 1949–50, 9d.; 1950–1, 7s. 9d.; 1951–2, 14s.; 1952–3, 12s. 6d.; 1953–4, 10s. 6d.; 1954–5, 17s.; 1955–6, 35s.; 1956–7, 42s. 6d.; 1957–8, 17s. 6d.; 1958–9, 23s. 6d.; 1959–60, 21s.;

Metal sales year ending 30 June 1960: £15,257,668. *Net profit*: £4,895,213 (after deducting £1,996,924 for S.W.A. taxation).

Directors: M. D. Banghart, U.S.A., A. Chester Beatty, U.K., W. Hochschild, U.S.A., Albert Livingstone, Plato Malozemoff, U.S.A., John Payne, jr, U.S.A., Ernest T. Rose, U.S.A., Fred Searles, jr, U.S.A., H. Dewitt Smith, U.S.A., Charles E. Stott, U.S.A., T. P. Stratten, F. Coolbaugh, U.S.A.

THE SOUTH WEST AFRICA COMPANY LTD: major shares held by Anglo-American Corporation of South Africa, New Consolidated Goldfields, and the British South Africa Company· Has the sole right to prospect for minerals within an area of 3,000 square miles forming part of the original Damaraland Concession area. Prospecting by geophysical and other methods is being carried on by Tsumeb Exploration Co. Ltd, a company formed for this purpose by arrangement with Tsumeb Corporation. Holds mining areas in the Otavi and Grootfontein districts, among others; produces lead vanadium ores and zinc sulphides at the Berg Aukas mine. The Abenab lead-zinc mine closed in 1958.

Capital: £2,000,000.

Other Investment

GENERAL MINING CORPORATION is involved in a concession granted by the South West African Administration for prospecting for minerals over a 1,400 square mile area between the Brandberg Mountains and Cape Cross and lying west of *Iscor's tin mine at Uis*. Deposits of copper and other base materials are said to be proven.

RIO TINTO, the Canadian uranium and mining finance corporation which merged with Consolidated Zinc, has a copper project at Onganya in conjunction with Japanese interests.

SELECTION TRUST has 12 per cent of its assets in South West Africa, and makes 13 per cent of its income there. The company has vast interests in West Africa, in Northern and Southern Rhodesia, and in the U.S.A.; it is linked with American Metal Climax, Roan Antelope Copper Mines, Mufulira Copper Mines, Rhodesian Selection Trust, Tsumeb Corporation, and others.

CONSOLIDATED GOLDFIELDS OF S.A. is a holding company of the South West Africa Co.

SOUTH AFRICAN MINERALS CORPORATION owns manganese

mining properties in the Okahandja district, where operations are presently suspended. A subsidiary, Gobabis Manganese, holds rights for five years to prospect over 2,800 square miles in the Gobabis district. The company holds chrome properties in the Rustenburg district.

ASSOCIATED ORE AND METAL CORPORATION LTD operates a wolfram property in the Omaruru district.

BETHLEM STEEL CORPORATION is surveying for oil.

Smaller companies – Industrial Diamonds; S.W.A. Salt Co.; South African Minerals Corporation Ltd (interested in manganese); S.W.A. Lithium mines – are South West African companies for the most part, but their investments are from South Africa, Britain, and the U.S.A.

Appendix E: Education in South West Africa

Population of South West Africa

Total: 520,000. *Whites*: 73,200; *Africans*: 428,000; *Coloureds*: 23,900.*

Of the *Africans*, about 170,000 are inside the Police Zone; the rest outside. The 1951 figures were – Ovamboland, 205,000; the Okavango, 28,000; the Kaokoveld, 12,000; the Eastern Caprivi Zipfel, 16,000.†

Schools in South West Africa, 1960

Within the Police Zone		*Beyond the Police Zone*
No. of schools	*No. of pupils*	*Ovamboland*:
93 (10 Govt)	9,732	103 mission schools with 15,834 pupils;
		20 State-subsidized with 822 pupils
83 mission		*Okavango*:
		10 mission schools;
		28 Bush schools with a total of 2,742 pupils.

Average cost per scholar, 1958–9		*No. of scholars*
White Government schools (excluding hostel expenses)	£42 19s. 0d.	12,740
Coloured schools	£24 19s. 3d.	

* Administrator's 1961 budget speech.   † 1951 Population figures.

253

African schools within the Police Zone	£13 19s. 4d.	13,437
African schools outside the Police Zone	£1 16s. 2d.	19,398

Expenditure on Education, 1958–9
Total: £1,372,982.
Whites: £1,121,585.
Coloured, and African inside Police Zone: £216,358.
African: £35,039.

(Source: *South African Yearbooks*).

References and Sources

Parts 2 and 3: THE PEOPLE OF SOUTH WEST AFRICA, AND THE EARLY HISTORY OF THE COUNTRY

Material on the peoples is scattered over numbers of publications, including the following:

Dr H. Vedder's *South West Africa in Early Times* (Oxford University Press, 1938), translated by Mr Justice Hall, is compiled largely from German missionary sources, and goes up to 1890, the year of the death of the Herero Chief Samuel Maharero and four years before the German occupation.

The Native Tribes of South West Africa, prepared in 1928 (published by the *Cape Times*) by the South Government for use at the Permanent Mandates Commission of the League of Nations, contains contributions by Dr Vedder on the Herero, Nama, and Berg-Damara, by C. H. L. Hahn on the Ovambo, and by L. Fourie on the Bushmen. These articles concentrate on ethnological material and old-time tribal custom.

On the Herero, the Reverend Michael Scott collected, largely through on-the-spot interviews, a considerable amount of material which he collated (in mimeographed form) in *Documents Relating to the Appeal to the United Nations of the Herero and Other South West African People against Incorporation in the Union of South Africa and for the Restitution of their Tribal Lands* (published in Johannesburg, 1948). Much of this material is also contained in Freda Troup's *In Face of Fear* (Faber and Faber, 1950). Following on the submission of the Scott material to the United Nations there was the Reply of the South African Government to the 1948 Questionnaire of the Trusteeship Council, *U.N. Document T/175*, 1948.

Gunter Wagner has written on 'Some Economic Aspects of Herero Life' in *African Studies* (Vol. 13, Nos 3 and 4, 1954).

On the Bushmen, see Elizabeth Marshall Thomas's sympathetic

work *The Harmless People* (Secker & Warburg, 1959); and an article by Dr P. V. Tobias 'The Survival of the Bushmen' (*Natural History* 70 (2), February 1961). South African Government plans for the Bushmen have been announced in copies of *Bantu*, a publication of the Bantu Affairs Department.

On the Bergdama people there is material in the Vedder books, and in O. Kohler's *Study of Omaruru District* (Government Printer, Pretoria, 1959).

A version of the *Ancestral Law of the Rehoboth Community* (dated 1 January 1874, being a revision of the 1868 Law) is available in the Windhoek Archives. A Commission probed the Rehoboth community in 1926: *Report of the Rehoboth Commission* (U.G. 41 of 1926), and produced a considerable amount of material on all the peoples of S.W.A. and on early history, reproducing among other things the lively exchanges between Chief Hendrik Witbooi of the Nama and the Imperial German Commissioner, Dr Göring.

The Report on the Tour to Ovamboland by Major Pritchard (U.G. 38 of 1915) is the account of the first South African government contact with these people. Lawrence Green's *Lords of the Last Frontier* (Timmins, 1952) describes the Ovambo as seen through the eyes of their government commissioners, and carries material on the other peoples too.

The South West Africa Commission (U.G. 26 of 1936) records the deadlocked views of three commissioners appointed to report on the South African administration of the territory up to 1936, and carries most available published material on the relations between the German and South African sections of the White population up to the mid-thirties.

Records of early White contact with the country include:

Expedition of Discovery into the Interior by Sir James Alexander, 1836 (reproduced from the Royal Geog. Soc. Jnl, January 1838).

Narrative of an Explorer in Tropical Africa by F. Galton (Murray, 1853).

Journal of Joseph Tindall 1839-55 (Van Riebeeck Society, 1959).

The Early Hunters and Explorers in S.W.A. 1760-1886 by A. D. Watts is a thesis submitted in 1926 to the University of South Africa.

The Windhoek Archives Lemmer collection contains *Letters written by Samuel Maharero, Hendrik Witbooi* and others.

Chief Witbooi's Journal, *Die Dagboek van Hendrik Witbooi*, was captured during a German attack on the Nama stronghold and was published by the Van Riebeeck Society in 1929.

The *Report of W. Coates Palgrave, Special Commissioner to the Tribes North of the Orange River, on his Mission to Damaraland and Great Namaland* was published in 1876.

There is also the *Cape Bluebook of Native Affairs* (1879) presented to both Houses of Parliament in Cape Town.

The *Robert Lewis Papers on Concessions* in Damaraland are preserved in the Windhoek Archives.

On the scramble for colonies and German colonization see:

P. T. Moon's *Imperialism and World Politics* (Macmillan, New York, 1930), which quotes from British State papers.

M. E. Townsend's *The Rise and Fall of Germany's Colonial Empire* (Macmillan, New York, 1930).

W. O. Addelotte's *Bismarck and British Colonial Policy* (University of Pennsylvania Press).

Germany's Claim to Colonies (Royal Institute of International Affairs, 1938).

A. J. P. Taylor's *Germany's First Bid for Colonies* (Macmillan, 1938).

The German period is recorded with thoroughness and frankness in:

K. Schwabe's *Der Krieg in Deutsch-Sudwestafrika 1904–6* (Berlin, 1907).

T. Leutwein's *Elf Jahre Gouverneur in Deutsch-Sudwestafrika* (Berlin, 1907).

P. Rohrbach's *Deutsche Kolonialwirtschaft* (Berlin, 1907), *Deutsche Kolonialpolitik* (Berlin, 1907), and *Aus Sudwestafrika Schweren* (Berlin, 1909).

Die Kämpfe der Deutschen Truppen in Sudwestafrika: Der Feldzug gegen die Hereros, based on official files, edited by the Department of History of War of the General Staff, Berlin, 1906.

Gustav Frenssen's *Peter Moor's Journey to South West Africa* (English ed., Constable, 1907).

There are also articles in the *Cambridge History of the British Empire* (Vol. 8, 1936); Dr H. Vedder's 'The German Occupation of 1883–1914'; and Prof. Valentin's 'S.W.A., Spoiled Child of the German Colonies'.

The British Bluebook *Report on the Natives of South West Africa and Their Treatment by Germany* prepared in the Administrator's office, Windhoek (H.M.S.O., London, 1918) was the official dossier on German rule. (Interestingly, there was a German antidote to this Report, alleging British imperialist crimes in India and during the Boer War in South Africa. It was published with the same title in Berlin in 1919.)

The S.W.A. Administrator's Report for 1922 contains some material on the aftermath of the German occupation, as does S.W.A.: Special Criminal Court Papers relating to Cases dealt with for the Military Protection of S.W. (U.G. 22 of 1917).

Part 4: THE SOUTH AFRICAN OCCUPATION

H. F. Trew in Botha Treks (Blackie & Co., 1936) has written a light-hearted version of the military campaign. See also Eric A. Walker's History of South Africa (Longmans, 1959).

On the Versailles period see Smuts, The League of Nations: A Practical System (Hodder, 1918) and Leonard Barnes, Empire or Democracy (Gollancz, 1939).

Invaluable for the years of the mandate are Reports of the Administrator of South West Africa (these were compiled for 1916 onwards, and the later reports were those submitted annually to the League of Nations); and the Minutes of the Sessions of the Permanent Mandates Commission of the League.

See also S.W.A. Administration, Report on Land Settlement (Windhoek, 1935); Native Reserves Commission (1928); The Boundary between Angola and South West Africa (1926).

Report on the Tour to Ovamboland by Major S. M. Pritchard (U.G. 38 of 1915).

Report on the Conduct of the Ovakuanyame Chief Mandume and on the Military Operations Conducted against him in Ovamboland (U.G. 37 of 1917).

Report of the Administrator on the Bondelswarts Rising 1922 (U.G. 30 of 1922).

Report of the Commission Appointed to Enquire into the Bondelswarts (U.G. 16 of 1923).

The Union Government's Treatment of the S.W.A. Mandate 1920–1944 is a thesis submitted by Pauline Rita Taylor to the University of Cape Town in 1944.

H. W. Dowd contributed to the Fletcher School of Law and Diplomacy (Harvard), as a thesis for a Ph.D. degree, a painstaking examination of The Non-White Land and Labour Policies of the South

African Administration of South West Africa 1918–1948. This contains detailed analyses of comparative expenditure on White and non-White services.

Part 5: SOCIAL AND ECONOMIC CONDITIONS

Official sources include:

S.W.A.: Long Term Agricultural Policy Commission (1950).

Report of the Minimum Area of Farms Commission (Meinert, Windhoek, 1946).

Report of the Commission on the Economic and Financial Relations between S.A. and S.W.A. (U.G. 16 of 1935); also the 1951 Inquiry (U.G. 26 of 1952) on the same subject.

Report of the Government on the Administration of S.W.A. for 1946 (U.G. 49 of 1947), the only report on the territory submitted to the United Nations.

South West Africa Legislative Assembly: Votes and Proceedings 1949–1962.

S.W.A. Native Labour Commission 1945–8 (Unie Volkspers, 1950).

Report of the Health Commission (Meinert, Windhoek, 1946).

Commission of Inquiry into Non-European Education in S.W.A. (1958).

Yearbooks of South Africa (these include chapters on South West Africa).

S.W.A. *Estimates* presented to the Legislative Assembly; S.W.A. *Accounts.*

South Africa's *Senate Hansard* and *House of Assembly Hansard.*

For the most part, government publications are out-dated and government departments reluctant to supply information. For example, approaches by the writer to three different government authorities and questions asked in Parliament for figures of land distribution (the last published figures are for 1956) went unanswered.

United Nations documents on South West Africa, compiled from primary, official sources, abound with detailed material analysing expenditure, tax policy, trade, tribal funds and trust monies, cattle census figures, health statistics, education statistics, and so on. The most useful U.N. documents are:

United Nations General Assembly, Committee on South West Africa: *Information and Documentation in Respect of the Territory of S.W.A.*: A/AC 73/L3 & 4; A/AC 73/L7, 13 May 1955; A/AC 73/L10, 19 August 1957; A/AC 73/L13, 2 September 1959; A/AC 73/L15, 9 August 1961; and others in the same series.

REFERENCES AND SOURCES

United Nations General Assembly, Fourth Committee: A/C 4/266, 29 November 1949 and A/C 4/512, 8 December 1961.

United Nations General Assembly, Committee on S.W.A.: Petitions and Communications Relating to *S.W.A.*: A/AC 73/3, 9 September 1960; A/AC 73/4, 30 October 1961.

Reports of the Committee on South West Africa to the General Assembly:

9th session: supplement No.	14	A/2666
10th	,,	,,	12	A/2913
11th	,,	,,	12	A/3151
12th	,,	,,	12	A/3626
13th	,,	,,	12	A/3906
14th	,,	,,	12	A/4191
15th	,,	,,	12	A/4464
16th	,,	,,	12	A/4957

Labour statistics cited were obtained from the S.W.A. Native Labour Association (in letters to the writer) and from Replies to Questions in the South African House of Assembly (Hansard).

D. C. Krogh in *National Income and Expenditure in S.W.A. 1920–1956* (*S.A. Journal of Economics*, Vol. 28, March 1960) has calculated a national income figure.

The ethnological publications of the Department of Bantu Administration and Development are studies by O. Kohler of the *Omaruru District* (1959), the *Grootfontein District* (1959), the *Gobabis District* (1959), the *Karibib District* (1958), the *Otjiwarongo District* (1959); and by Gunter Wagner of the *Okahandja District* (1957). All are published by the Government Printer, Pretoria, as, too, *Notes on the Kaokoveld and its Peoples* by N. J. van Warmelo (1951).

Part 6 : MANDATES AND TRUSTEESHIP

On the Mandate system see: Quincy Wright, *Mandates under the League of Nations* (University of Chicago, 1930); R. W. Logan, *The Operation of the Mandate System in Africa 1919–1927* (Washington, 1942).

On United Nations trusteeship: John McLaurin, *The United Nations and Power Politics* (Allen & Unwin, 1951); James N. Murray Jnr, *The United Nations Trusteeship System* (University of Illinois, 1957); R. N. Chowduri, *International Mandates and the Trusteeship System*, a comparative study (The Hague, 1955); B. T. G. Chidzero, *Tanganyika and International Trusteeship* (O.U.P., 1961).

S.W.A. and S.A.: The History of a Mandate (published by authority of the South African Government in New York, 1946) is the South African Government case for incorporation.

Other booklets published at this time were:

Dr A. B. Xuma, *S.W.A.: Annexation or Trusteeship* (1946).

The Case for Bechuanaland (April 1946), the representations of the chiefs of Bechuanaland against incorporation.

Sir C. Dundas, *S.W.A.: The Factual Background* (South Africa Institute of International Affairs, 1946).

J. D. Rheinallt Jones, *The Future of S.W.A.* (South Africa Institute of Race Relations, 1946).

The *Annual Survey of U.N. Affairs*, edited by Clyde Eagleton (1949–62), summarizes debates and decisions year by year, as do the *Afro-U.N. Bulletins* of the American Committee on Africa.

Records of *United Nations General Assembly* and *Fourth Committee Discussions* and *Proceedings* are invaluable, though mountainous. Oral statements by petitioners are part of these records.

On the legal issues see *International Court of Justice: Reports, Judgments, Advisory Opinions and Orders*, for example, the Advisory Opinion of 11 July 1950 on the International Status of S.W.A. Also United Nations sixth session: *Report of the S.W.A. Committee on Legal Questions to the Committee on S.W.A.* A/AC 73/2.

See also Dr T. E. Donges's speech before the plenary session of the U.N., Paris, 18 January 1952: *The Greater Issue behind the Dispute over S.W.A.*, S.A.'s appeal to the U.N. to destroy this evil which threatens to destroy the organization (South Africa House, London, 1952).

Useful booklets are: Adv. I. Goldblatt's *The Mandated Territory of S.W.A. in Relation to the U.N.* (Struik, 1961); and R. B. Ballinger's *The Case against the Union* (South Africa Institute of Race Relations, 1961).

Periodicals and newspapers consulted included the *Windhoek Advertiser*; *South West News* (the first and only African publishing enterprise, no longer in existence); *Financial Mail*; *Contact*; *Guardian* (banned); *New Age* (banned); *South West Africa Annual*; *South African Mining and Engineering Journal*; also reports of the Land Bank and Consolidated Diamond Mines of S.W.A.

Index

Alexander, Ray, 196–7
Algeria, 241
Aminuis Reserve, 144
Andersson, Charles, 64–6
Anglo-American, 156, 237
Angola
  border traffic, 12, 41
  clash with Ukuanyama, 98–100
  labour from, 128, 132, 133–4
  nationalist hopes, 238
Angola Boer project, 107–8, 116
Apartheid, 12–17, 127–8, 140,
  229–35, 239–44
Appolus, Putuse, 219
Archimbault, Mr, 181
Aukeigas, 146

Balfour, Lord, 74
Banghart, M.D., 151
Bantu Authorities, 31
Basson, 'Japie', 54
'Basters'; see Rehobothers
Belgian Congo, 54, 206, 238, 241
Benson, Mary, 236
Berg-Damara
  grievances of, 35–6
  numbers of, 35
  origins of, 34
  Reserves of, 36, 146
Bethlem Steel Corporation, 152,
  252

Beukes, Hans, 194
Beukes, Hermanus, 41, 45
Beukes, Johannes, 45
Beukes, Timothy, 101, 103
Bismarck, 64, 69–73
'Black diamond' sheep, 154
Boers, 67, 72
Bondelswarts
  history of, 101
  risings of, 75, 81
  S. A. punitive expeditions
    against, 98, 101–4
Botha, Gen. Louis, 42, 88–90
Bushmen
  character of, 47
  numbers of, 46
  origins of, 46
  Reserves of, 46, 48
  White opinions of, 46
  work of, 46–7
Buxton, Lord, 110

Caprivi Strip, 223
Carpio-de Alva mission, 221–4,
  240
Cecil, Lord Robert, 94
Chief, status of, 127
Clarke, E. P. Courtney, 162
Coetzee, Jacobus, 62
Colonization (of S. W. Africa),
  61–83

Coloured population, 48
Congo; see Belgian Congo
Consolidated Diamond Mines, 151–2, 155–6, 249
Cope, R. S., 131
Copper production, 154
Courtney, Winifred, 22, 213–14

Diamond production, 155–6, 237
Diaz, Bartholomew, 62
Dönges, Dr, 185, 188
Drew, Dewdney, 104
Drought, 33, 153

Education, 15, 163–5, 253–4
Epikuro Reserve, 143
Etosha Petroleum Company, 152

Fabregat, Professor, 189, 218, 219
Farming, 15, 19, 38–9, 106–9, 152–3, 154, 157–8, 247, 248
Federale Volksbeleggings, 152
Finance, 151–66, 171–2, 249–52
Fines, 137
First World War, 88–93
Fishing industry, 152, 156
Food and Canning Workers Union (Cape Town), 196
Foreign Investments, 249–52
Fortune, Ismail, 194
France, 187, 191, 238
Francois, Captain von, 73–4
Frey, Dr Karl, 124

Galton, Sir Frances, 39, 63
Gariseb, Fritz, 35
Germany community
    after Second World War, 50–53
    and Nazis, 50, 53
    internment in Second World War, 50
        outnumbered by South Africans, 50
    present political significance, 56–7
    size, 49
    Smuts's attitude towards, 49
German occupation, 49, 69–83
    and Rhenish Mission Society, 64
    British reaction to, 71–2
    economic development during, 72–3, 75, 87
    in First World War, 88–93
    summarized, 92–3
    treatment of tribes, 82–3, 87
Getzen, Erich; see Kerina, Mburumba
Gold mining, 233–4
Goldblatt, Advocate, 186
Goraseb, Cornelius, 36
Goraseb, David, 36, 37
Göring, Dr, 73, 245–6
Grazing fees, 163
Great Britain, 179, 187, 191, 214, 217–19, 221, 224, 238, 241
Green, Frederick, 66

Hall Commission of Inquiry, 200–201, 211
Haybittel, 66
Hahn, Hugo, 65
Hahn, Commissioner of Ovamboland, 100, 126
Health services, 160
Herbst, Major, 103–4
Herero
    and Aminuis land-shuttle scheme, 147–8
    and cattle-raising, 28, 29, 163
    character and appearance of, 27
    dispute with Mbanderu, 203

education of, 165n.
effect of mandate on, 110–16
exiles, 29, 182
in First World War, 91
in German occupation, 72–3, 75–7
numbers of, 28
origins of, 27–8
petitions to U.N., 188, 196, 200, 202–3
Reserves of, 30, 110–16
war with Germany, 28, 30, 78–83
wars with Nama, 32, 66–8
Hofmeyr, G. R., 103, 169
Hottentots; see Nama

India, 214
International Court of Justice, 185, 187–9, 213, 215, 219, 224

Jonker Afrikaner, 63, 66

Kambonde, Johannes, 196, 199
Kandjo, Festus, 111–13
Kaokoveld, 141–2
Kapuuo, Clement, 22, 30, 31, 199, 201
Karakul sheep, 154
Katutura township, 16, 209–11
Kaukuetu, Vatja, 198, 200, 211, 219
Kauraisa, Charles, 219
Kerina, Mburumba (Erich Getzen), 22, 190, 192, 193–4, 198–202, 207, 211
Khama, Tshekedi, 182
Khoman, Thonat, 190
Kooper, Marcus, 147, 194, 202
Kozonguizi, Jariretundu, 22, 194, 198–202, 205–7
Kuhangua, Jacob, 194, 200

Kutako, Hosea, 22, 29–31, 80, 112–14, 148, 184, 196, 198–201, 203, 222, 236

Labour,
for gold mines, 132–4
in the Police Zone, 136–7
living conditions, 134–5
organization of, 119, 129–39, 234
recruitment of, 130–8
shortage of, 137–8
strike, 197
trade unions, 196–7
wages, 130, 138–9, 196, 233
working hours, 197
Land
distribution of, 142–3, 148, 247
loans and mortgages for, 149
South African expropriation of, 106–9, 116
Land bank, 149
League of Nations mandate
institution of, 94–7
pre-Second World War, 169–74
S.A. betrayal of, 17–21, 140, 169–225 passim
The Times on 18,
United Nations and, 175–95, 205–25
Leutwein, 74–81 passim
Lewin, Julius, 22
Lewis, Robert, 72, 73
Lindequist, von, 81, 154
London Missionary Society, 64
Lloyd George, 94
Louw, Eric, 19, 169, 181, 183, 191–4, 215, 218–21
Luderitz, 71
Lugard, Lord, 105

Maharero, 65, 67, 68, 73, 203
Maharero, Frederick, 29, 30, 113, 182, 196
Maharero, Samuel, 29, 76, 77, 113
Malan, Dr, 183, 184
Mamugwe, Werner, 22, 203
Mandate; *see* League of Nations mandate
Mandume, Chief of Ukuanyama, 98–100
Marengo, Jacob, 81, 82
Marine Diamond Corporation, 156
Maritz, General, 88
Marquard, Frank, 196
Mbaeva, Nathaniel, 219
Metal Climax Corporation, 206, 250
Minerals industry, 152, 154–6, 233
Missionaries, 64–8
    and education, 163–4
    and hospitals, 166
    and Herero-Nama wars, 66–8
    and tribes, 65
Moon, P. T., 173
Moor, Peter, 78, 79
Morris, Abraham, 90, 101–4
Munjuku II, 31, 203

Nama (Hottentots)
    appearance of, 34
    clans of, 32
    distribution of, 32
    during German occupation, 73–5, 81–3
    in First World War, 91
    organization of, 33
    petitions to U.N., 34, 188
    Reserves of, 33, 34, 141, 146
    war with Herero, 32, 66–8

N.A.T.O., 213–14
Nelengani, Louis, 194
Newmont Mining Corporation, 151
Ngavirue, Zedekia, 22, 198, 209–11, 219
Nujoma, Sam, 194, 200–2, 207

Okavango, 45, 142
Okombahe Reserve, 144
Oppenheimer, Sir Ernest, 155, 237
Oranjemund, 155–6
Otjimbingive Reserve, 144
Otjituuo Reserve, 144
Ovambo
    agriculture of, 38–9
    appearance and character of, 39
    defeat by Portuguese, 98–100
    numbers and distribution of, 37–8
    origins of, 38
    petitions to U.N., 196
    tribes of, 38
    work of, 40
Ovamboland
    administration of, 125–8
    apartheid in, 128
    as example of 'non-White contentment', 40
    as forbidden territory, 38, 40
    border with Angola, 40–41
    during German occupation, 39
    education in, 163–4
    geography of, 141
    hospitals in, 166
    labour in, 129–35
    nationalist movement, 199
    population of, 37–8
    taxes in, 163

Ovamboland Peoples' Organization (O.P.O.), 199, 200–202
Ovitoto Reserve, 144

Palgrave, William Coates, 43, 67, 68, 75
Pandit, Mrs, 183
Permanent Mandates Commission, 169–74
  origin of, 97
  and S. A. punitive expeditions, 98
  and the Bondelswarts shooting, 102–4
  and the Rehobothers, 105
  and Ovamboland, 126, 131
  composition and procedure of, 169
Police Zone, 121, 128, 136
Portuguese (defeat of Ukuanyama), 98
Pritchard, Major S.M., 98–9

Referendum (1946), 179, 181–3
Rehobothers ('Basters')
  grievances of, 41–2, 45
  history of, 42–4
  in First World War, 90–91
  missionaries and, 67
  origins of, 41, 42–3
  punitive expeditions against, 98, 104–5
  superior status of, 141
  territories of, 44
  treaty with Germans, 43
  White opinion of, 46
Reserves, 25
  farming in, 159–60, 163
  numbers in, 145
  siting of, 110–16, 140–50
Rhenish Mission Society, 64–5

Rio Tinto, 152

Salazar, 238
Schwabe, Captain, 77
Scott, Michael, 182–200 passim
Sears, Mason, 213
Sharpeville, 211–12
Shimi, Ushona, 196
Smuts
  and mandate, 94–7, 106, 172–3, 175, 178–9
  attitude towards German settlers, 50
South Africa
  administrative responsibilities of, 123–5, 159, 161–2, 171–2, 183
  and health services, 166
  and mandate, 17–21, 140, 169–225 passim
  and self-government, 178–9
  armed forces of, 230–31
  defeat of Germany in First World War, 89
  economic benefits from mandate, 159–63, 235–7
  expropriation of land during mandate, 106–9
  future policy of, 231
  policy on Reserves, 145–6, 170
  punitive expeditions, after First World War, 88–105
  report to U.N., 114
  S.W.A.N.U. and S.W.A.P.O. oppose, 204
  S.W. Africa mandated to, 94–7
  White settlers from, 157–8
South West Africa
  administration of, 14, 123–8, 183
  economy of, 151

exports of, 157–8
geography of, 141–2
population of, 25, 50
size of, 25
tribes of, 25; *see* Berg-Damara, Bondelswarts, Bushmen, Herero, Nama, Ovambo, Rehobother
South West Africa Affairs Amendment Act (1949), 124
South West Africa Company Ltd., 251
South West African National Union (S.W.A.N.U.), 198, 200–211
and Herero-Mbanderu dispute, 203
and tribal activities, 203
attitude to U.N., 204
plans for independence, 204–6
relations with S.W.A.P.O., 202, 206–8
South West African Native Labour Association (S.W.A.N.L.A.), 130, 132, 133, 138, 139, 156
South West African Peoples' Organization (S.W.A.P.O.), 198, 202–8
and U.N. petitions, 203
origins of, 200–201
relations with S.W.A.N.V., 202, 206–8
South West African Progressive Association, 198
South West African Student Body, 197
South West Party, 54
Stel, Simon van der, 62

Tambo, Oliver, 194
268

Taxes, 162–3
Toivo, Toivo Ja, 22, 194, 198–200, 202
Trade Unions, 196–7
Tribal levies, 163
Trotha, General von, 80, 81
Tsumeb Corporation, 151–2, 154–5, 249–50

Ukuanyama tribe (defeated by Portugal), 98
United Nations Organization
Ad Hoc Committee of, 187–8
African representation in, 212, 215
and 1946 referendum, 179, 181
and Sharpeville, 212
and shooting of Dec. 1959, 209–11
Carpio-de Alva mission, 221–4
Good Offices Committee, 190–96, 213
petitions to, 11, 188, 193–5, 196, 198, 199, 204, 209, 216–17, 240
South West African Committee, origins of, 188; attempt to enter S.W. Africa, 19, 217–18; recommendations of (1961), 219
Special Committee of Seven, 20, 220–21
U.S.A., 187, 189, 191, 213, 215, 217, 238
U.S.S.R., 192

Vedder, Dr H., 37, 124
Verwoerd, 19–21, 166, 222–3, 229–30

Wagner, Dr Gunter, 28

Walvis Bay, military installations at, 223
Waterberg East Reserve, 144
Welensky, 237–8
White settlement, statistics, 248

Wilson, President, 95
Witbooi, David, 182–3, 202, 222
Witbooi, Hendrik, 32, 66, 73–4, 78, 81, 82, 245–6
Witbooi, Moses, 66